IMAGES
of America

EAST PROVIDENCE

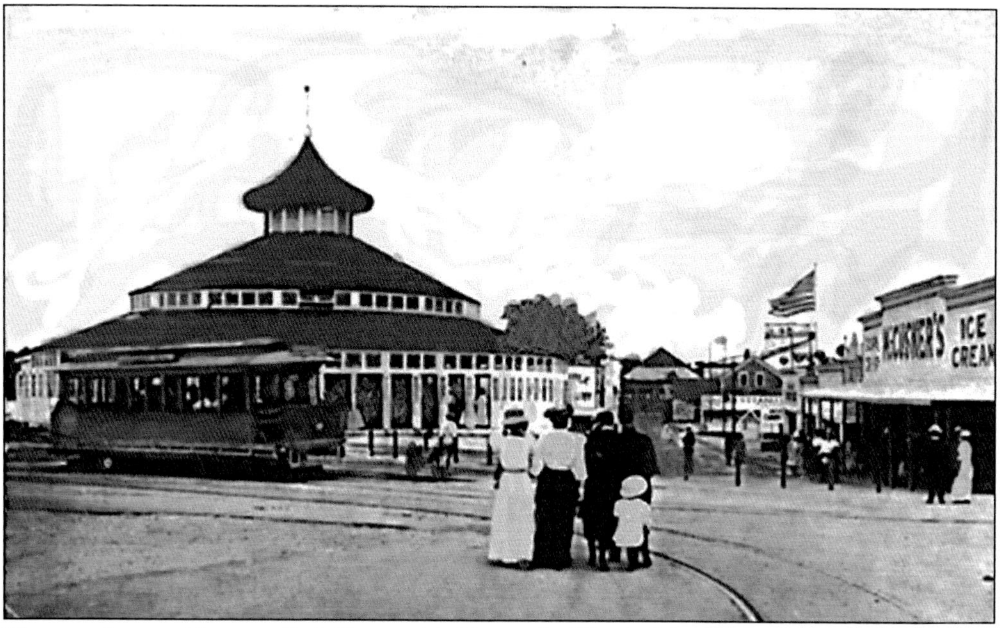

The very famous Crescent Park Carousel in Riverside, Rhode Island.

IMAGES
of America

EAST PROVIDENCE

East Providence Historical Society

ARCADIA
PUBLISHING

ISBN 978-0-7385-4457-1

Published by Arcadia Publishing
Charleston, South Carolina

Printed in the United States of America

Library of Congress Catalog Card Number: 2005935865

For all general information contact Arcadia Publishing at:
Telephone 843-853-2070
Fax 843-853-0044
E-mail sales@arcadiapublishing.com
For customer service and orders:
Toll-Free 1-888-313-2665

Visit us on the Internet at www.arcadiapublishing.com

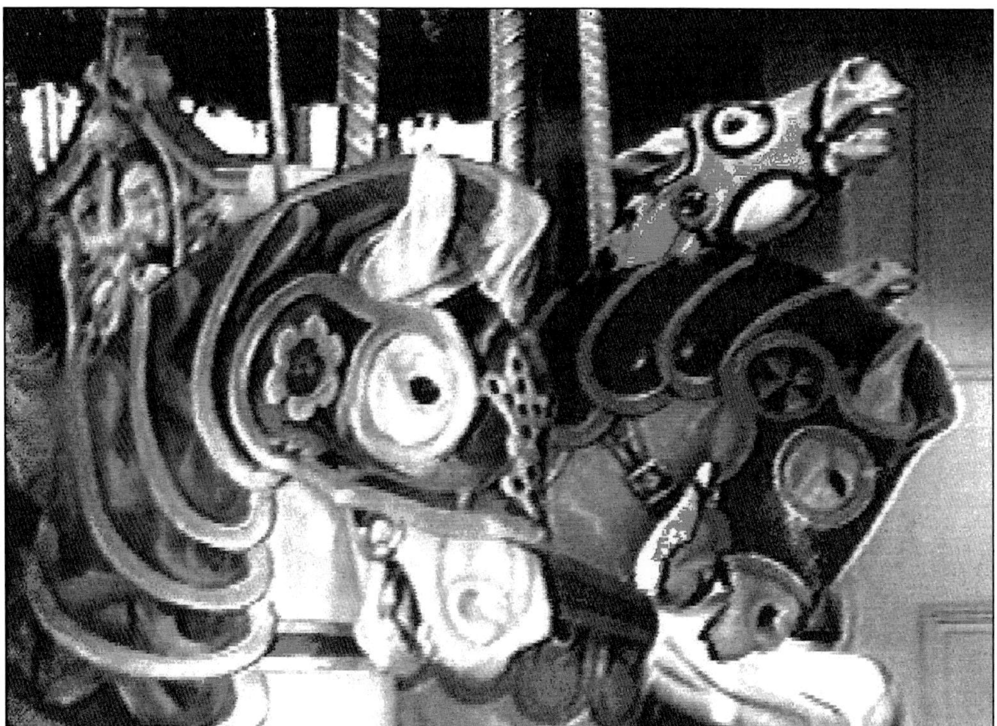

The famous Charles I.D. Looff horses can be seen at the Crescent Park Carousel in Riverside.

Contents

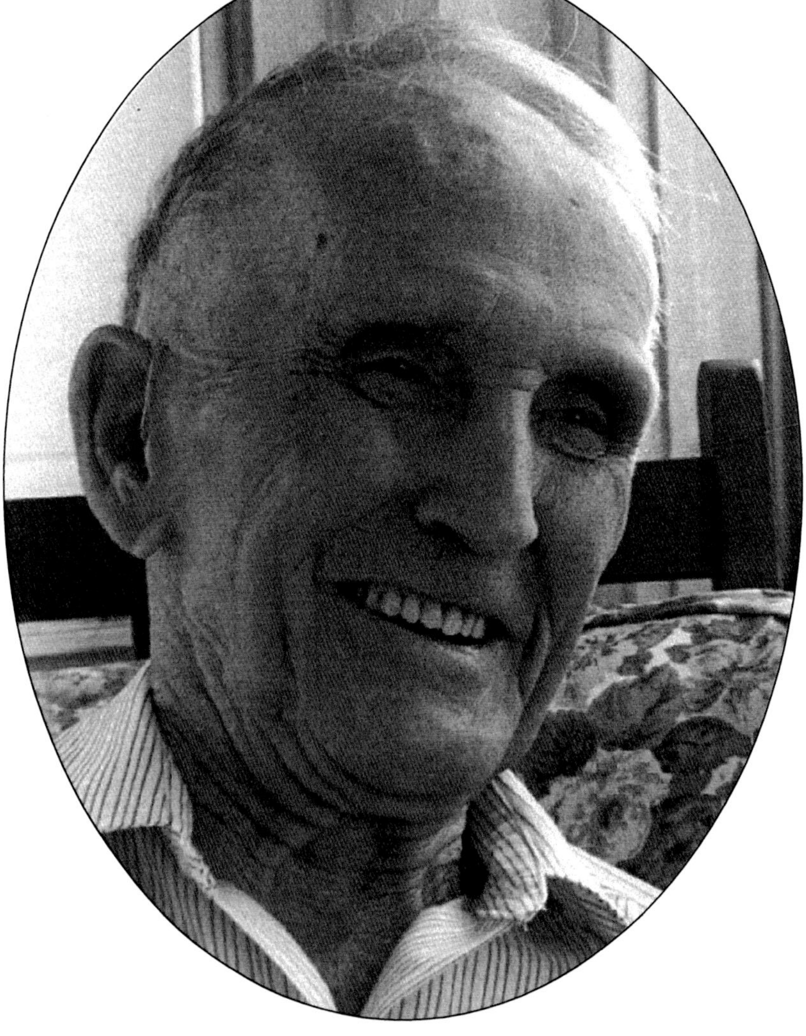

Dedicated to the memory of Jess Welt (1890–1981).
His images of the past have brightened our future.

Many of the photographs in this book were taken by Jess Welt, who was born in Waldoboro, Maine, in 1890. His family moved to East Providence in 1899. He worked with his father, Simon, as a shipbuilder at the East Providence Drydock and Marine Railway Company.

He later became a building contractor and built many of the houses in the East Providence area. During those years Jess was an active amateur photographer, making pictures of much of the town, especially the Watchemoket section where he lived and worked. He used view-type cameras, with both 4x5 and 6x8-inch glass plates, which he processed in his cellar workshop.

Although he was a highly competent builder and finish carpenter, he is best remembered as a photographer. Many of the hundreds of pictures that he made have been reproduced as postcards, book illustrations, calendar pictures, etc., and are highly prized by collectors. We are pleased to dedicate this book to his memory.

Introduction

This history of East Providence in pictures was truly a joint project of the East Providence Historical Society and community members with an interest in history. East Providence has a long and complicated history, extending to 1636 when Roger Williams first briefly stayed here.

The community has persevered through years of struggle under the British Crown, through King Philip's War and the American Revolution as part of the Massachusetts Bay Colony, and finally through acceptance as part of the State of Rhode Island. The community has moved forward first as the Seekonk Plantation, then as the Town of Rehoboth from 1643 until 1812, when part of Rehoboth along the Seekonk River and the Bay took on the name Seekonk. In 1862, when part of Seekonk was first annexed to Rhode Island, the citizens voted to call their town East Providence. In 1962 the town was chartered as a city.

This pictorial history attempts to capture the early vitality and transformation of the town from a quiet farming community to a multi-faceted city with three distinct purposes: industrial, commercial, and recreational. Yet all three sections meld as a cohesive, interdependent, and flourishing community.

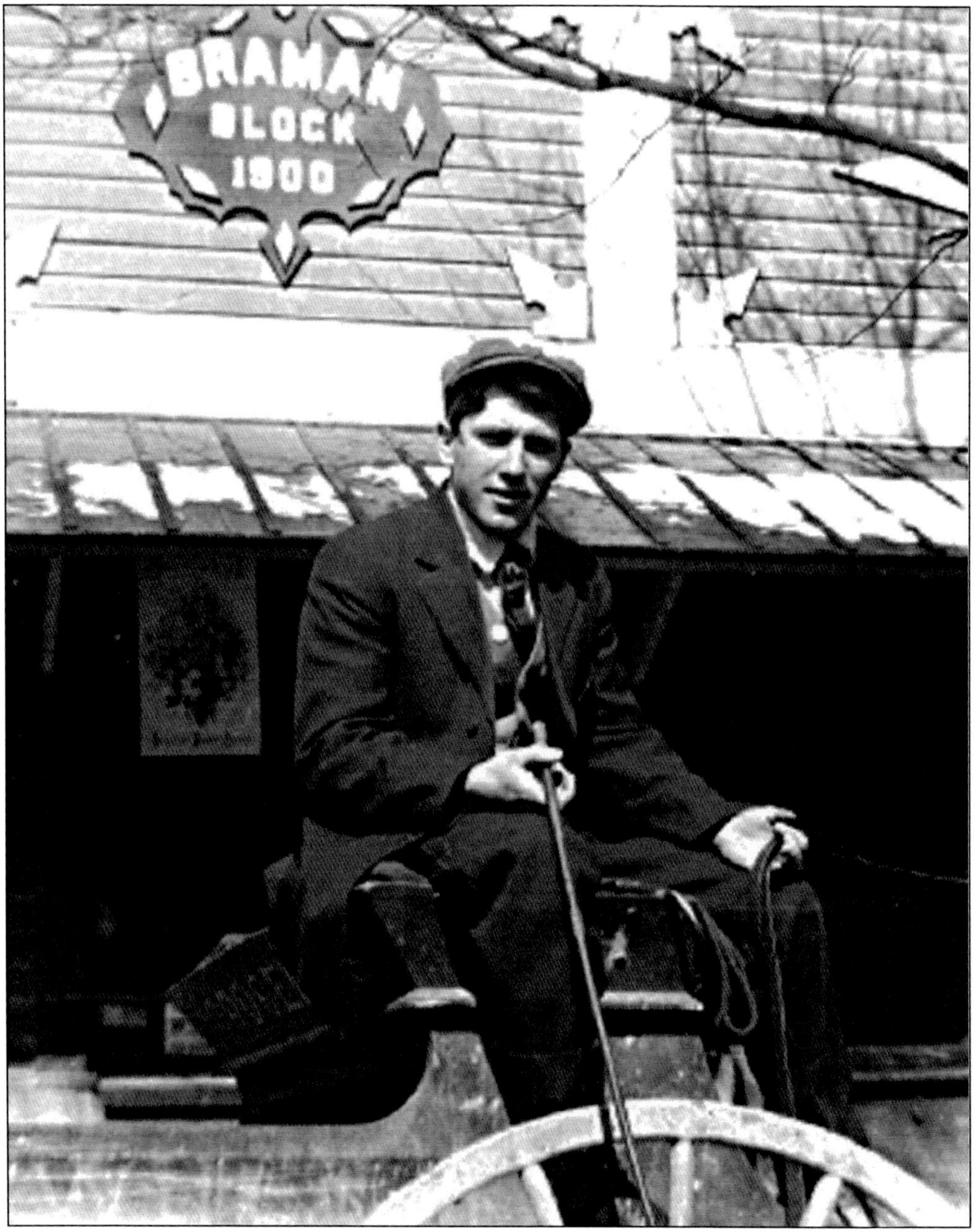

Jess Welt is sitting on a wagon in front of a market in the Braman Block in 1910. The Braman Block was at the corner of Burgess Avenue and Juniper Street. As a young man, Jess delivered groceries. There is a convenience store in this building today.

One

Watchemoket

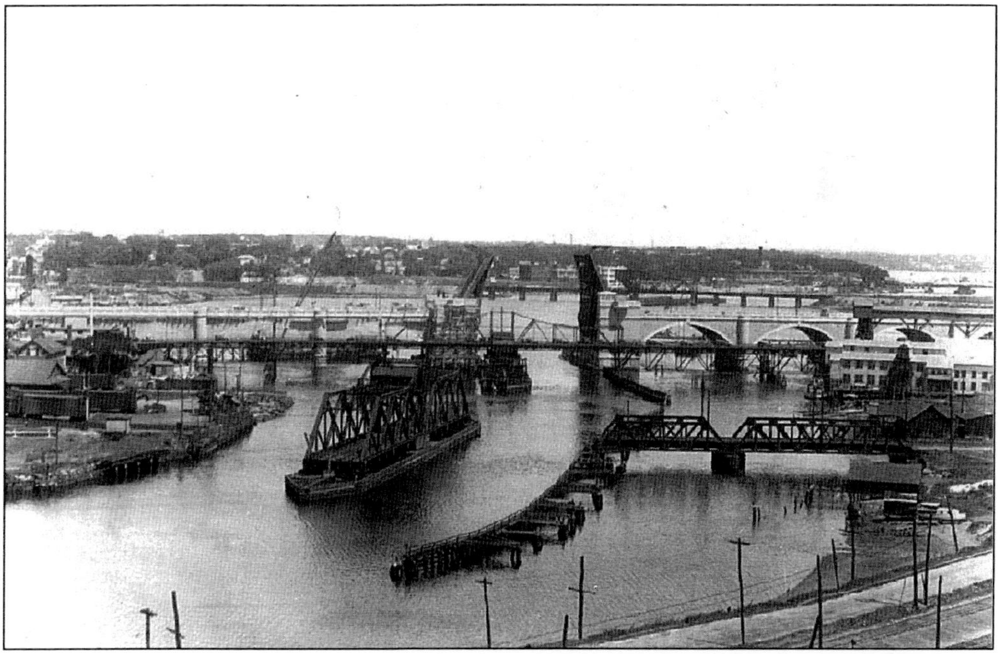

Len Erickson, the historian of Watchemoket, has written that "Watchemoket is an Indian word meaning the proximity of the river and the tidal marsh with the feel and smell of that area . . . Watchemoket Square started at the place known as Bold Point which was a fording place of the Wampanoag Indians across the Seekonk River. In the early years of East Providence the best crossing place on the river was this same crossing place. In 1793 John Brown of Providence built a bridge from Fox Point to Bold Point in what was then Rehoboth. In 1885 a high level iron bridge was built. This caused all kinds of building in the area. Early on horses and stagecoaches followed by autos and electric trolleys flowed over the bridges. An inn was built near the bridge area and some 100 businesses eventually opened. By 1906 the Square became the central business district of East Providence. Watchemoket Square covered about nine acres of land in the central section of the town."

In the photograph we see the old railroad bridge in the foreground. Behind it are the old 1885 iron bridge and the "new" concrete Washington Bridge, built in 1931. These are followed by another railroad bridge and, in the far distance, the Red Bridge.

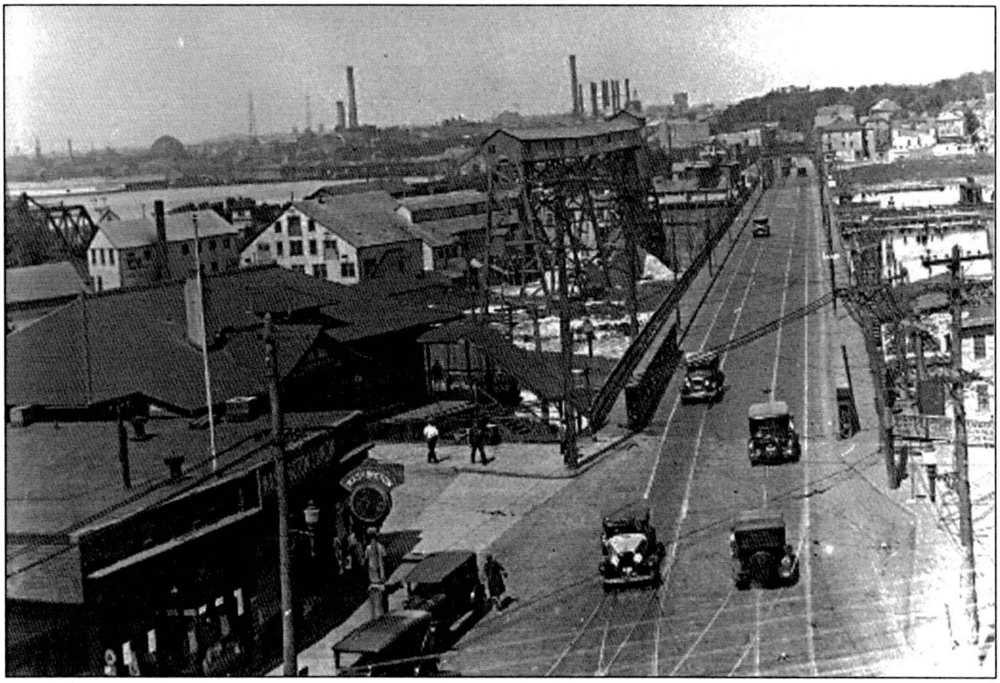

This is the view west toward Providence across the Washington Bridge. The railroad station is on the far left corner and the oyster house is behind it. The time period is the 1920s.

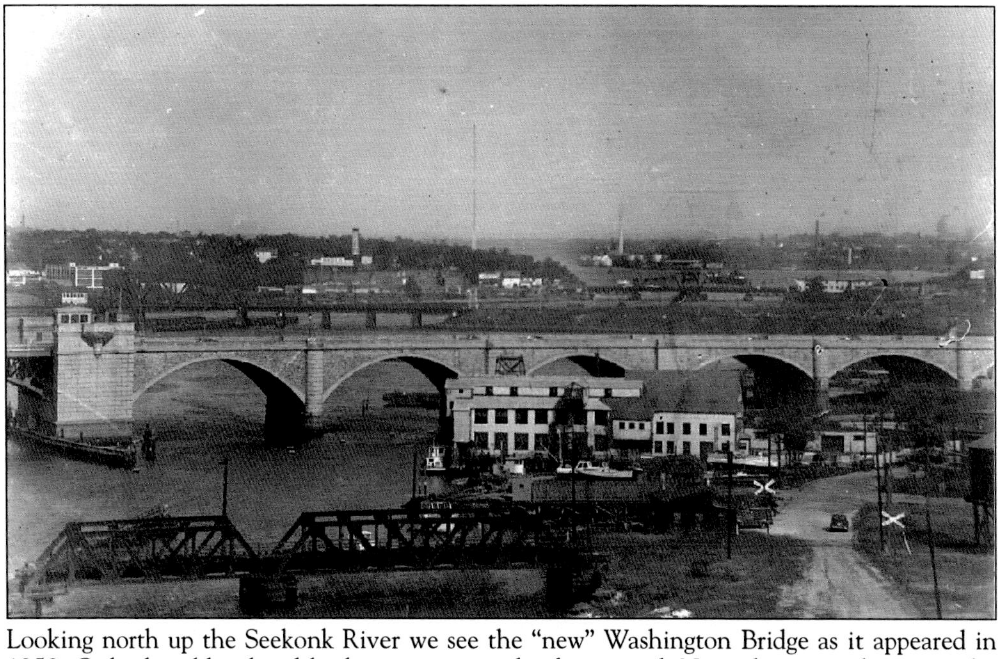

Looking north up the Seekonk River we see the "new" Washington Bridge as it appeared in 1950. Only the old railroad bridge remains in the foreground. Note the oyster house in the foreground. In the distance are another railroad bridge and the Red Bridge.

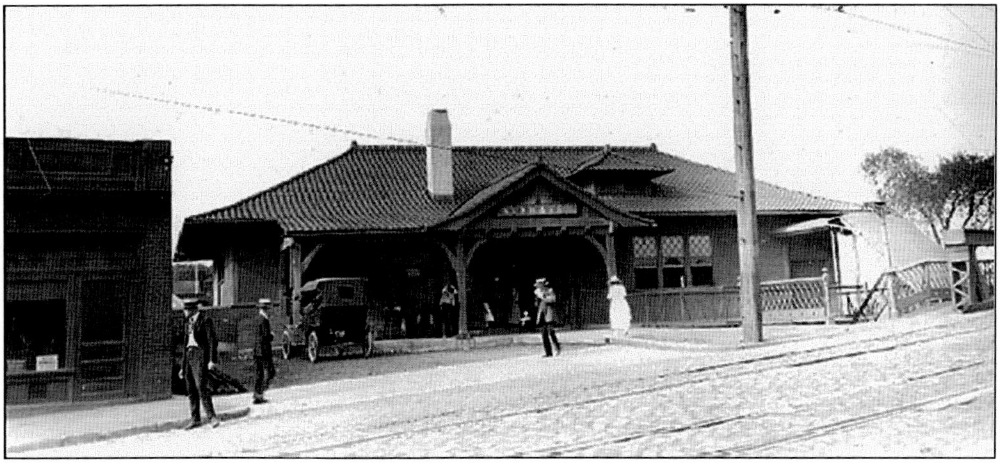
The railroad station served the Consolidated Line. The station was built in 1910.

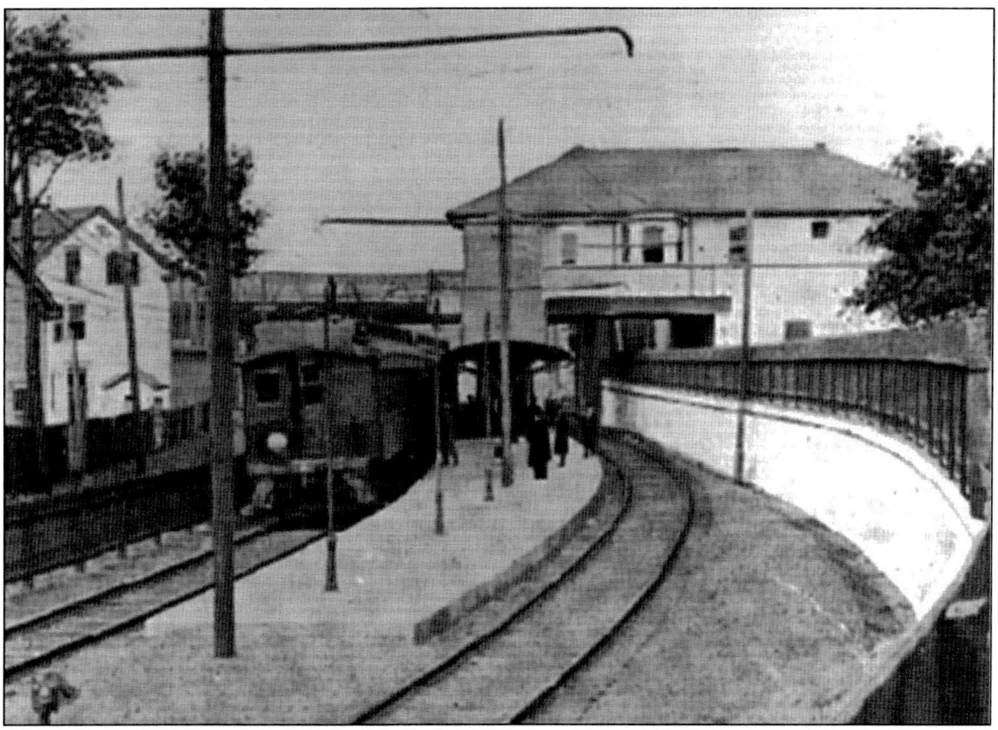
This rear view of the tracks behind the railroad station shows the sharp curve necessary to enter the station.

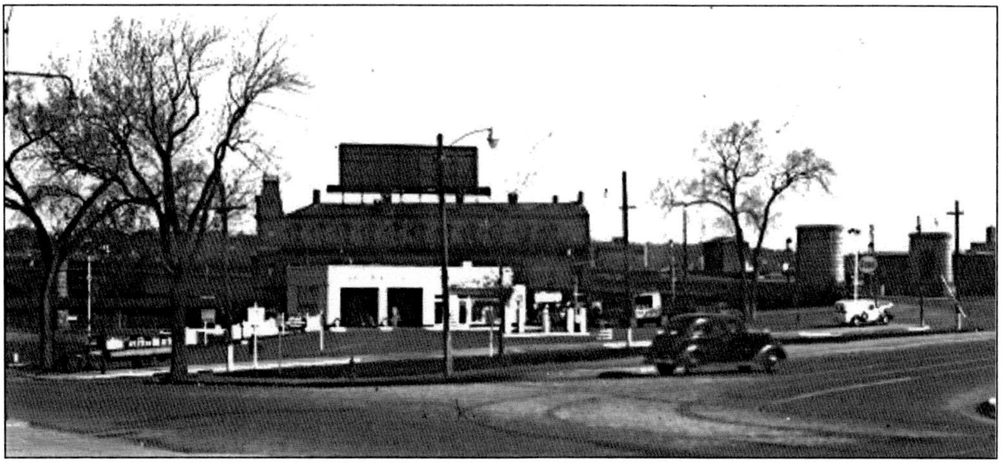

Esso operated a gas station on this site beside the Washington Bridge until the Rte. 195 expressway went through. Previous to Esso, the old Lyric Theater was on this site, a block east of Watchemoket Square.

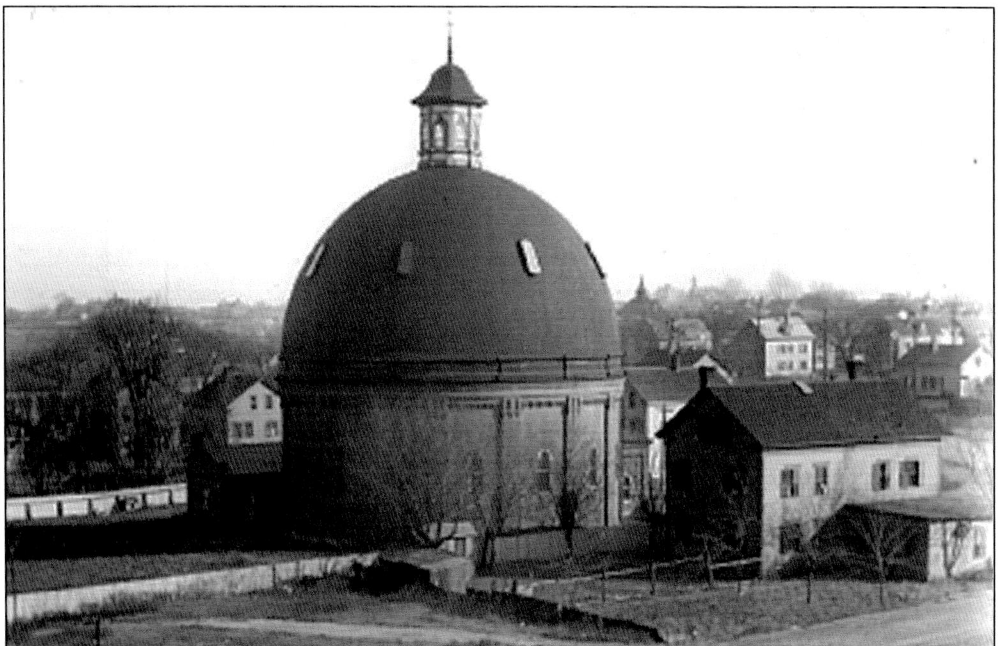

The Providence Gas Company used the Gasometer for gas storage at the foot of Fort Hill. The structure was destroyed during the 1938 hurricane.

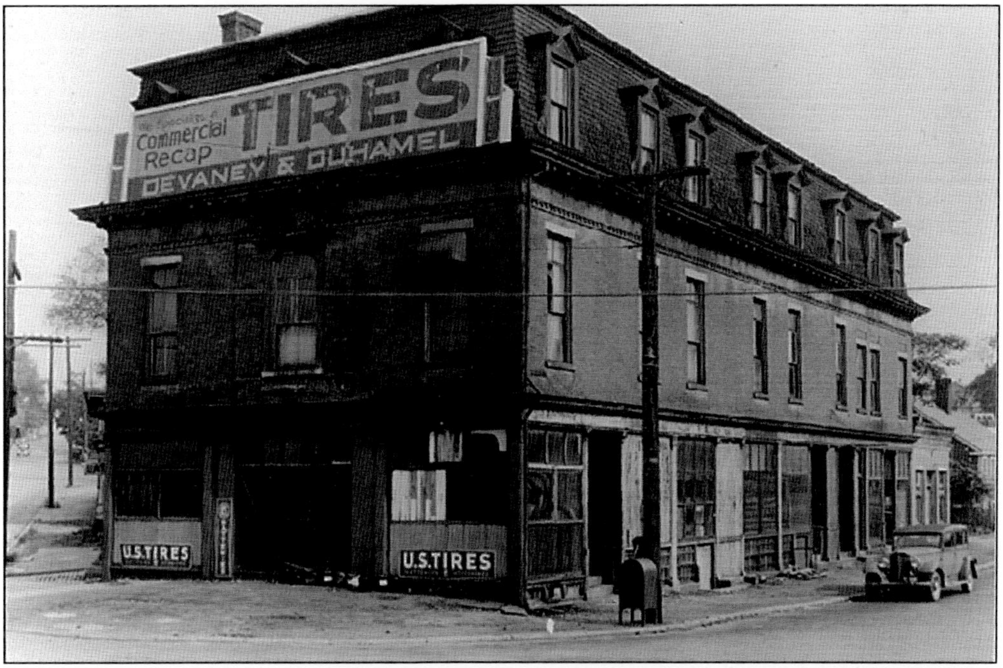

The Ingraham Building was built in 1870 by John Ingraham, a prominent businessman in town. It faced the 1885 Washington Bridge between Taunton and Warren Avenues. There was a large staircase to a grand hall on the second floor. A horse once climbed the stairs for a wild west show. Town meetings were held here just before the "new" town hall was built.

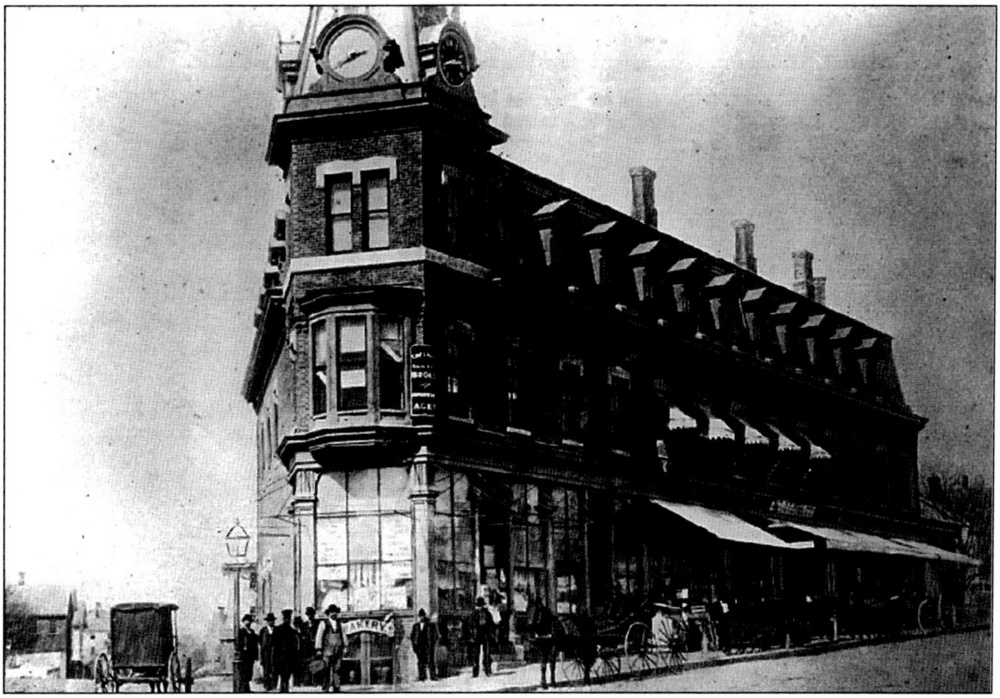

In 1875 another businessman, Thomas Ray, built our only "skyscraper," on Taunton Avenue and Valley Street. The tower clock was a special attraction.

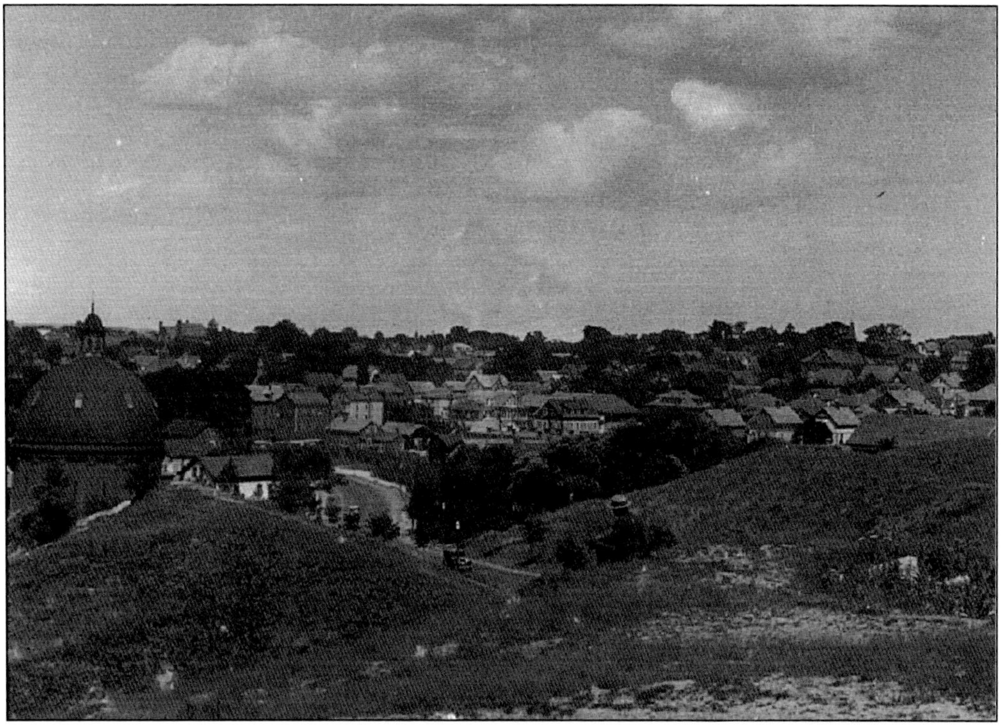

Fort Hill on the shore of the Seekonk River is the highest point in Watchemoket. This view is looking northeast with the Gasometer at the left.

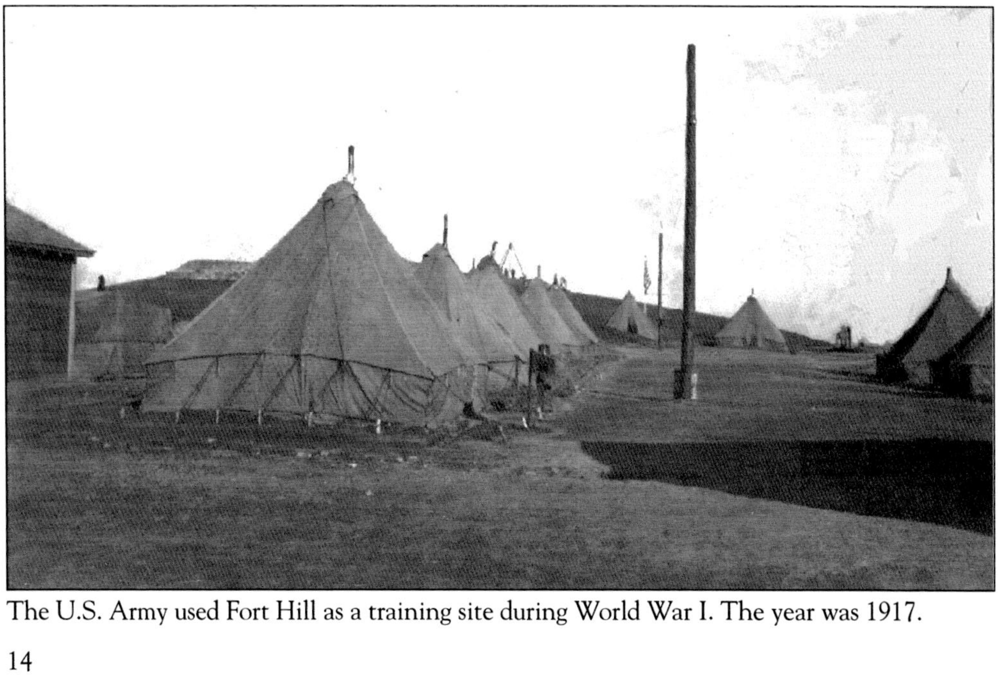

The U.S. Army used Fort Hill as a training site during World War I. The year was 1917.

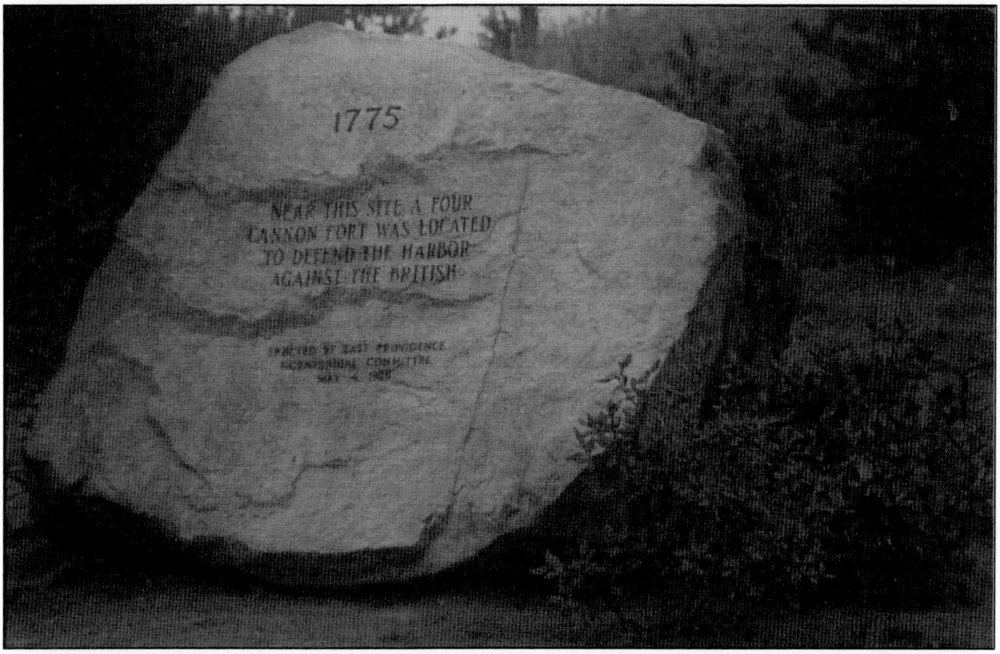

In 1775 four cannons were erected on Fort Hill facing south toward Newport, where the British were located. A memorial was erected during the American Bicentennial of 1976 on the corner of Mercer Street and the Veteran's Memorial Parkway to mark the site.

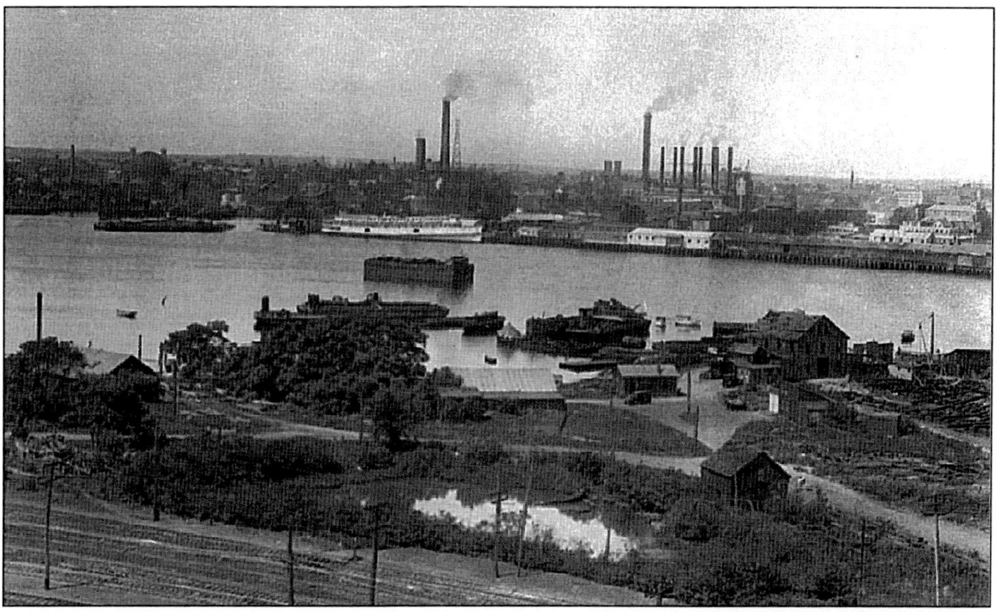

This view from Fort Hill is looking west to Providence. In early evenings people gathered here to watch the sunset and the New York boat start its passage from Providence into the night.

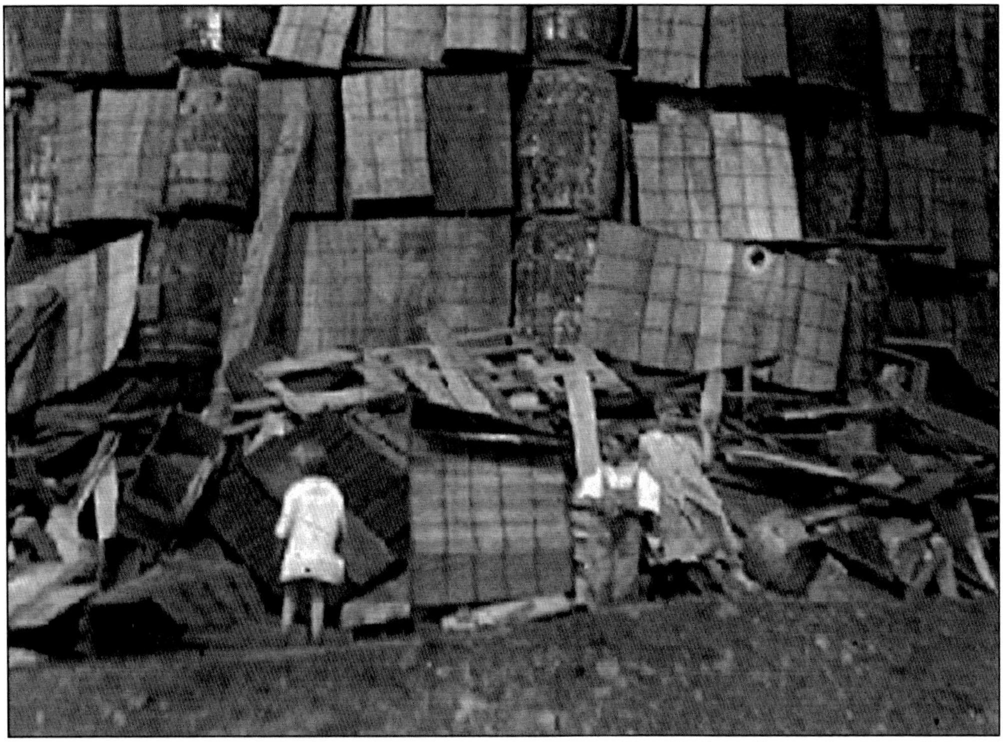

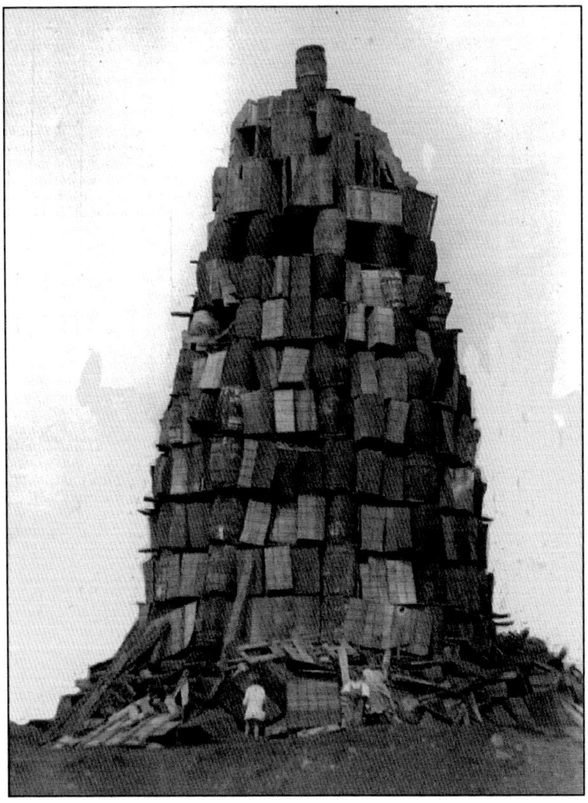

Two little girls are fascinated by the debris which is piled up to form the bonfire in the lower photo in 1918. The fire pile was built on top of Fort Hill every Fourth of July. The bonfires were eventually stopped, for flying embers were becoming hazardous to the surrounding neighborhood.

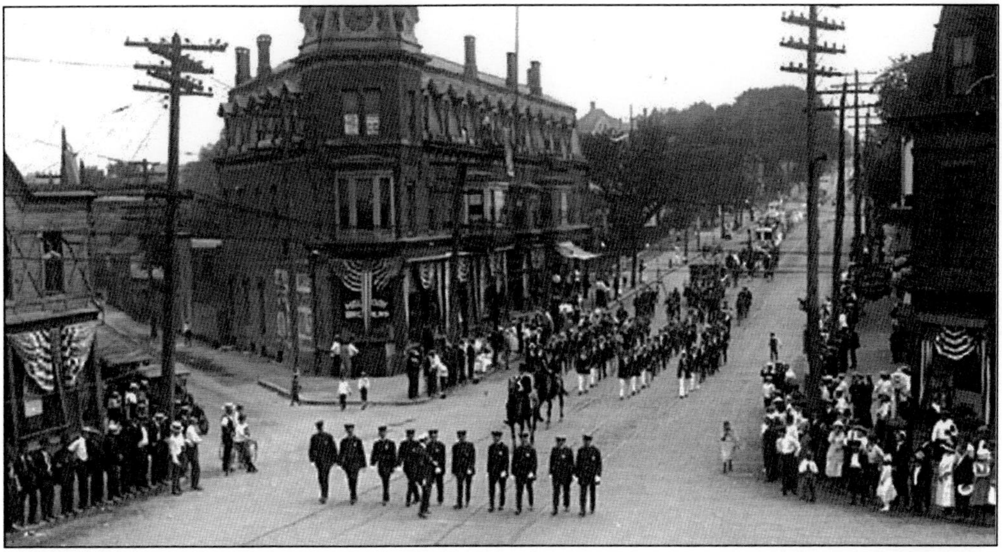

This photograph of the 1921 Fourth of July Parade shows parade units marching down Taunton Avenue. They would turn here in Watchemoket Square and parade east up Warren Avenue.

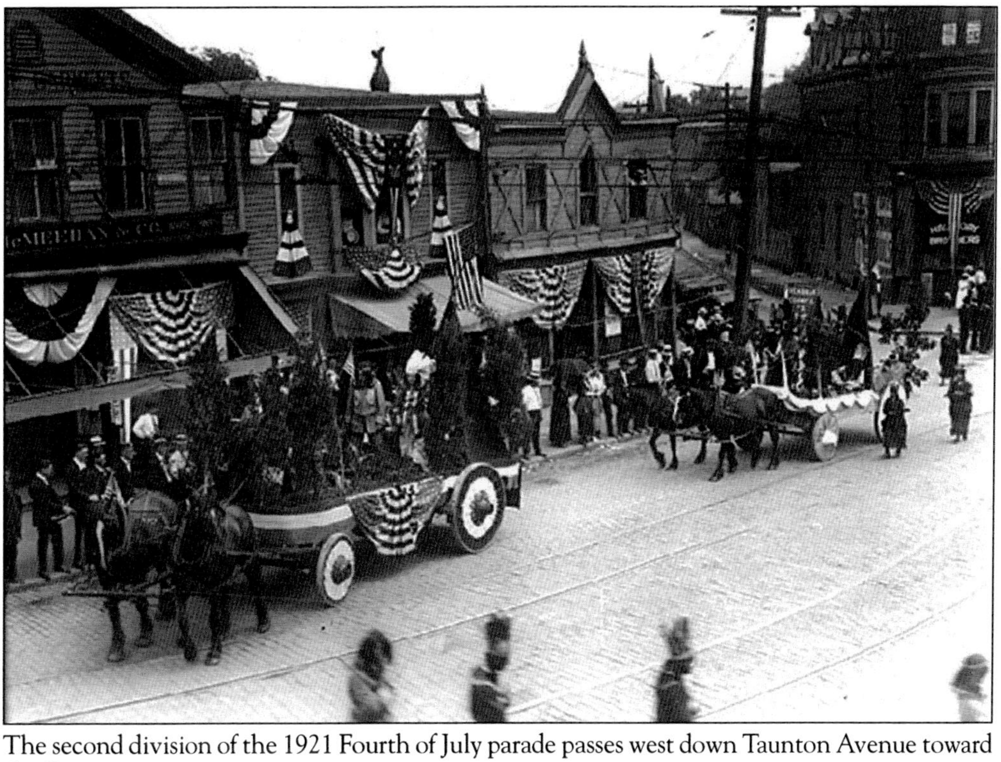

The second division of the 1921 Fourth of July parade passes west down Taunton Avenue toward the Square.

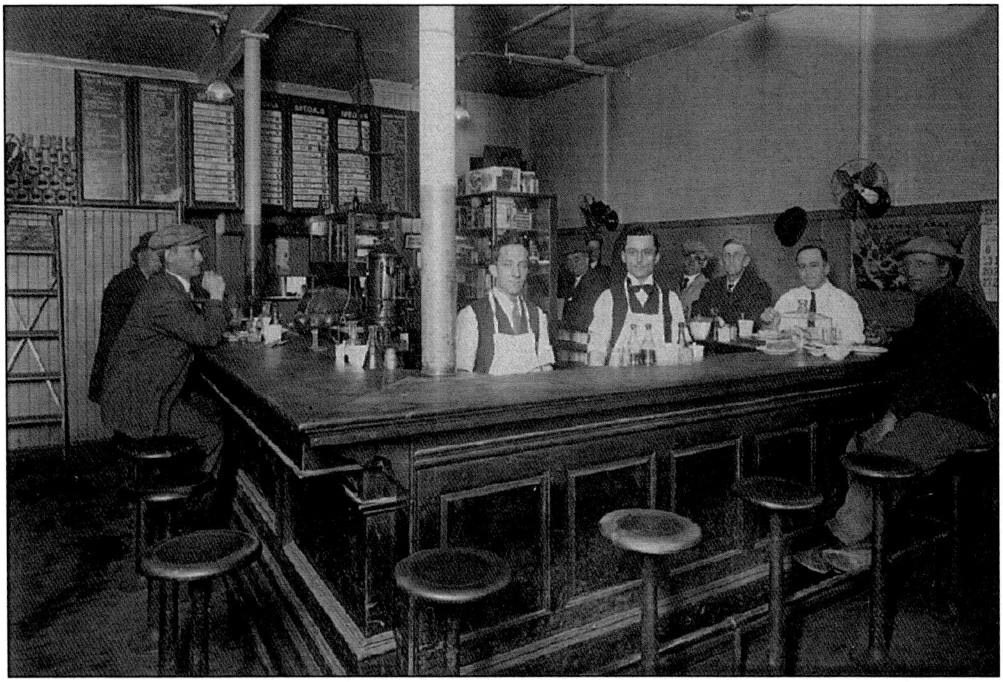

Jacques Lunch started out c. 1885 as Sullivan's Bar. In the early 1920s it became known as Jacques Lunch. Hughes and Leo Jacques are manning the counter in the photograph. Peter Rougas opened here as the Washington Lunch and continued until 1931, the year after the new bridge was built.

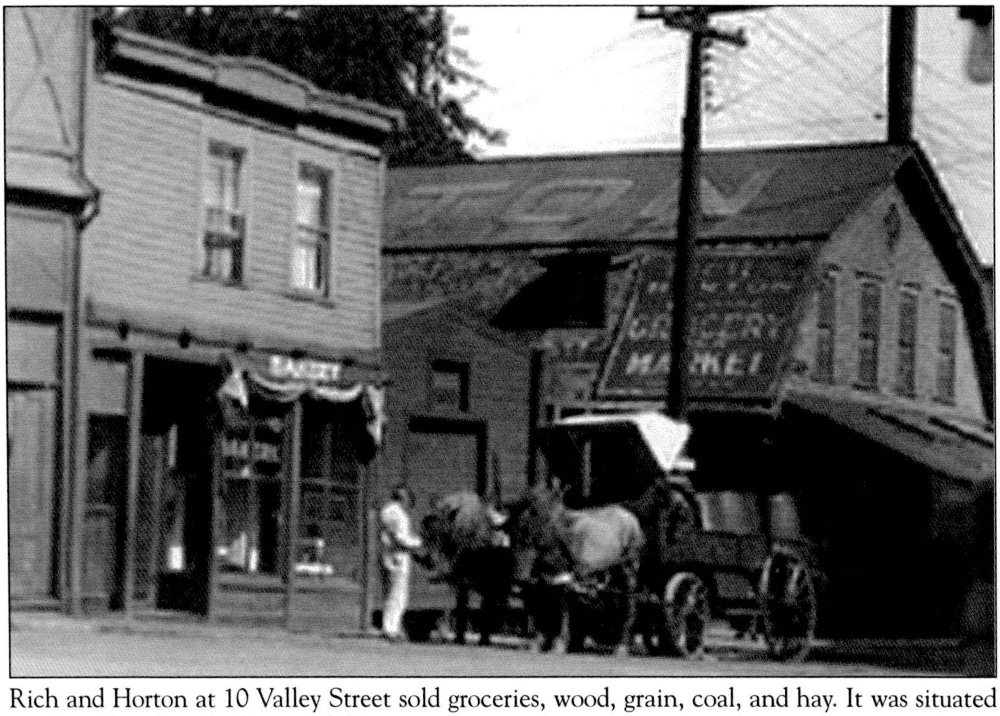

Rich and Horton at 10 Valley Street sold groceries, wood, grain, coal, and hay. It was situated on the railroad tracks for easy delivery.

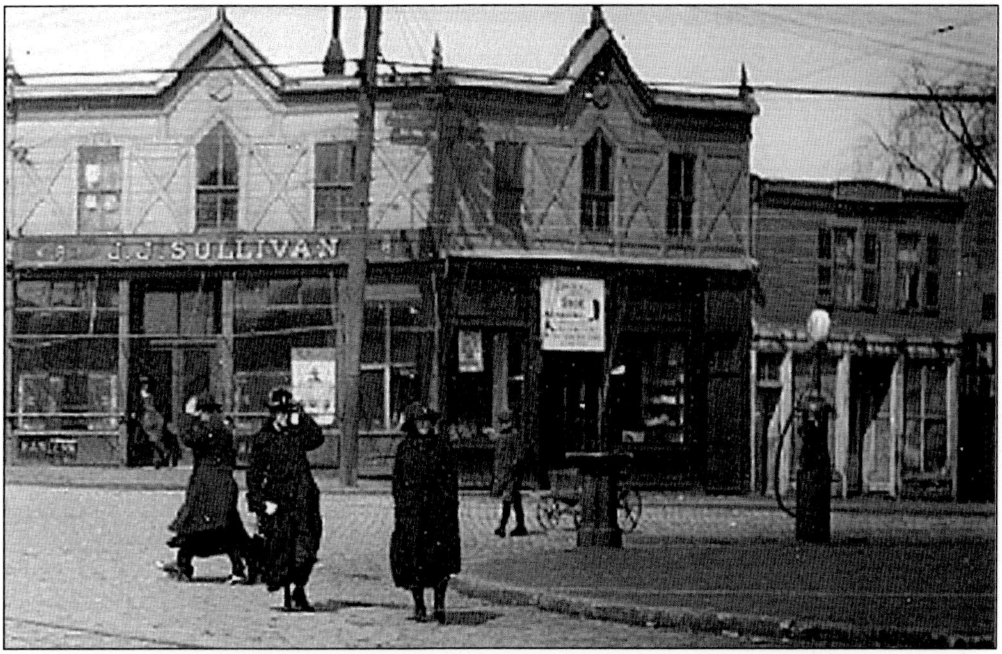

Two ladies stroll by the horse trough and the gas pump at the junction of Taunton and Warren Avenues in about 1910.

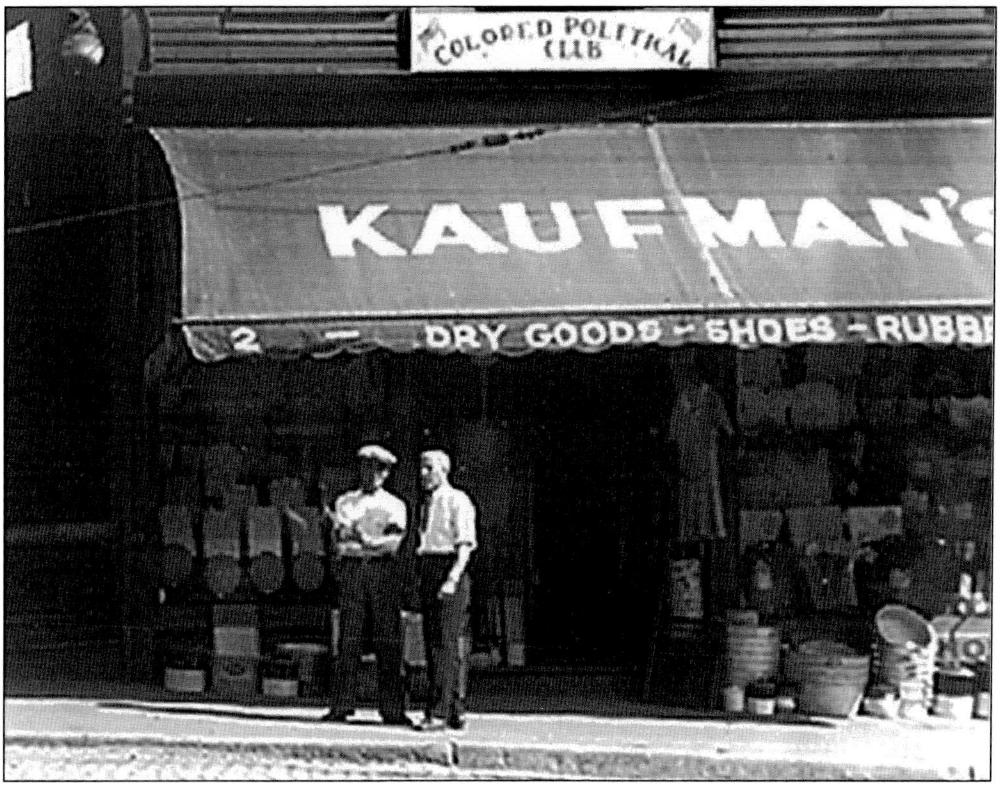

Kaufman's Dry Goods was located on Warren Avenue.

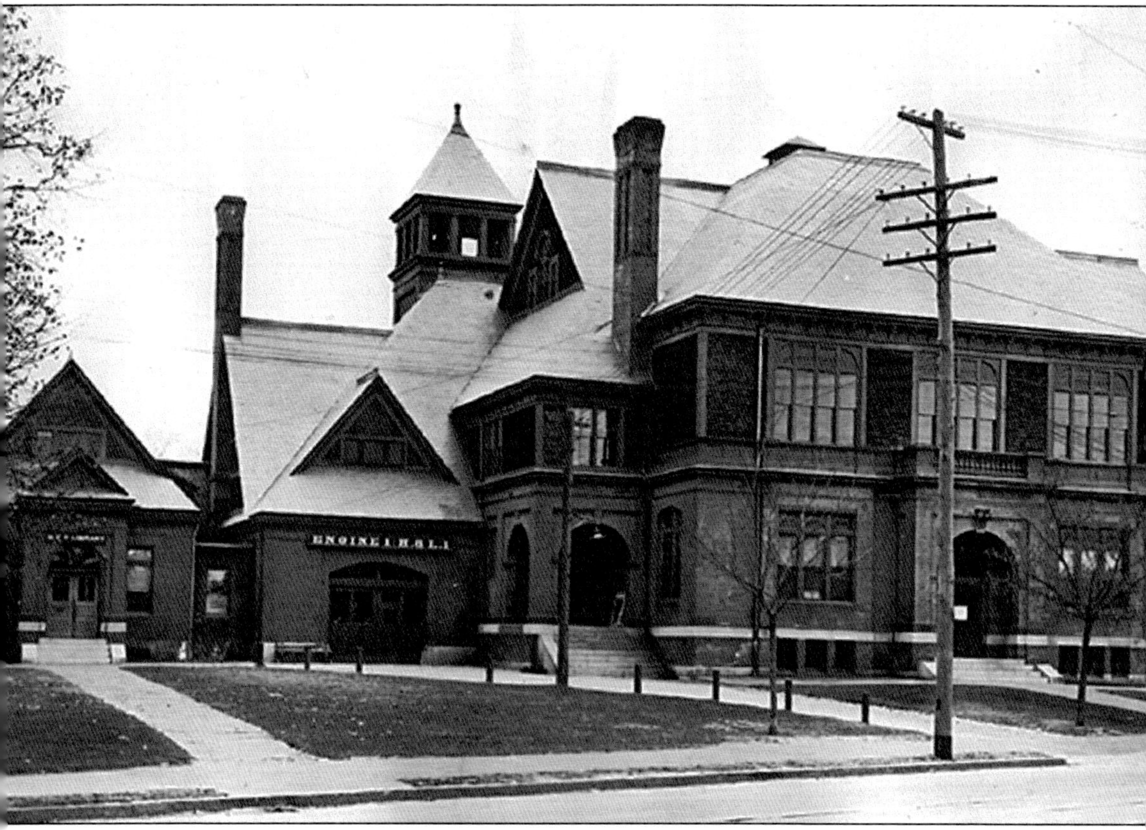

With the Watchemoket part of town becoming an important business and commercial area, it was decided to move the center of government from town hall in the Rumford area to a more central location on Taunton Avenue. The building, built in 1888–89, was designed by architect William Walker & Son. It housed the Town Council Chamber, which also served as a movie theater on Saturdays for many years. In addition to town offices there was a fire station to the left and a small ell which at one time served as a library and later as the police station. Balls and high school graduations were held in the council chambers, town meetings were held in the chambers until the early 1950s. In 1962 it became the city hall after East Providence received its city charter. The building burned in 1976 and was replaced by a modern structure on the same site.

The Civil War Memorial in front of the town hall was dedicated on July 4, 1919. The 8-foot statue stands on a 46-ton boulder from Kent Heights. Two hundred seventy-six soldiers and sailors of Bucklin Post #20 who fought during the Civil War are listed. Theo Alice (Ruggles) Kitson was the sculptor and the Gorham Company of Providence cast the figure in bronze.

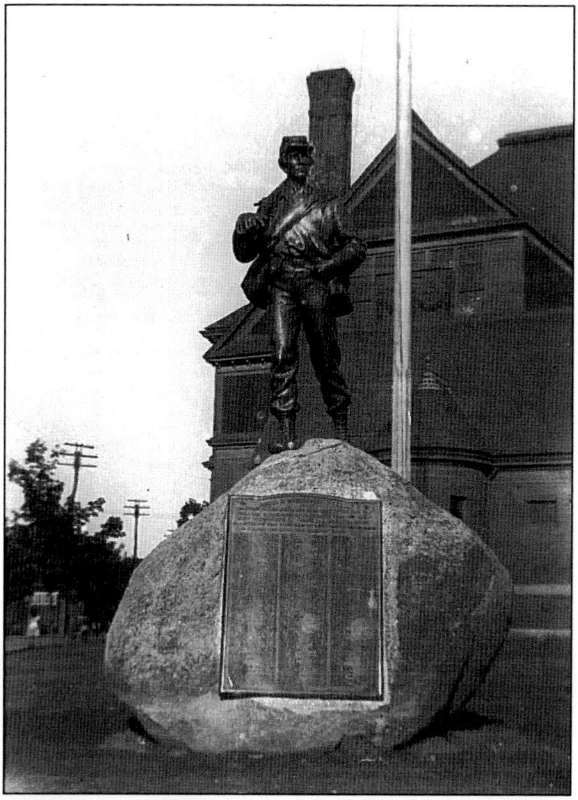

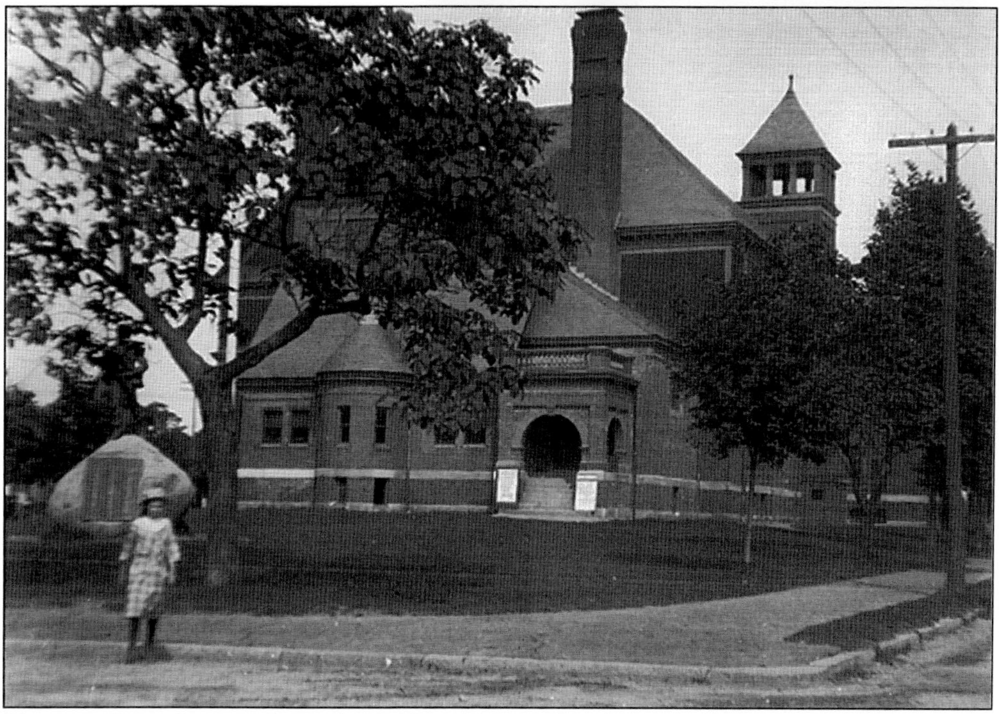

This view from the west shows the Soldiers Memorial and town hall in 1924.

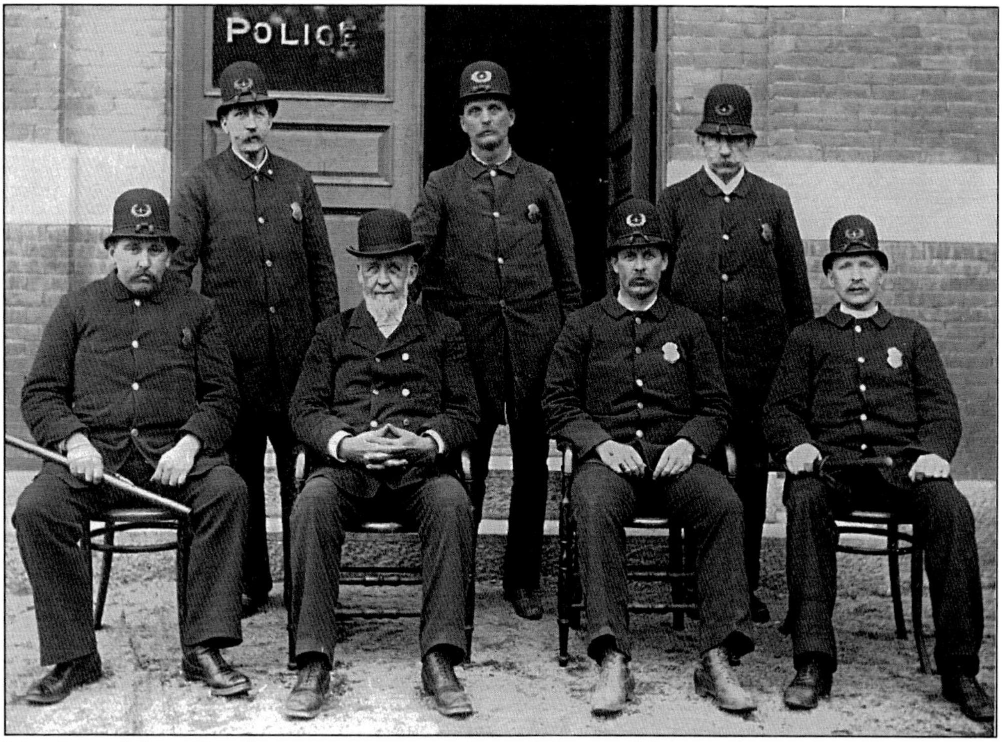

Members of the police department, organized in 1862, posed for a group picture in front of the town hall station c.1900. Chief Rufus Adams is in the derby; to his left is Everett Adams, who later became chief; and in the open doorway is Walter Taggert .

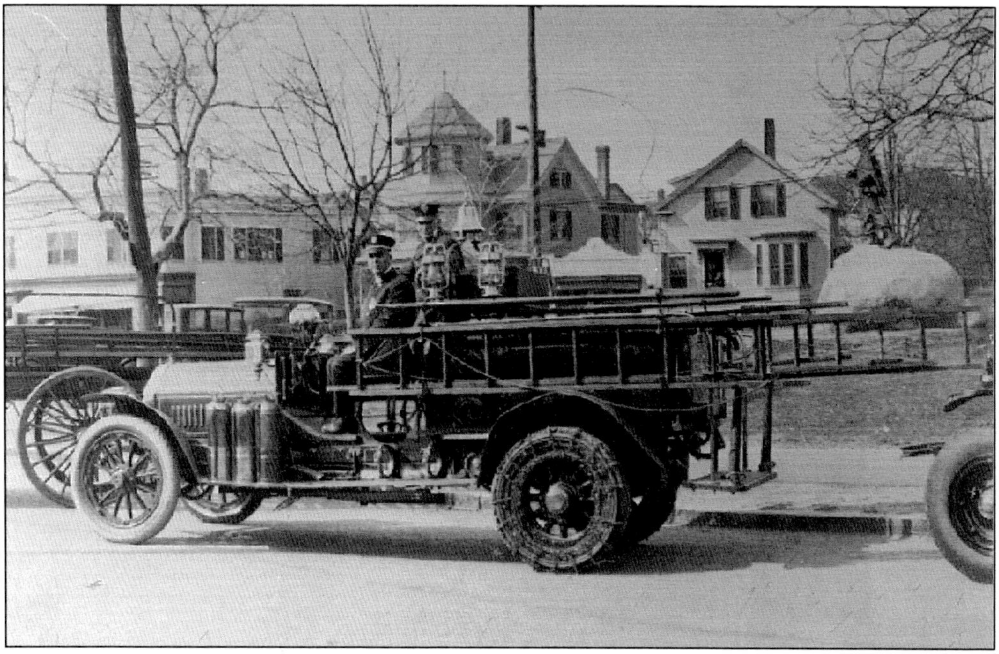

Captain Walter Reynolds and Fred Harris pose in a 1911 Alco firetruck c. 1914 on the west side of the town hall. The truck dates from 1911.

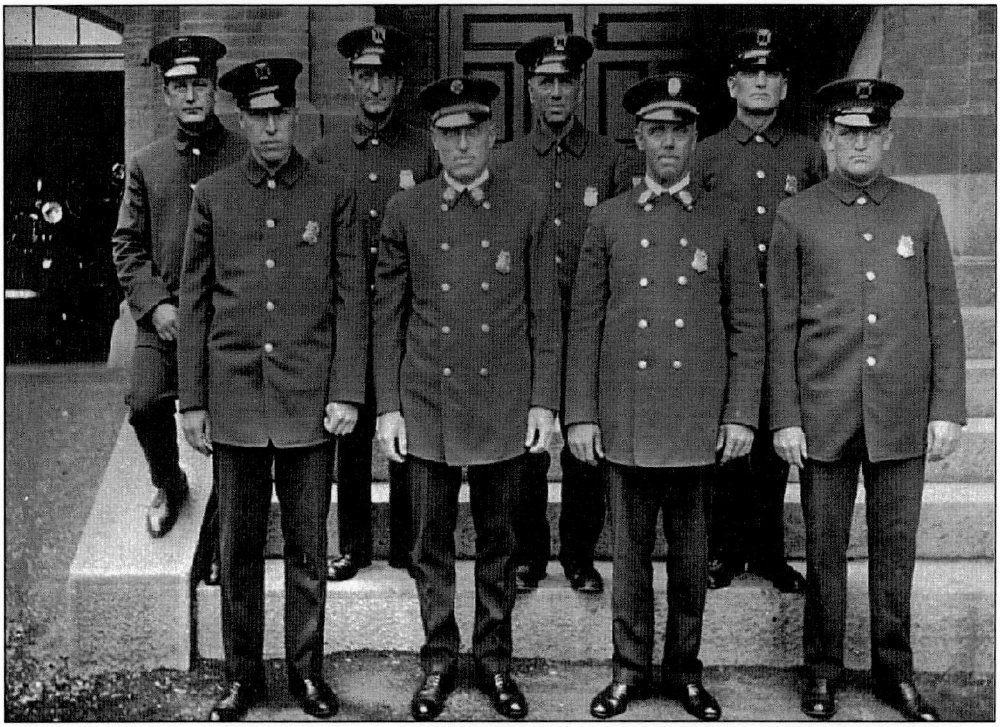

East Providence fire fighters in front of the town hall fire station c. 1926. From left to right are: (front row) Leonard Anderson, Chief Arthur Griswold, Captain Warren Reynolds, and Everett Bowden; (back row) Percy Hutson, Harry Grant, Charles Roderick, and Fred Harris.

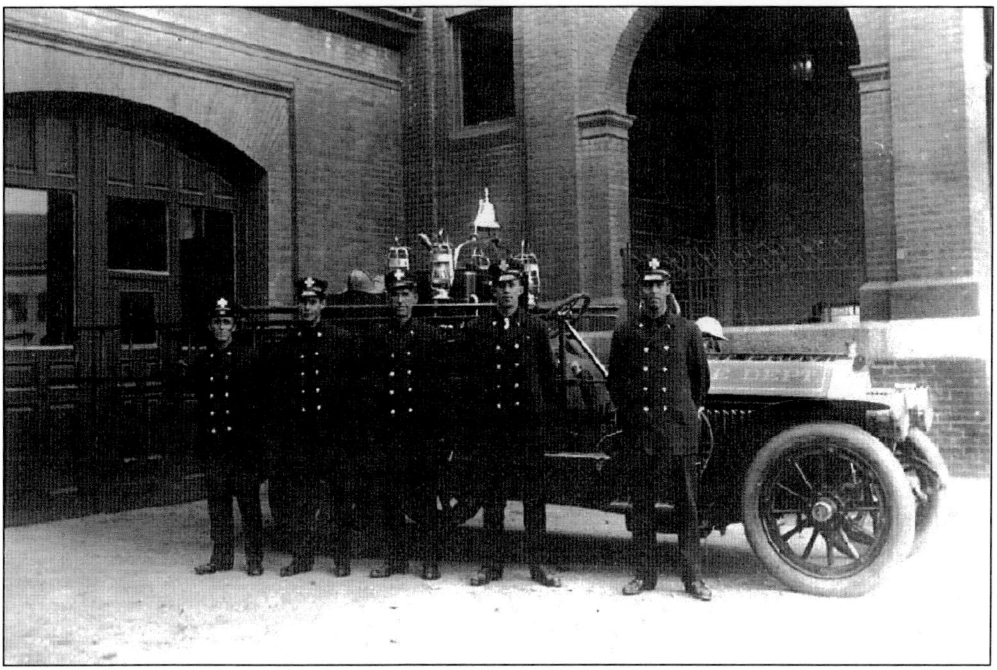

Pictured in front of the town hall fire station in 1914 are, from left to right, John Reynolds, Edward Feid, Frederick Provencher, Everett Brown, and Warren Reynolds.

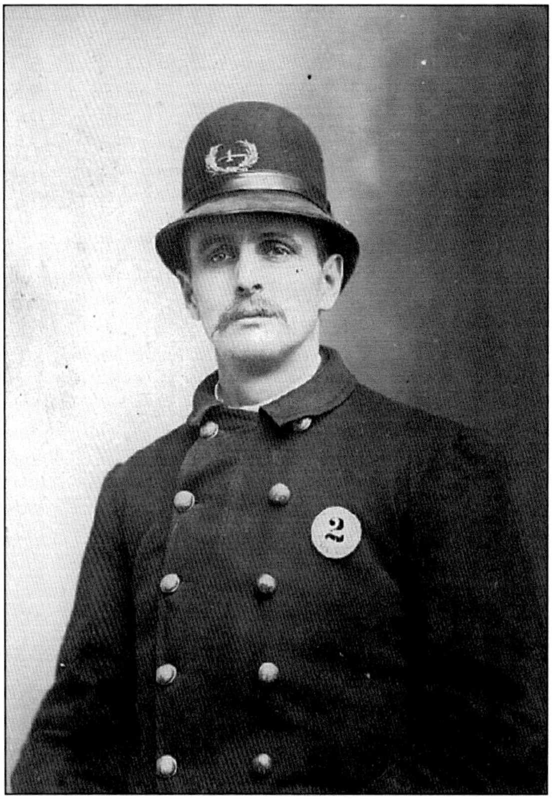

Policeman Walter Taggart served in the Watchemoket Square for forty-nine years. He directed traffic across the old wooden covered bridge when he started in 1883. The new Washington Bridge was built in 1885 and the "new" Washington Bridge was built in 1930–31 before he retired. He also patrolled on foot along the waterfront south to the Wilkesbarre Pier from 6 pm to 5 am each night.

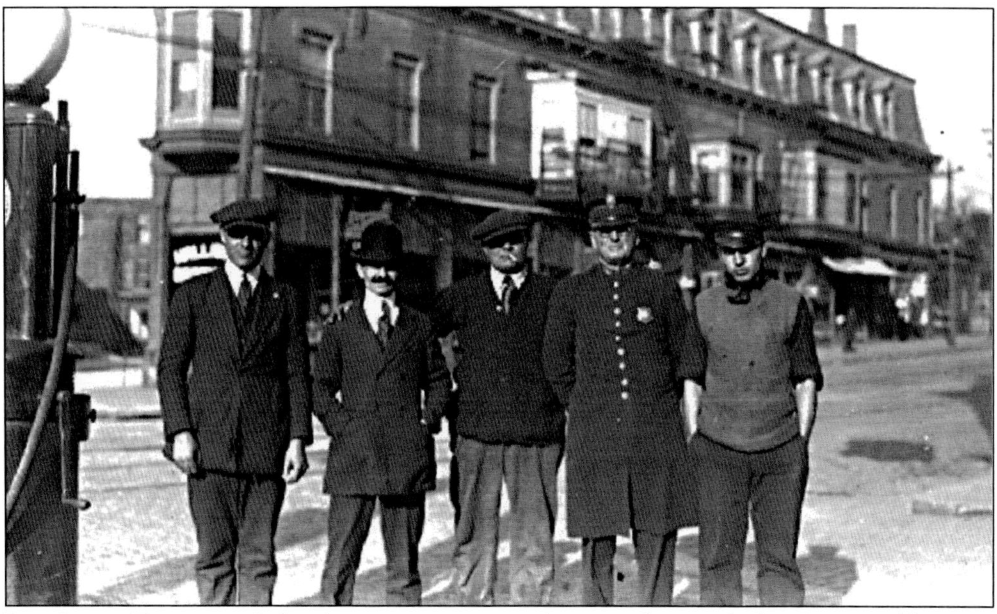

Patrolman Taggert and local citizens are standing in front of the Ray Building on Taunton Avenue.

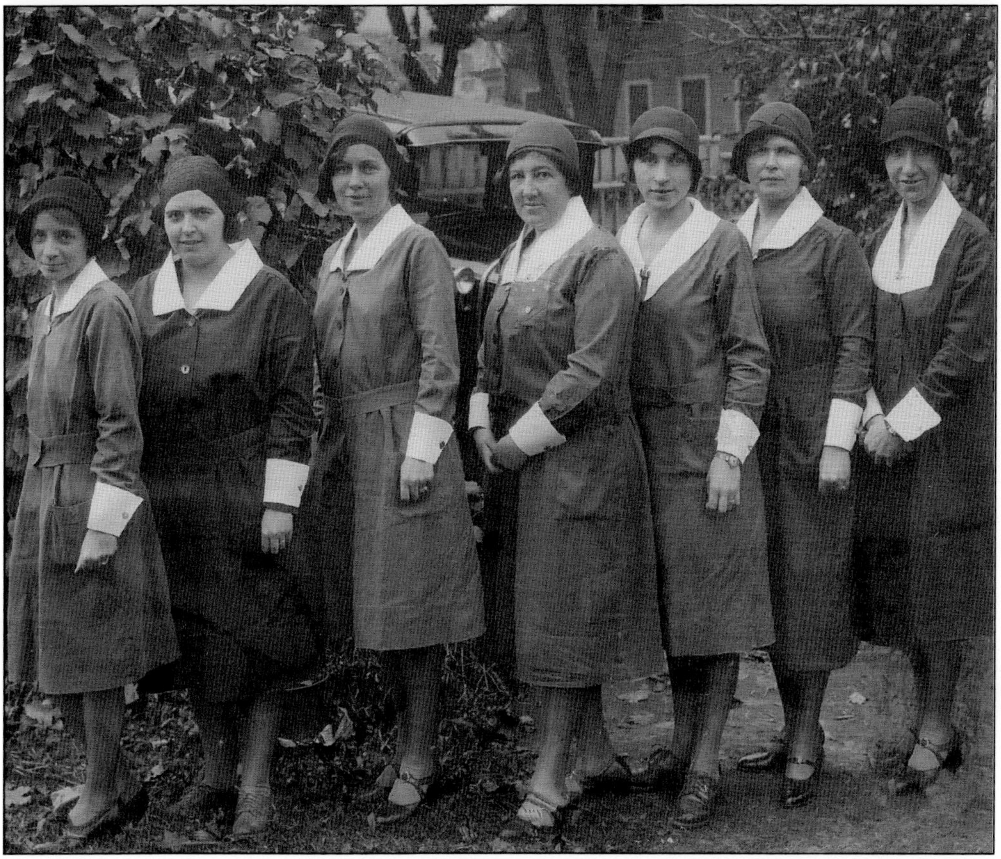

The Visiting Nurses were organized in 1910 and their office was located for many years in the old Weaver House on Grove Avenue. Pictured from left to right are Elsie Butler, Florence Blake, Ebba James, Anna McGuire, Jean Ross, Violet Deconti, and Effie Dalton, who was the first school nurse.

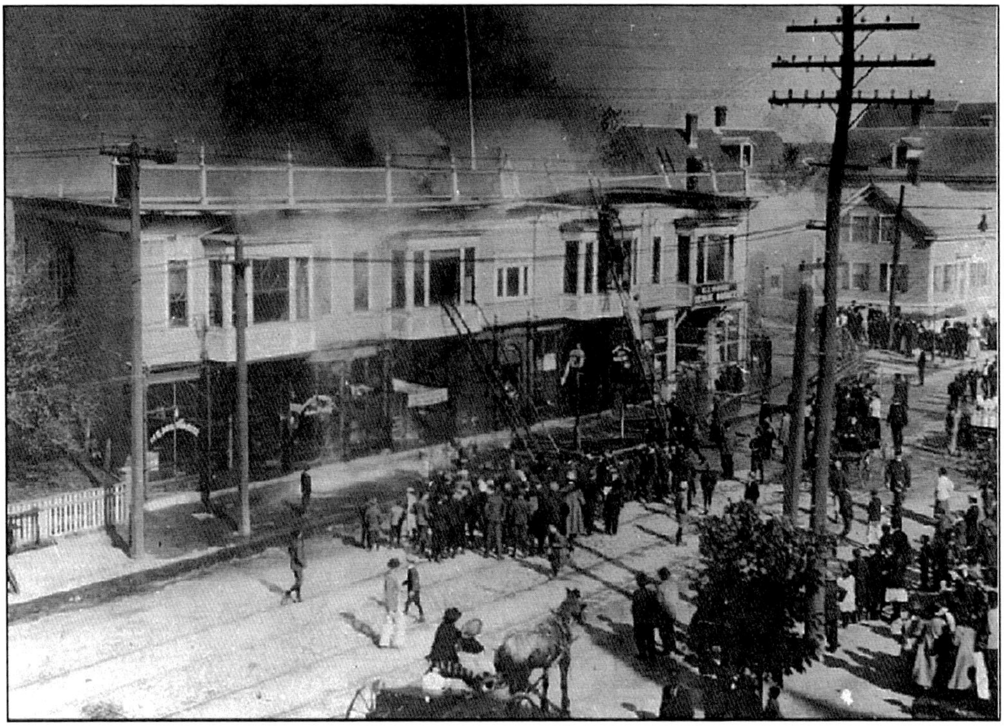

Our fire team fighting a fire in a block of stores at the corner of Taunton Avenue and James Street across from the fire station and town hall.

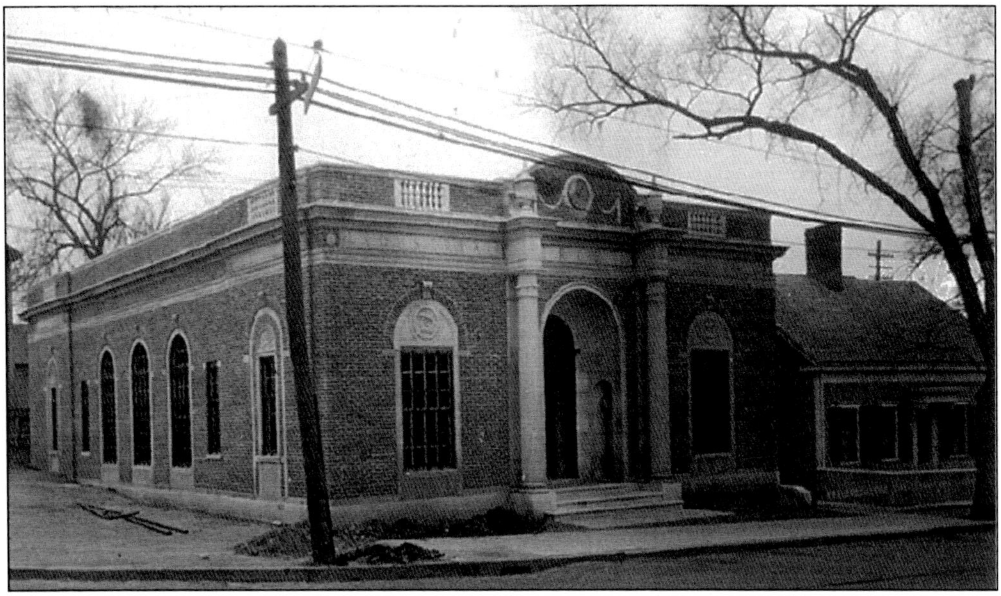

One of the first banks in Watchemoket was the Industrial Trust Bank on Warren Avenue on the right as one drove off the Washington Bridge into East Providence. In 1926 it was a necessary component in a busy business district.

By the late 1920s movies were so popular that the Saturday movies had outgrown the Town Hall Council Chamber. The Hollywood Theatre was built across from the town hall on Taunton Avenue and is seen here in 1942.

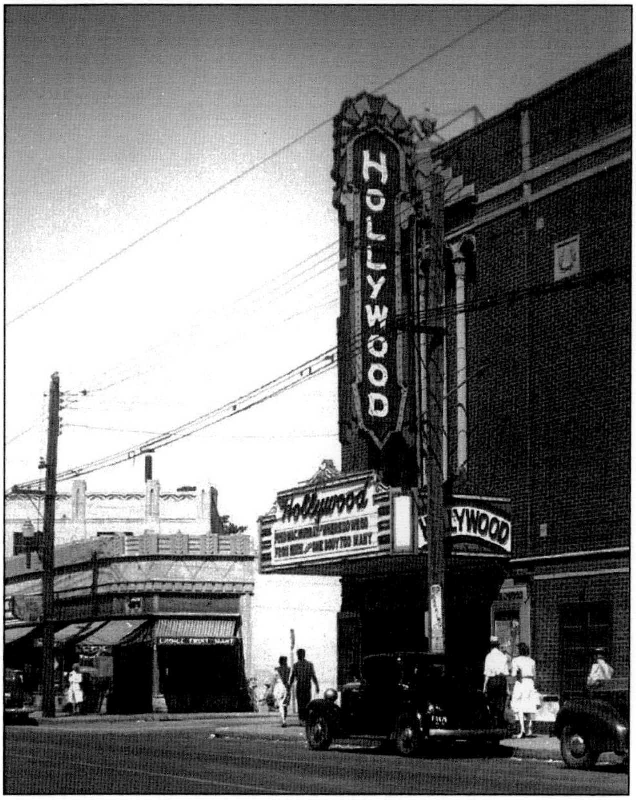

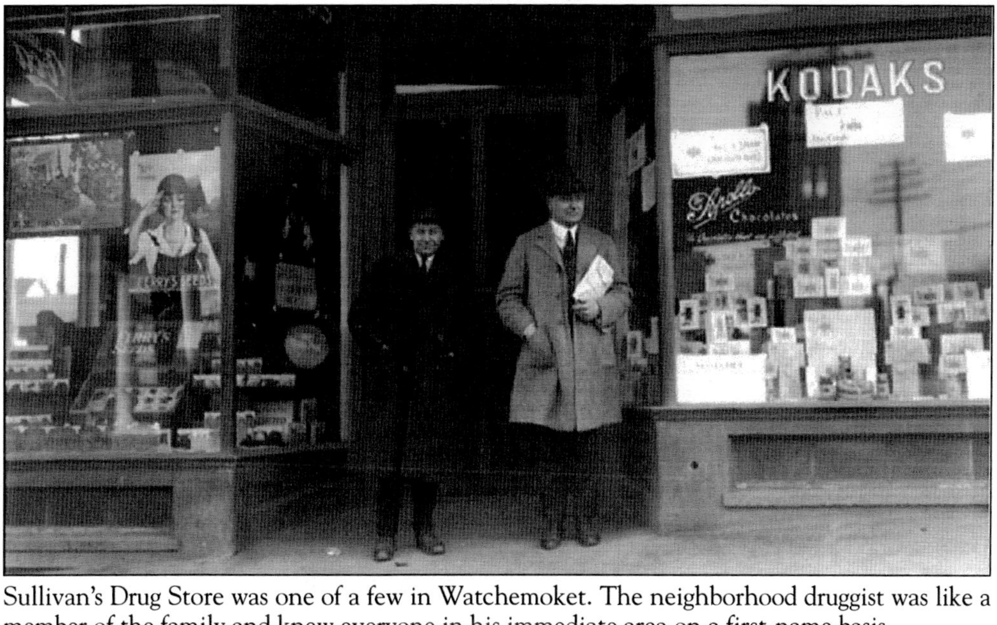

Sullivan's Drug Store was one of a few in Watchemoket. The neighborhood druggist was like a member of the family and knew everyone in his immediate area on a first-name basis.

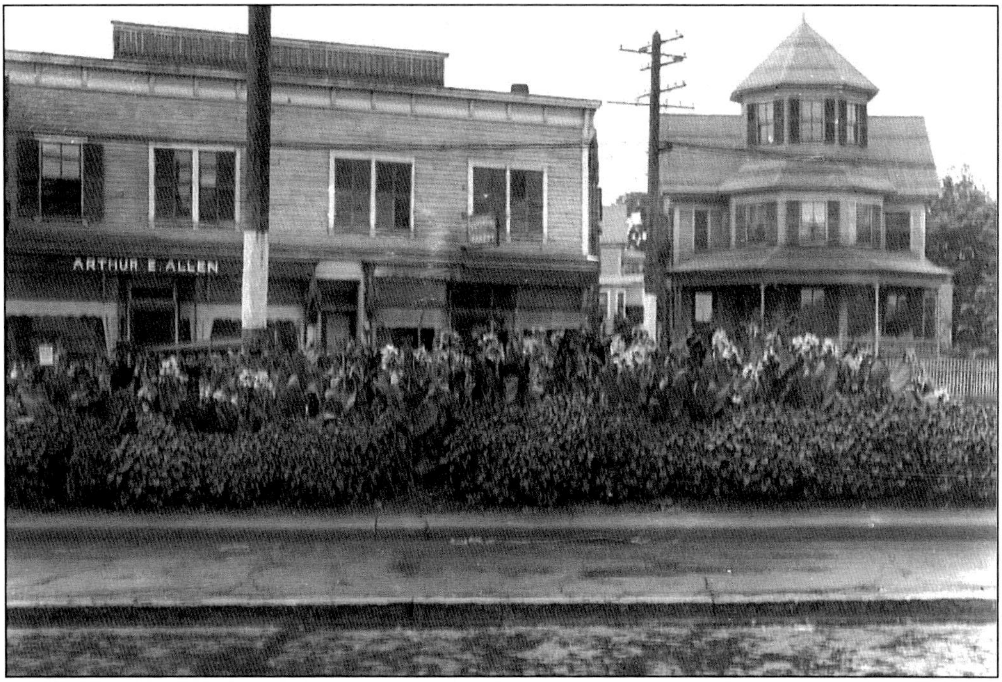

On Taunton Avenue across from the west side of the town hall was Allen's Drug Store. Medicines were not the only goods dispensed here. It was the most popular place to get a healthy dose of the best coffee ice cream in town. Little glass-topped tables on a black-and-white tiled floor beckoned when anyone stopped in to buy a newspaper.

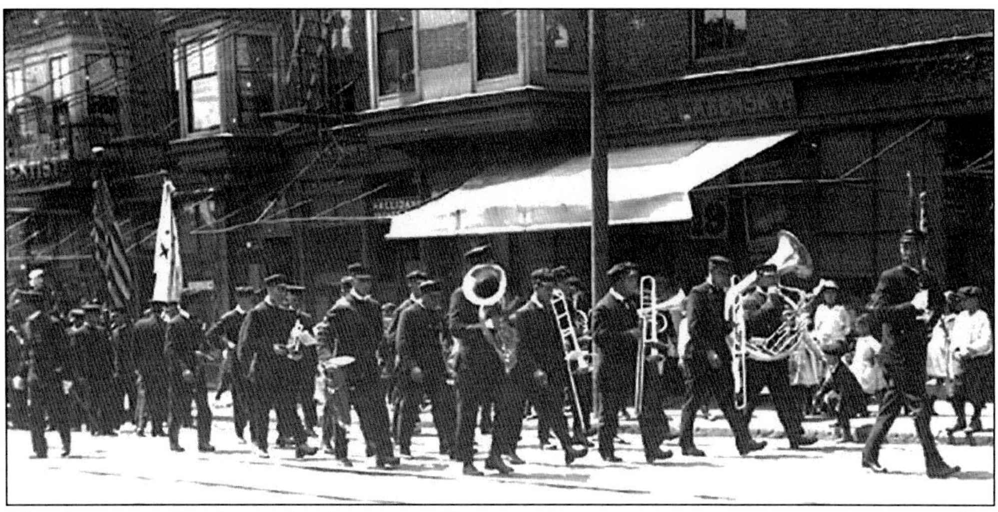

The American Band steps lively east on Taunton Avenue on its way to a reviewing stand in front of the town hall.

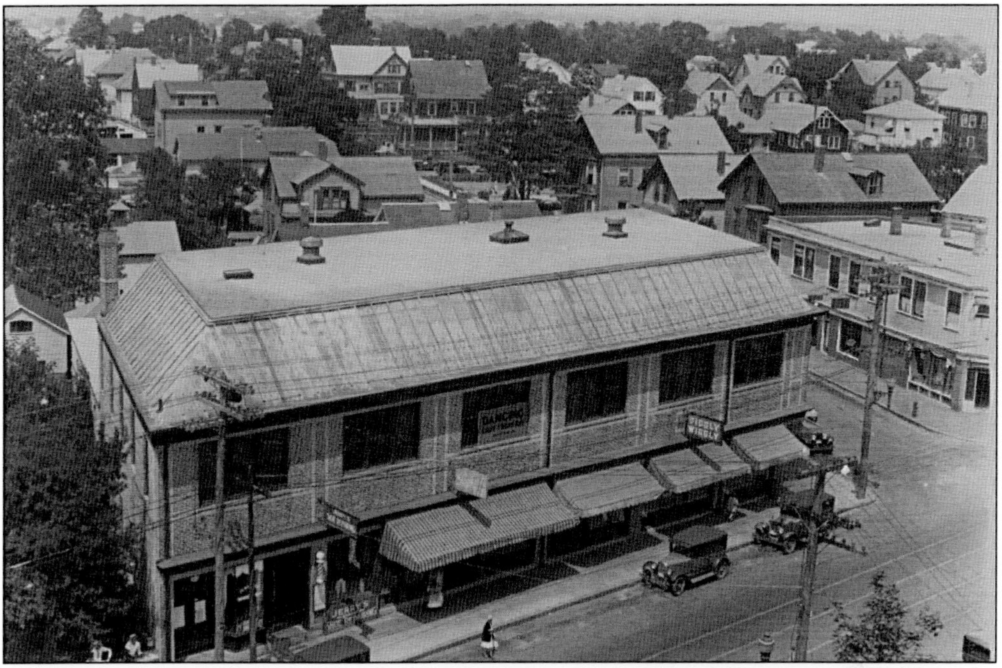

The Piggly Wiggly Market in 1934 was the first "self-serve" market. It was soon followed by the A&P and the First National, all on Taunton Avenue.

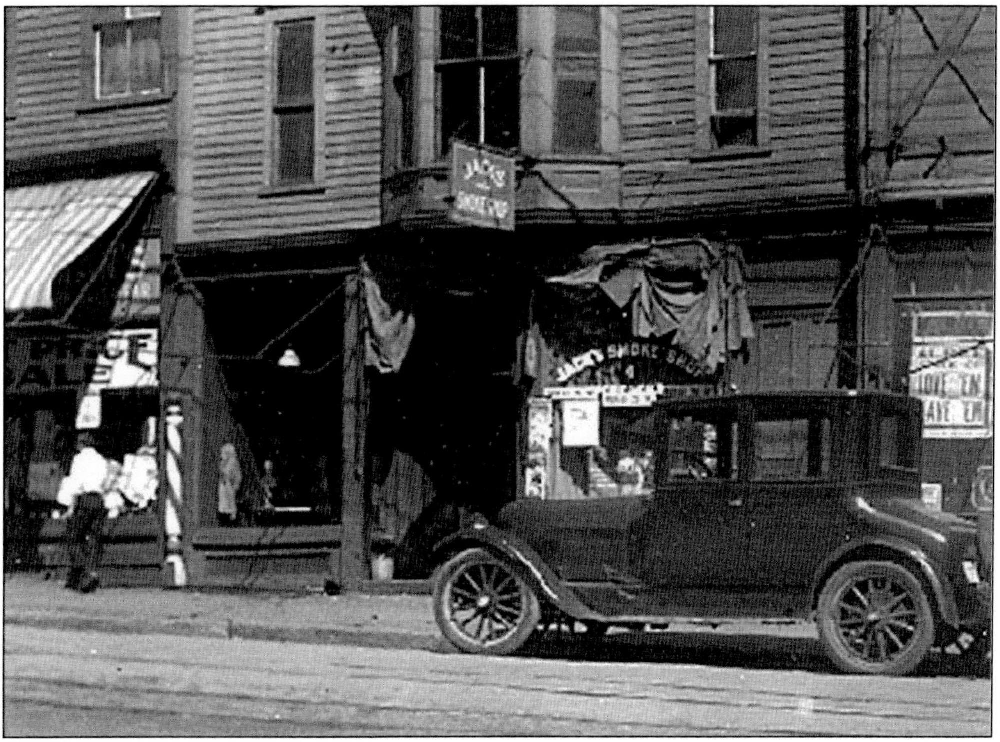

Jack's Smoke Shop was located at 6 Taunton Avenue in the Square.

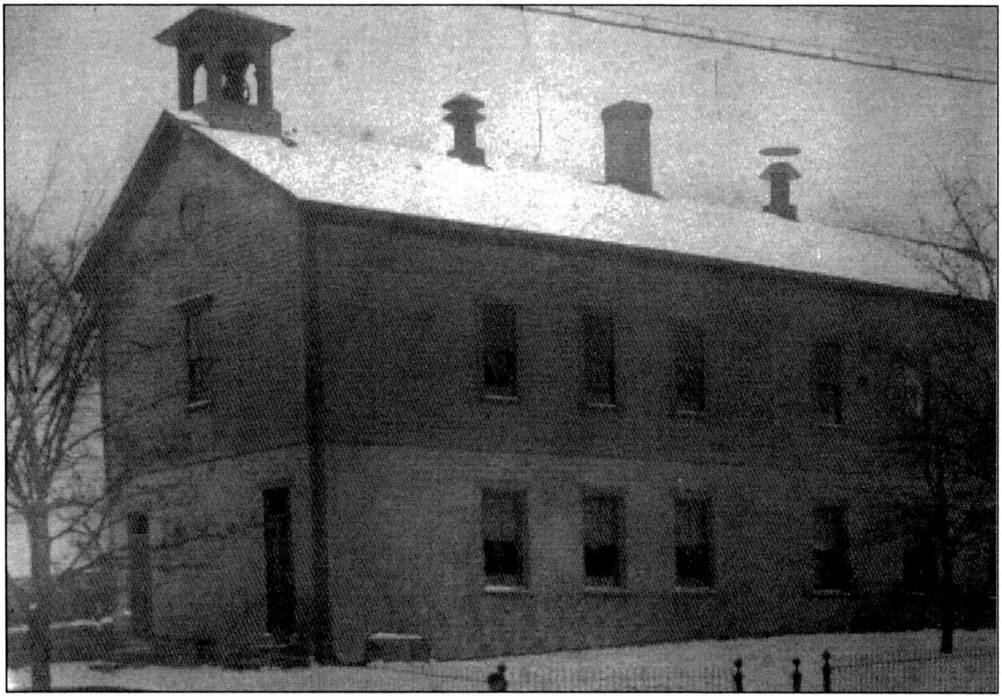

When East Providence separated from Massachusetts in 1862, the Potter Street School was inherited from the Town of Seekonk. At first a one-room school, it was soon enlarged to contain four school rooms. The town was growing. It was located at the corner of School and Potter Streets and was razed to make way for the Rte. 195 expressway.

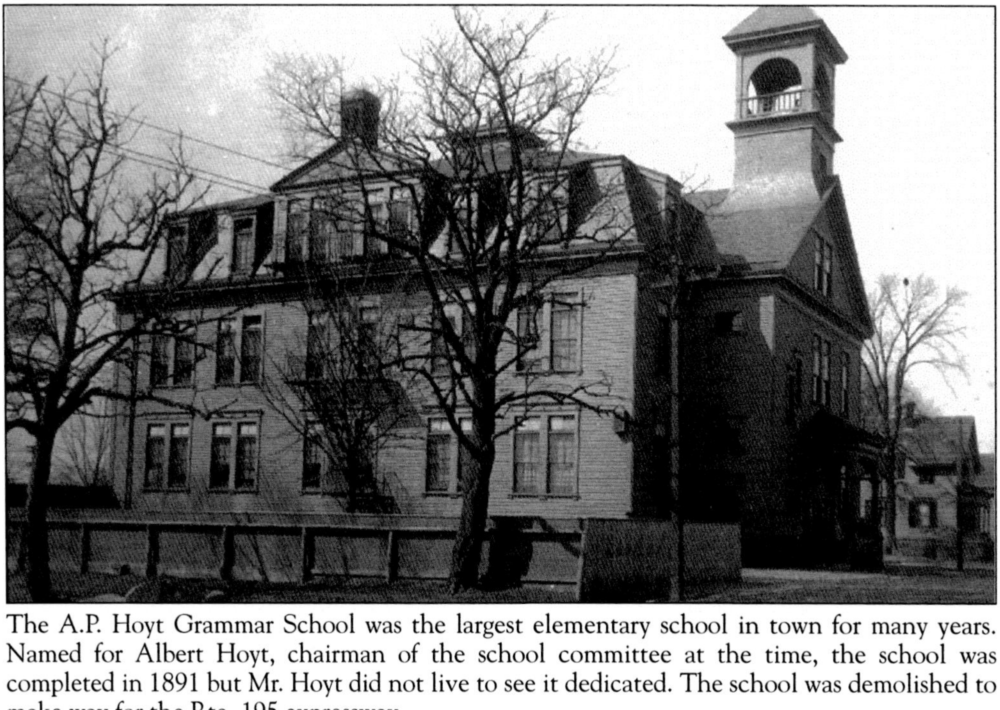

The A.P. Hoyt Grammar School was the largest elementary school in town for many years. Named for Albert Hoyt, chairman of the school committee at the time, the school was completed in 1891 but Mr. Hoyt did not live to see it dedicated. The school was demolished to make way for the Rte. 195 expressway.

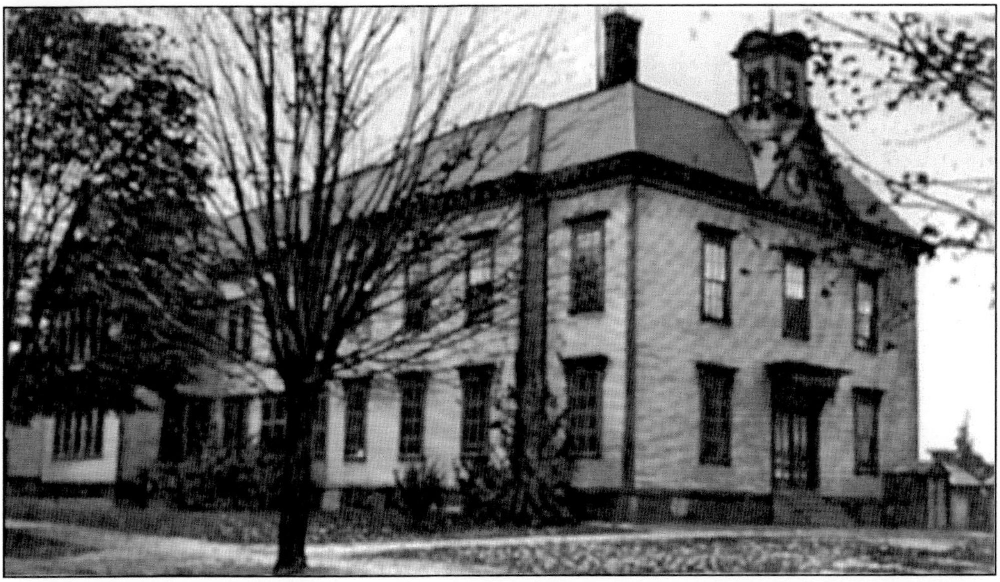

The East Providence High School, built in 1875 on Grove Avenue, was originally named Grove Avenue Elementary. In 1884 a high school was established on the first floor. Later, as more students enrolled, the elementary grades moved to the new Hoyt School and Grove Avenue was enlarged by a two-floor addition. When the new high school was built in 1910, the school returned to housing the elementary grades.

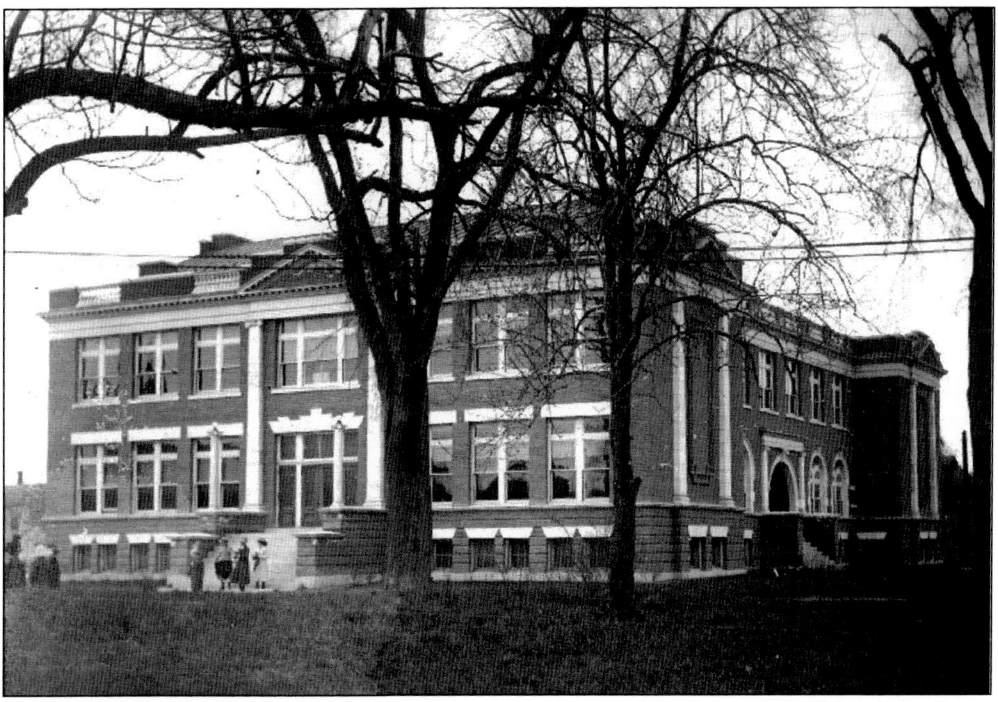

By 1910 the town had grown, the population increased, and a new larger high school was needed. The new high school was completed by 1912. It had two floors and before fourteen years had passed a third floor had to be added. It is now used for senior citizen apartments.

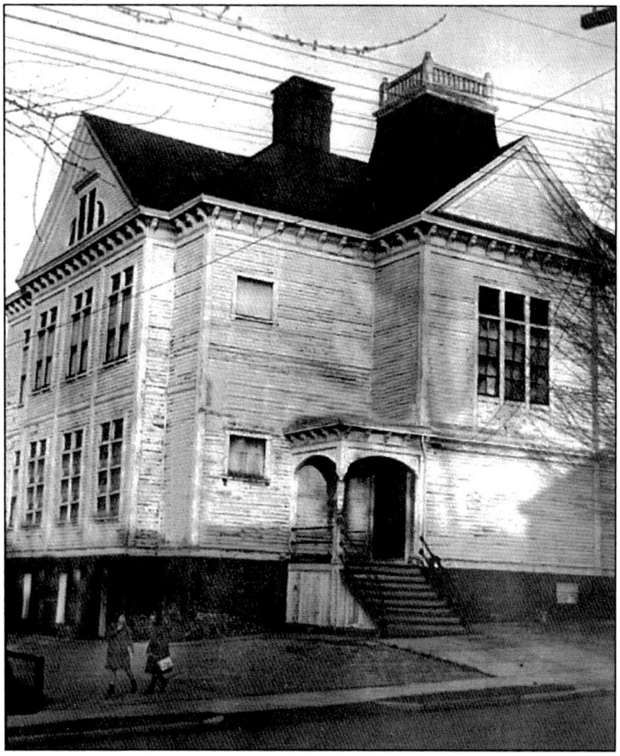

Originally known as the Mauran Avenue School, and later as the Hazard School, this building was erected at the corner of Mauran Avenue and Sixth Street in 1884. Mauran Avenue had been named for Joshua Mauran, another local businessman of repute. The site is now a playground.

The first area library was located in Lyceum Hall in lower Watchemoket. Later it moved to the town hall on Taunton Avenue. In 1938 this new Weaver Library opened on Grove Avenue. The land and building funds were provided under the will of Susan Anthony and named in honor of her mother, Susan Weaver, who was one of the founders of the Watchemoket Free Library.

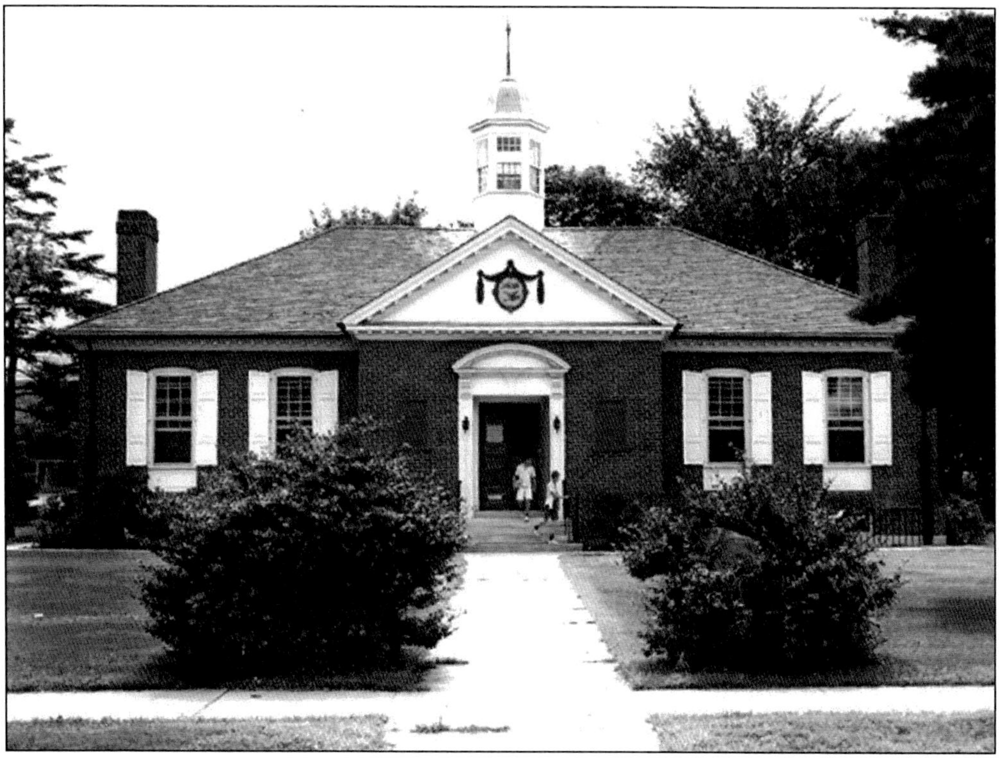

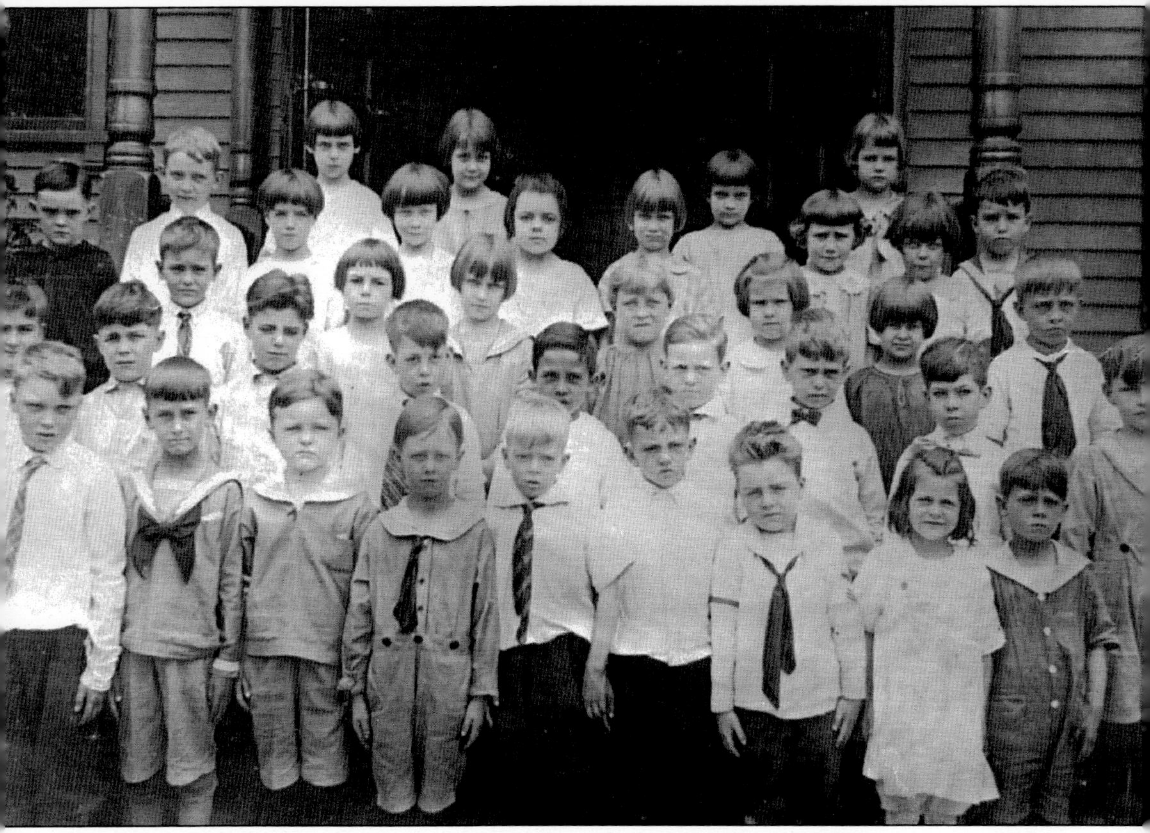

The James Street School was built in 1882. The fifth grade posed on the front steps in 1924. From left to right are: (front row) William Endicott, unidentified, Gordon McIntosh, Bertram Rodman, unidentified, unidentified, Francis McCarthy, Florence Ryan, and unidentified; (second row) unidentified, unidentified, Benjamin Harris, Fred Suggett, unidentified, unidentified, Henry Springer, Augustus Grocer, and Arthur Fishlock; (third row) Lloyd Johnson, Dorothy Baldwin, Evelyn Stark, Constance Fitzgerald, Frances Peck, Jean Hutson, and Louis Arnold; (fourth row) Earl Scott, Elmer Yeaw, unidentified, unidentified, Barbara Norton, Arlene Coombs, unidentified, unidentified, and Alfred Whitehead; (back row) Arlene Bond, Arlene Adams, Irene DelRossi, and Betty Chace. The building is still in use for other purposes.

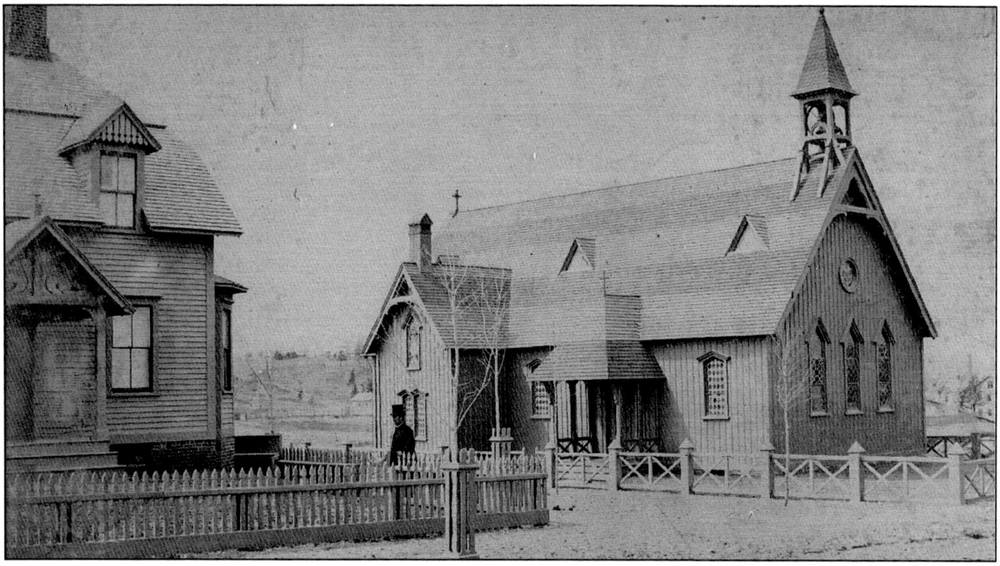

St. Mary's Episcopal Church was built on the corner of Warren Avenue and Fourth Street in 1870. It was one of the first churches built in the burgeoning community of Watchemoket. The group had organized in 1867 and until the new church was built had been meeting in the Potter Street School. The land for the church was donated by Mr. and Mrs. Edward D. Pearce.

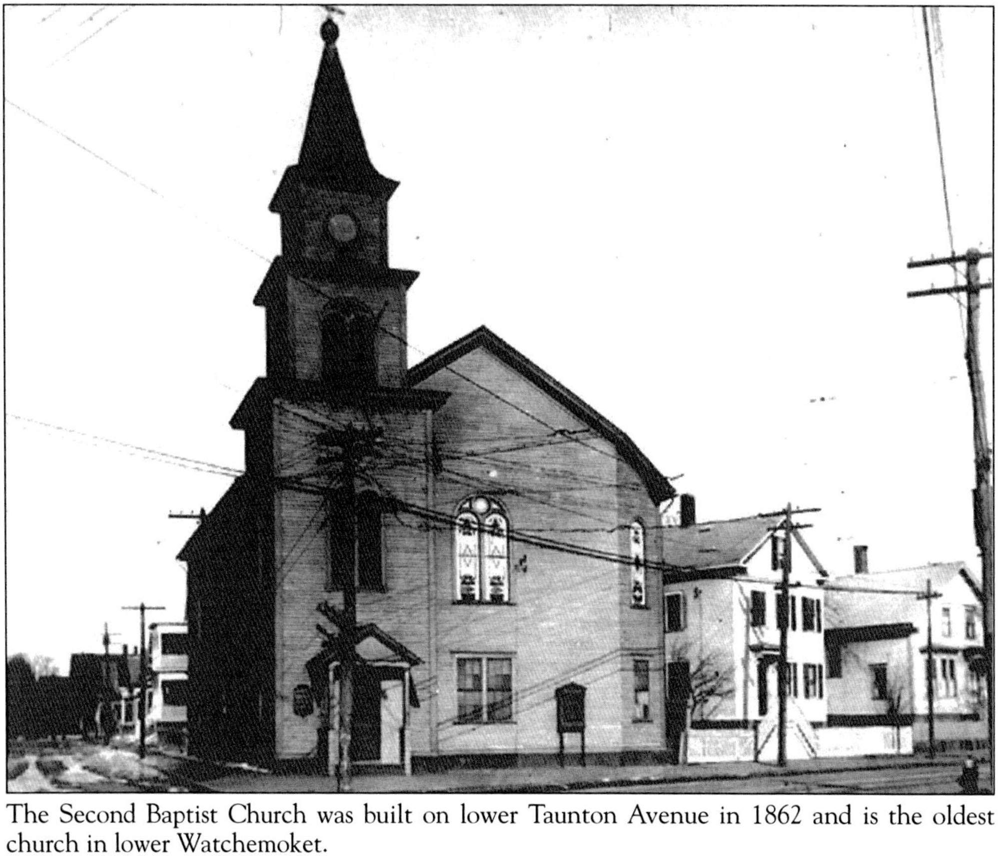

The Second Baptist Church was built on lower Taunton Avenue in 1862 and is the oldest church in lower Watchemoket.

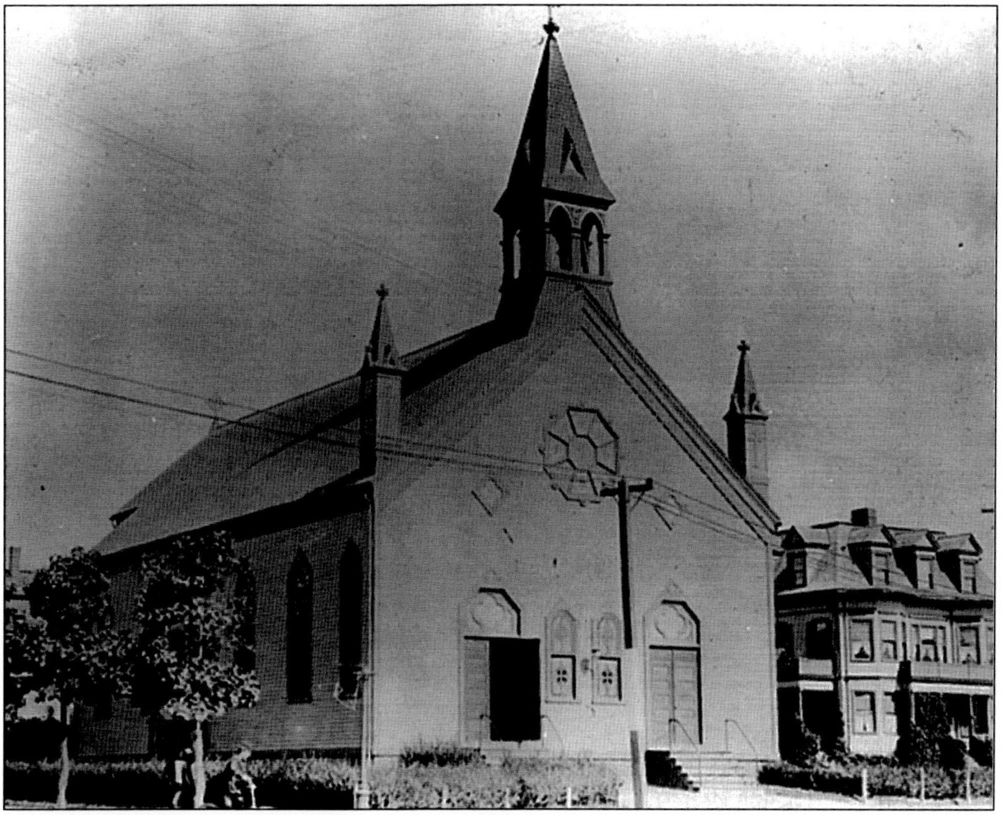

The Sacred Heart Catholic Church was established in the center of the town on Taunton Avenue in 1869.

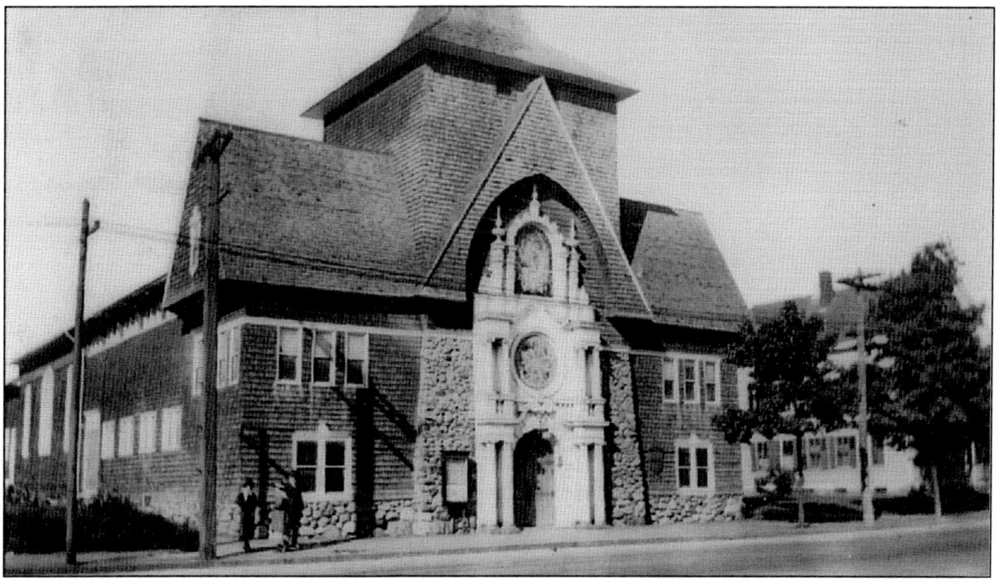

The second Haven Methodist Church (shown here) was built in 1900 and burned in 1929. It was larger then the first church, which was built on Taunton Avenue in 1883. The church presently standing was built in 1931.

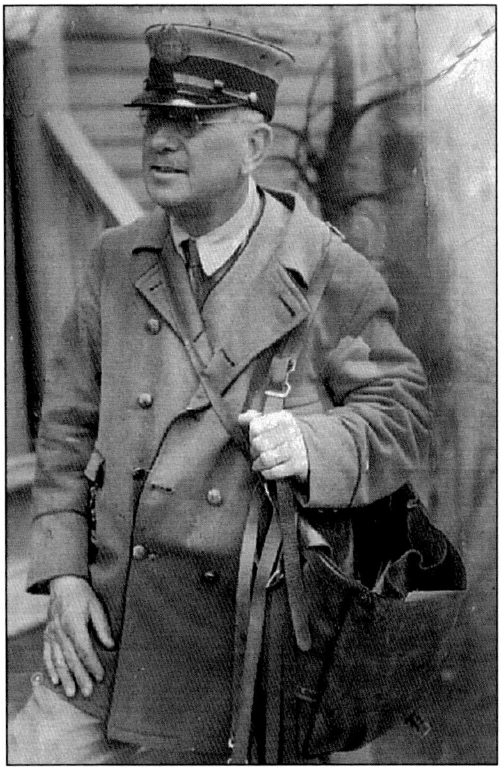

Postman Clarence Rich retired in 1933 after thirty-two years. He had the Taunton Avenue route, which included the town hall and high school. During World War I he would give a high sign to a girl in the high school whenever she had mail from her boyfriend overseas. She would then rush home on the lunch hour to get it!

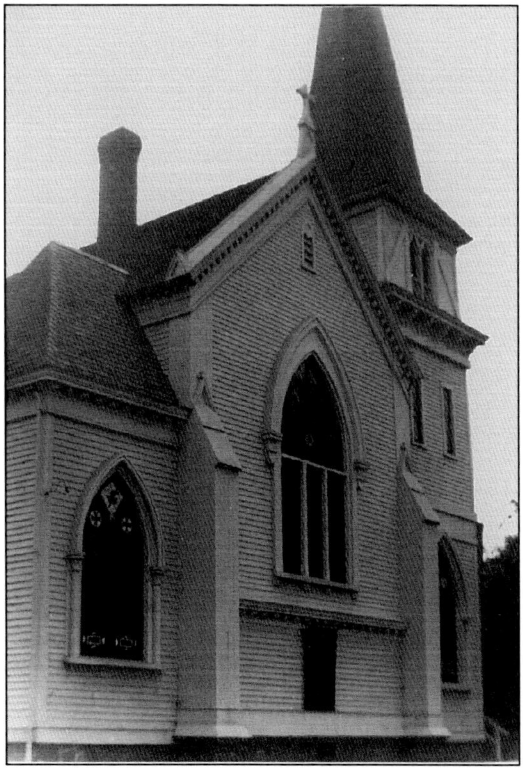

In 1858, before the town became East Providence, the First Universalist Church of Seekonk was organized in the old Seekonk Town Hall on Pawtucket Avenue. The church meetings were held there and later in Pierce Hall on Warren Avenue. In 1882 the church was loaned a lot on Alice Street by Thomas Ray. He lived next door in what is today the Scott Funeral Home. Seekonk had become East Providence, so the church name was changed to the First Universalist Church of East Providence.

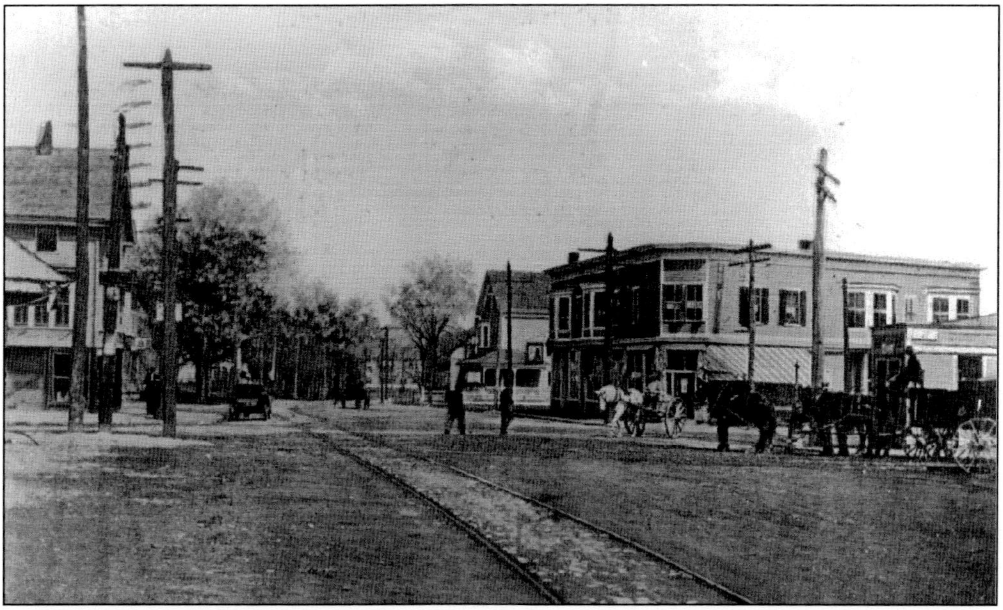

Farther east from the Seekonk River was a major crossroads in town known as Six Corners. Here three major streets intersected each other: Waterman Avenue and Taunton Avenue crossed each other like an "X," and North Broadway ran north and south through the midsection of town. Here in 1900 travel was by horse and buggy and trolley (note the tracks).

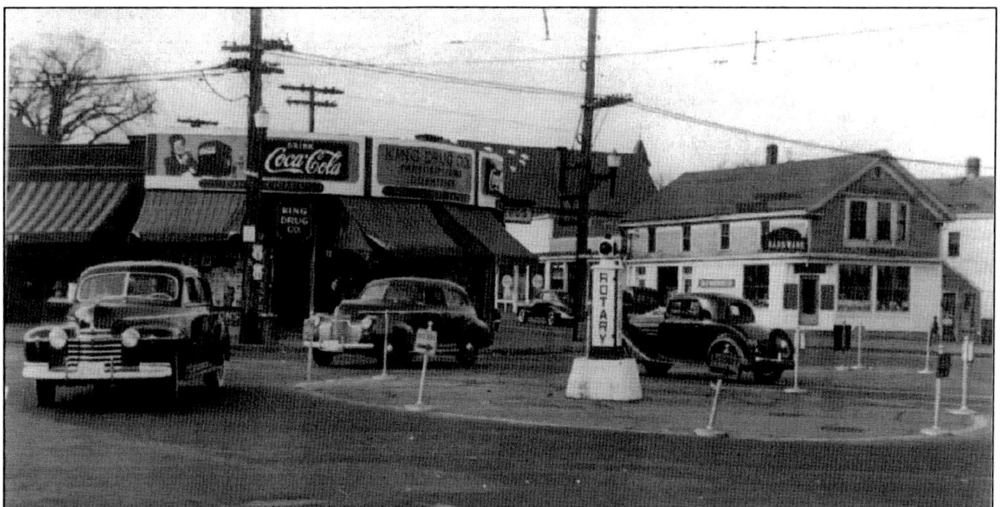

By 1941 heavy traffic had made a rotary at Six Corners necessary. As the town grew this crossroads became a flourishing shopping area until a modern underpass was built in the 1960s. Stores then began moving to the new malls.

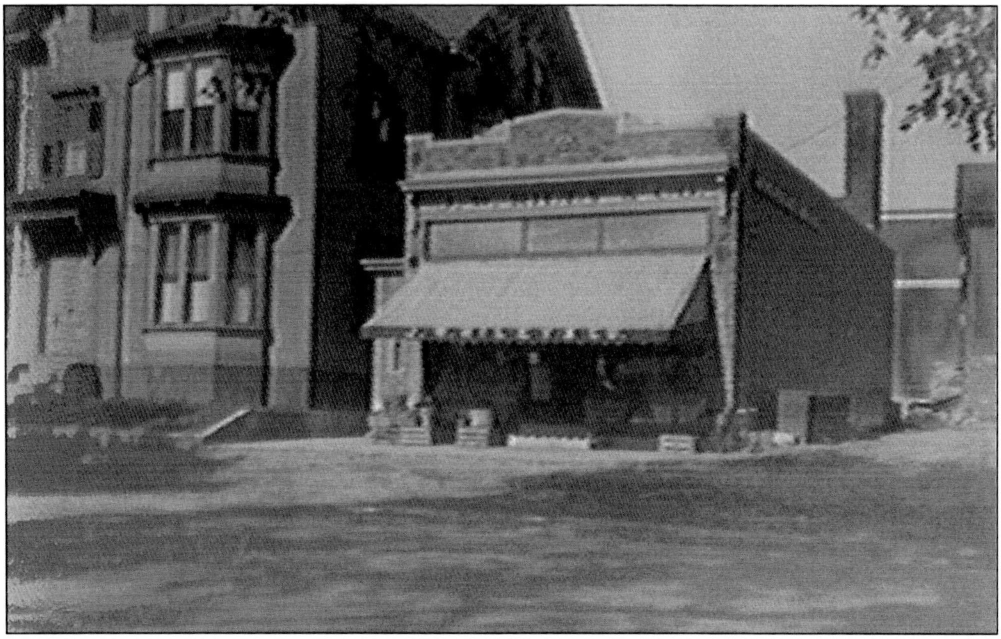

Riley's Market was one of many stores at Six Corners. It was located on Broadway in 1924, and survived when many buildings were torn down to make way for the "new" junior high school c. 1928. The junior high is now senior citizen housing and Riley's is Horton's Fish Market.

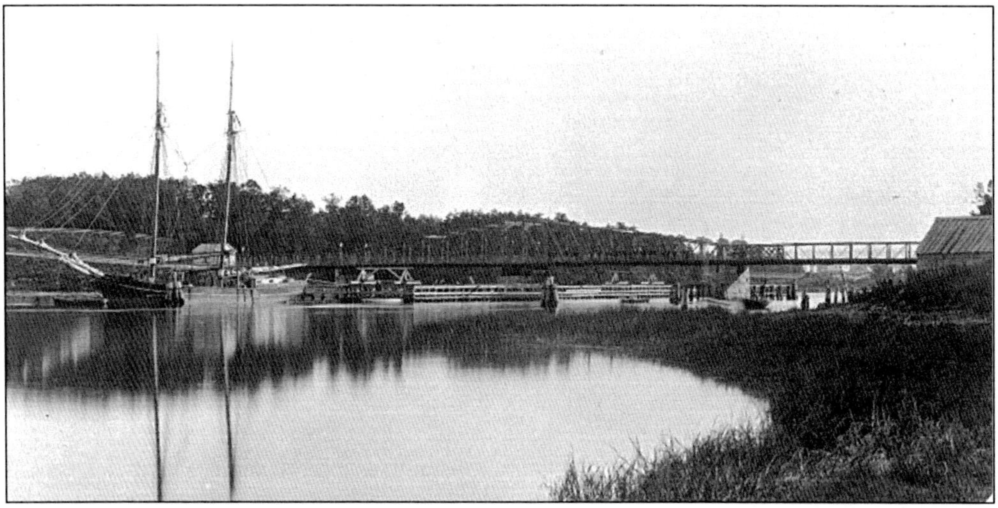

This Red Bridge was one of many crossing a narrow part of the Seekonk River between Waterman Street in Providence and Waterman Avenue in East Providence. This one was built in 1895. The first bridge at this location was built by Moses Brown in 1793, followed by one in 1807 and one in 1872. The bridge shown here was taken down when the new Henderson Memorial Bridge was built to the north in the 1960s.

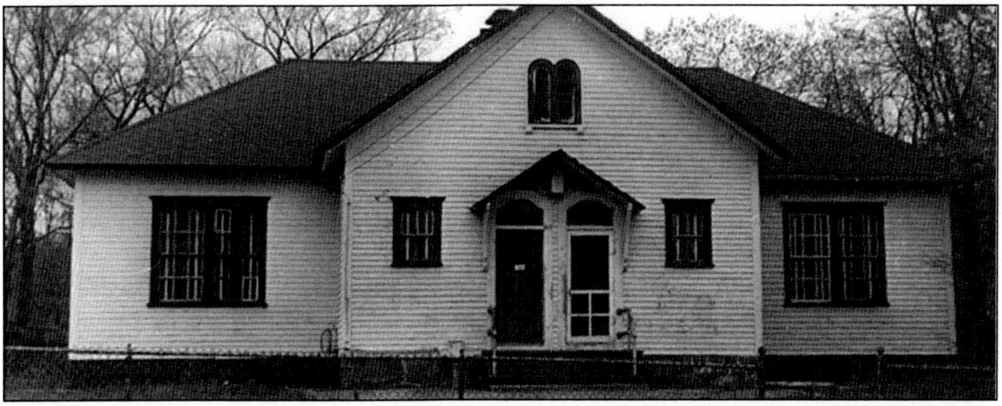

Broadway Primary was built as a two-room school on North Broadway in 1862, shortly after the town became East Providence. Originally it was called PS No. 3 and its neighbor was the Trolley Car Barn. Both were torn down when the connector ramp was built for the Henderson Bridge in the late 1960s.

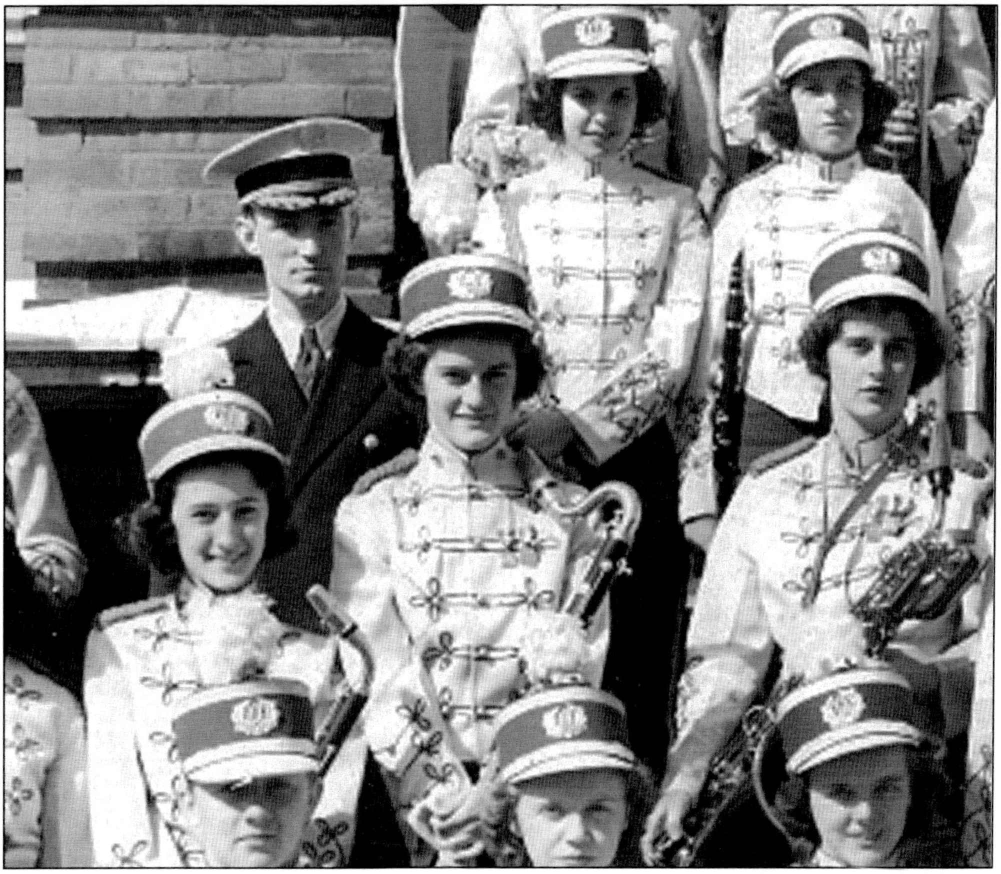

Stephen Farnum was a well-known band director for the East Providence High School when it was located on Taunton Avenue at Six Corners. This 1942 photograph shows a group of the students. From left to right are: (front row) William Bentley, Lucille Tucker, and Gladys Whitmarsh; (middle row) Jean Salter, Helen Wright, and Elizabeth Turner; (back row) Dr. Farnum, Anna Correia, and Elizabeth Drill.

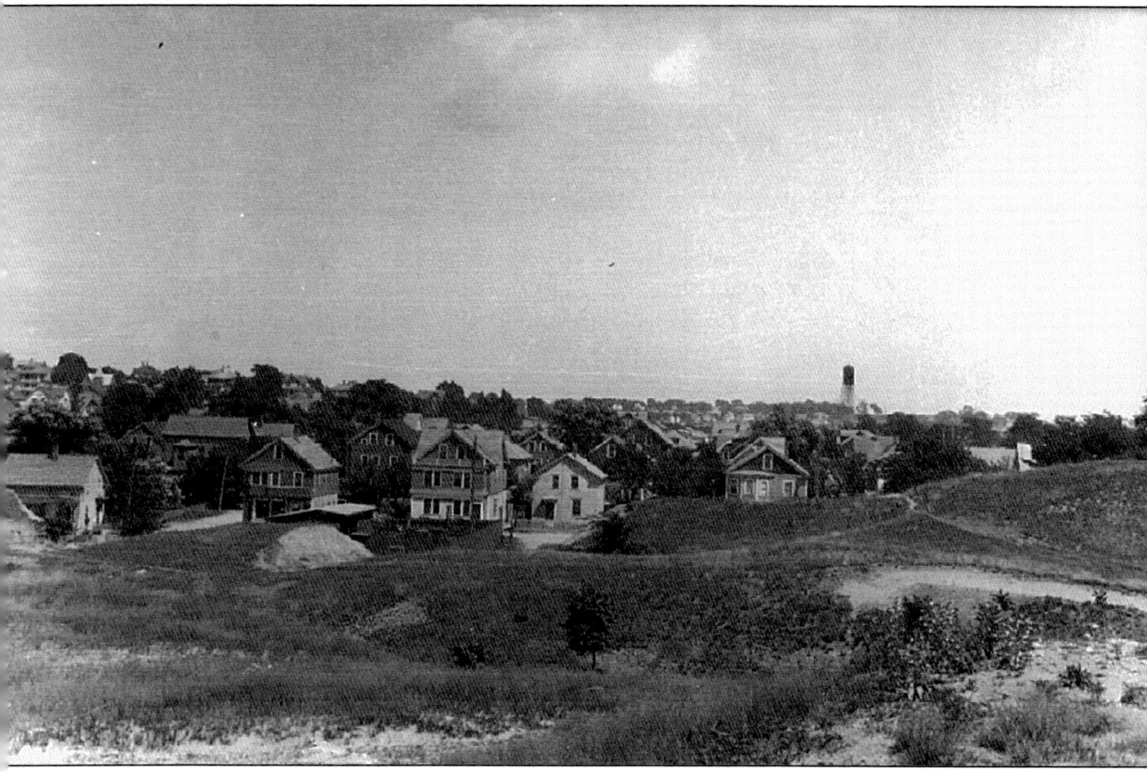

This view from the top of Fort Hill looks east across Watchemoket to the Kent Heights water tower on the horizon in the eastern part of central East Providence.

Two

Kent Heights

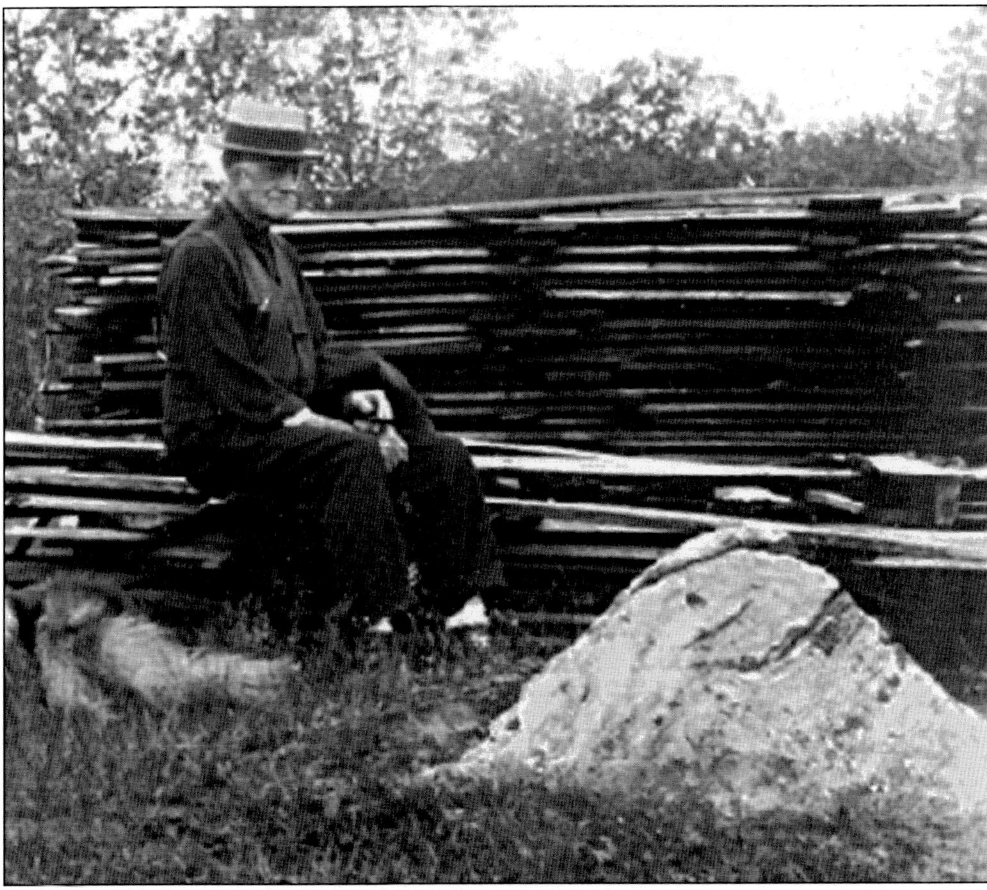

While the western part of Watchemoket was becoming the business center of town, the eastern part consisted of several farms. The largest farm was the White Rock Farm owned by Alfred J. Kent, seen sitting here by a woodpile. His farm consisted of 400 acres of orchards, potato, and corn fields, and a dairy farm with many head of cattle. Eight of his fifteen children were sons who worked the farm. Mr. Kent gave the name Kent Heights to the area in the 1920s and was responsible for getting a Kent Heights post office branch office in his store. During his life he was very involved with town government and was quite a force in local politics.

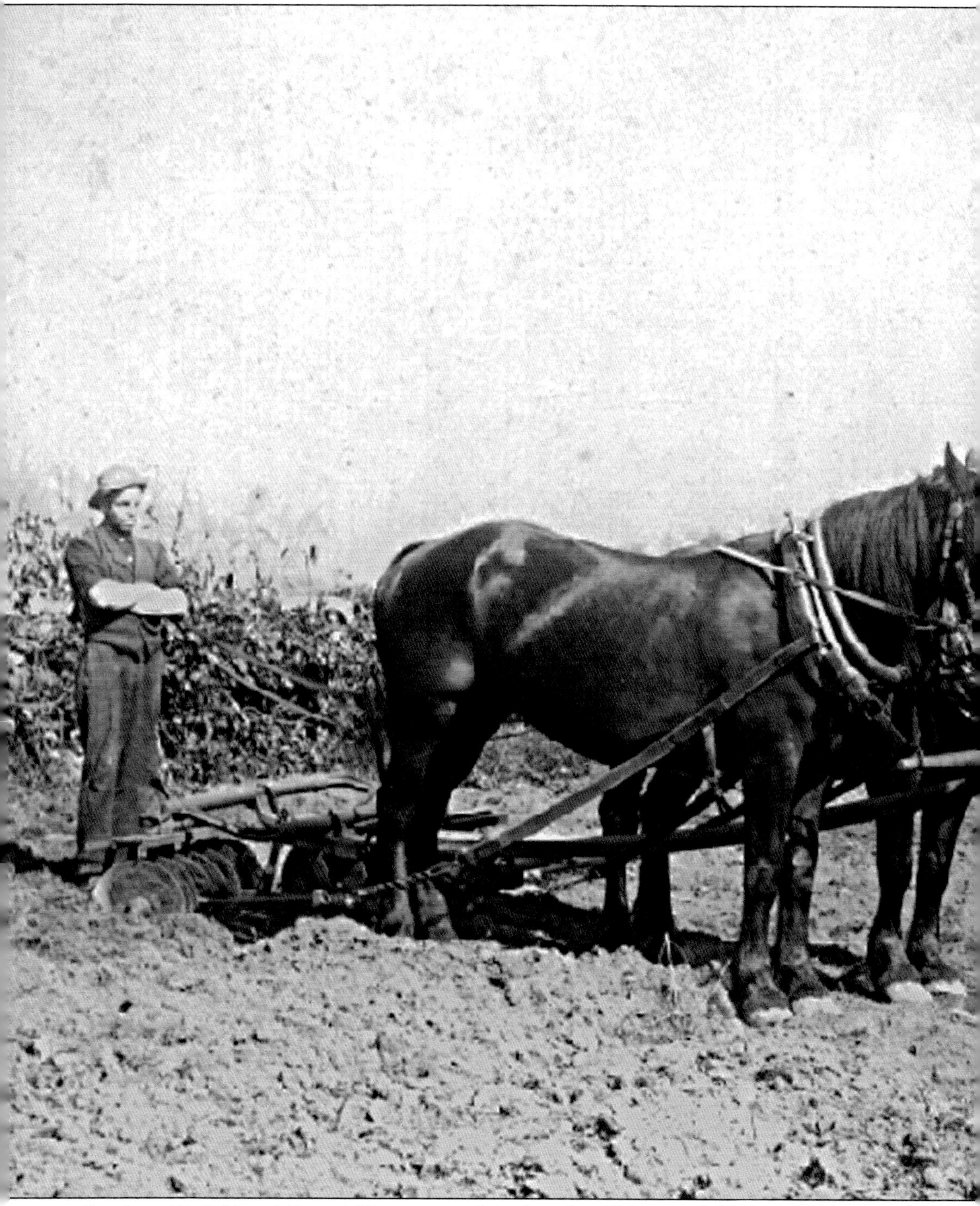

Brothers Garfield and Samuel Kent are tending their horses in the Kent Farm field along the Old Barrington Road, now called the Wampanoag Trail. Cornfields (left) and apple and peach

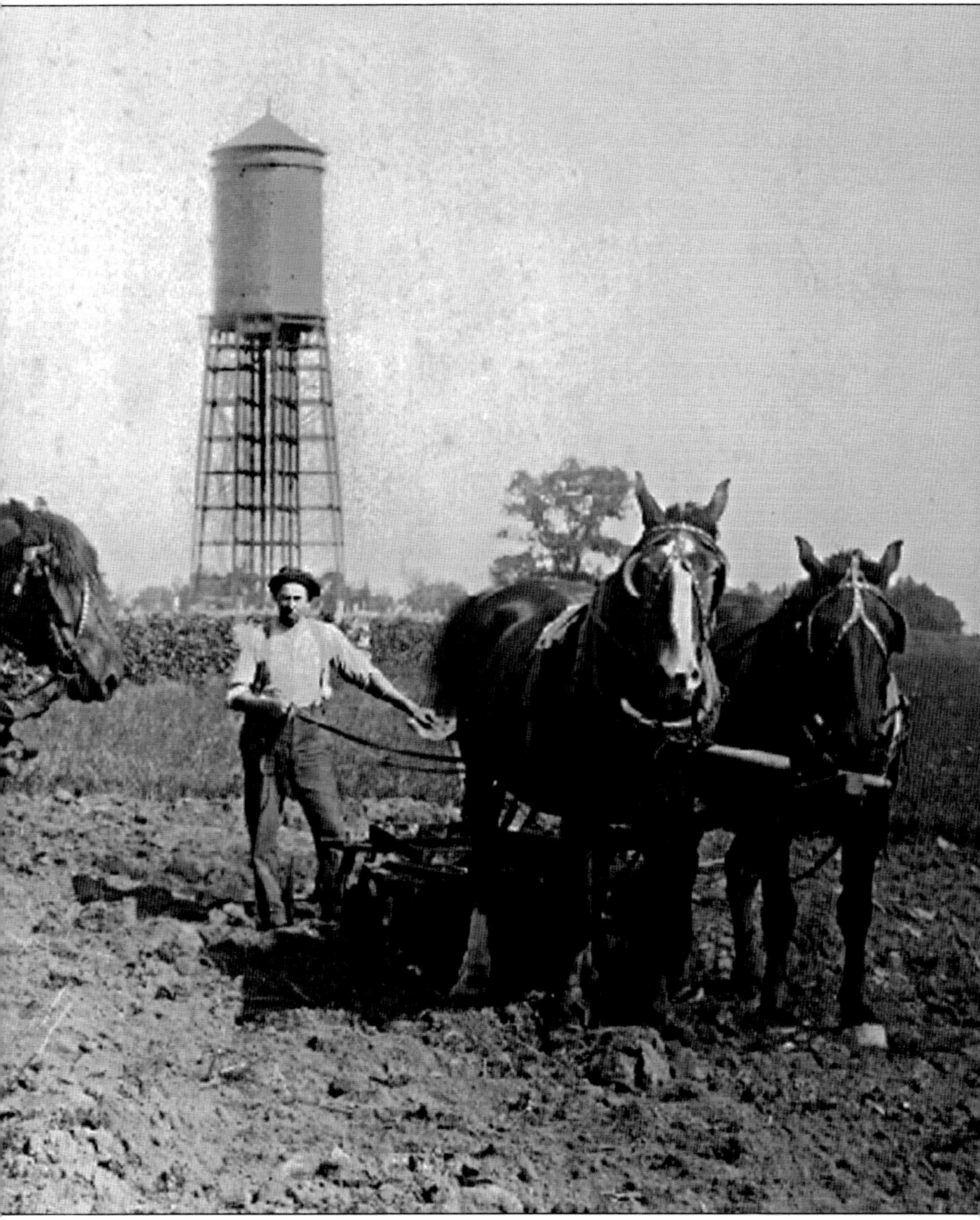

trees (far right) can be seen in the background. The standpipe in the center of the farm supplied water to East Providence.

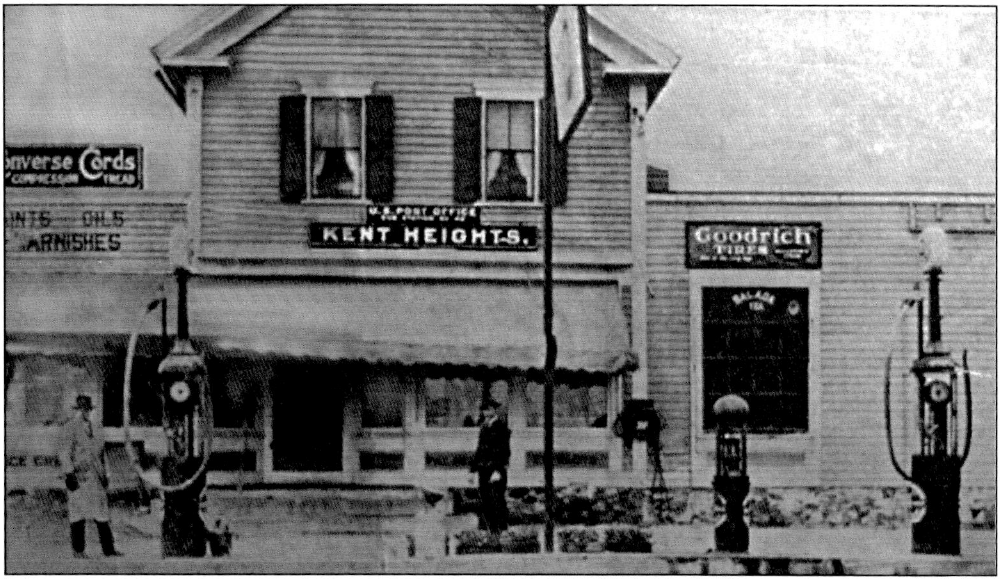

The Kent Heights Store was run by E. Everett Kent. His father, A.J. Kent, bought the store to sell his eggs, milk, and fresh vegetables. Everett eventually bought it. Eight men and one woman worked here along with eight of his children. He had the first gas pump in town put in by Standard Oil.

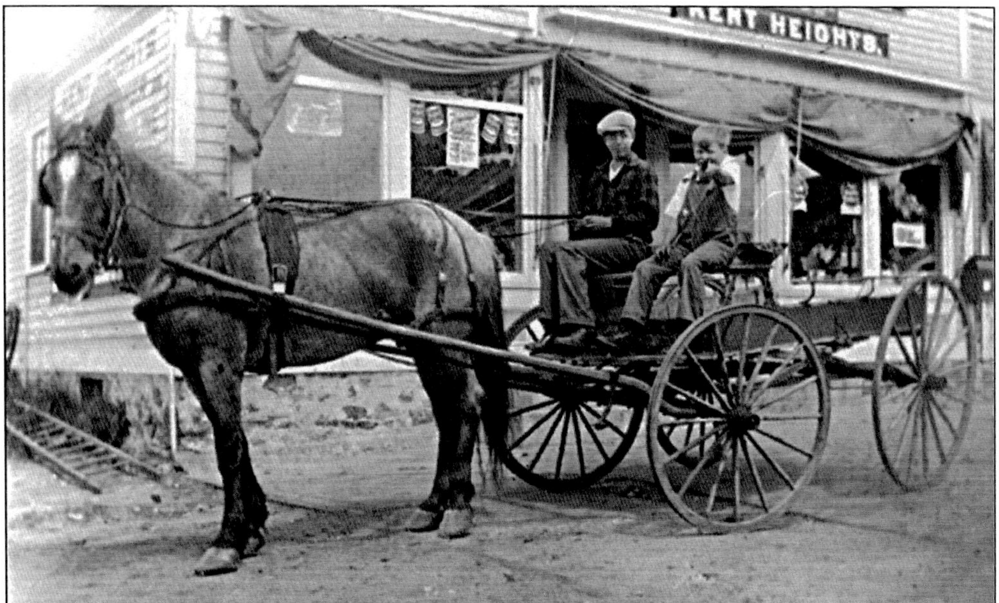

The Kent Store wagon with Norman Anderson and Ralph Kent seated in front was used to deliver groceries for the store. Later Everett bought the town's first automobile delivery truck, a 1907 Cadillac which cost $300.

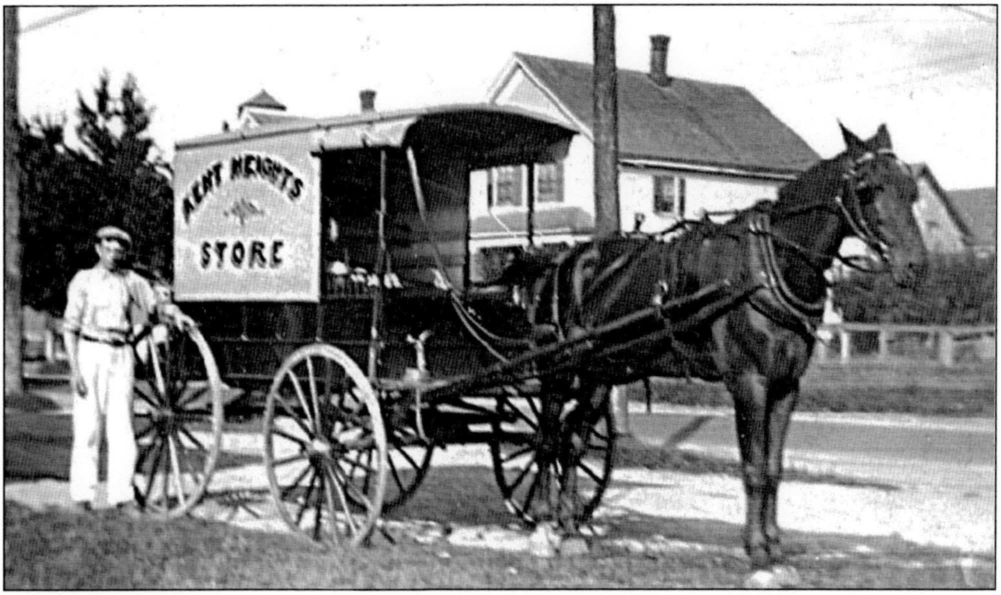

Customers would phone in their orders to the store and would receive delivery that day in this wagon with the name on the sides. All orders delivered on Saturday would have a bag of candy included if there were children in the family.

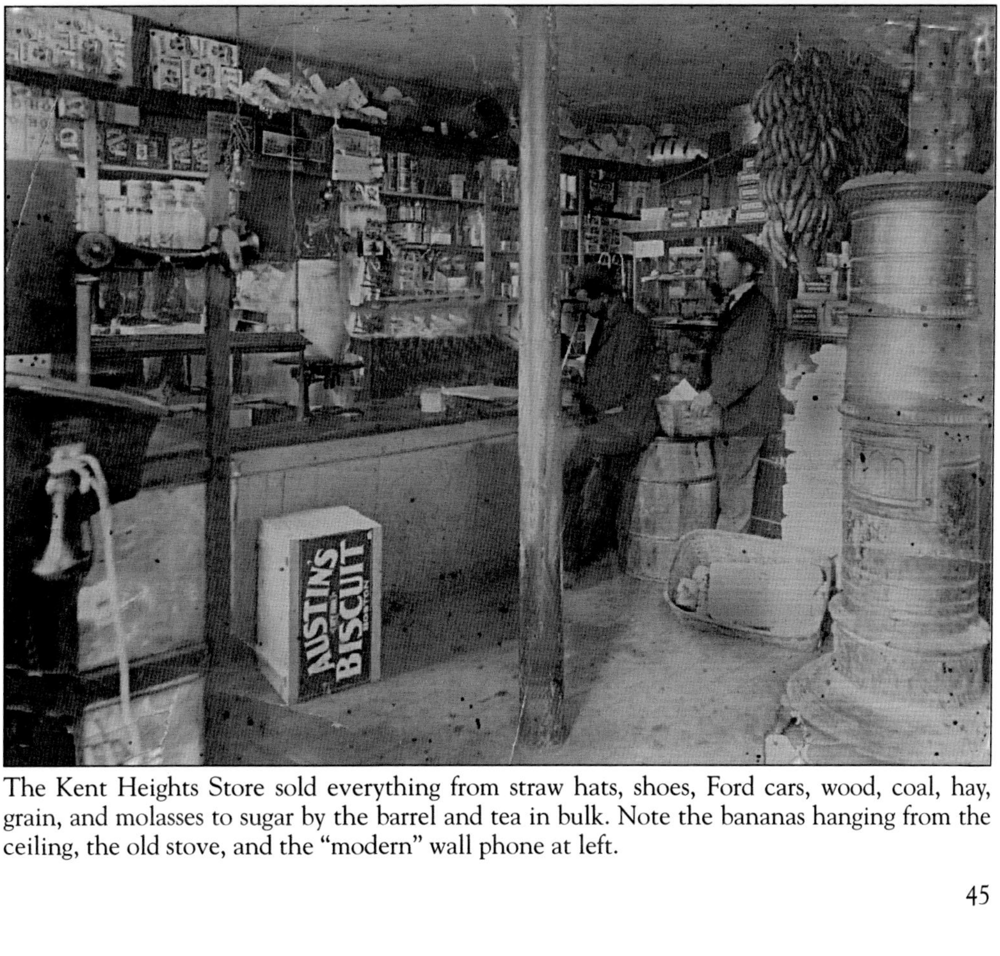

The Kent Heights Store sold everything from straw hats, shoes, Ford cars, wood, coal, hay, grain, and molasses to sugar by the barrel and tea in bulk. Note the bananas hanging from the ceiling, the old stove, and the "modern" wall phone at left.

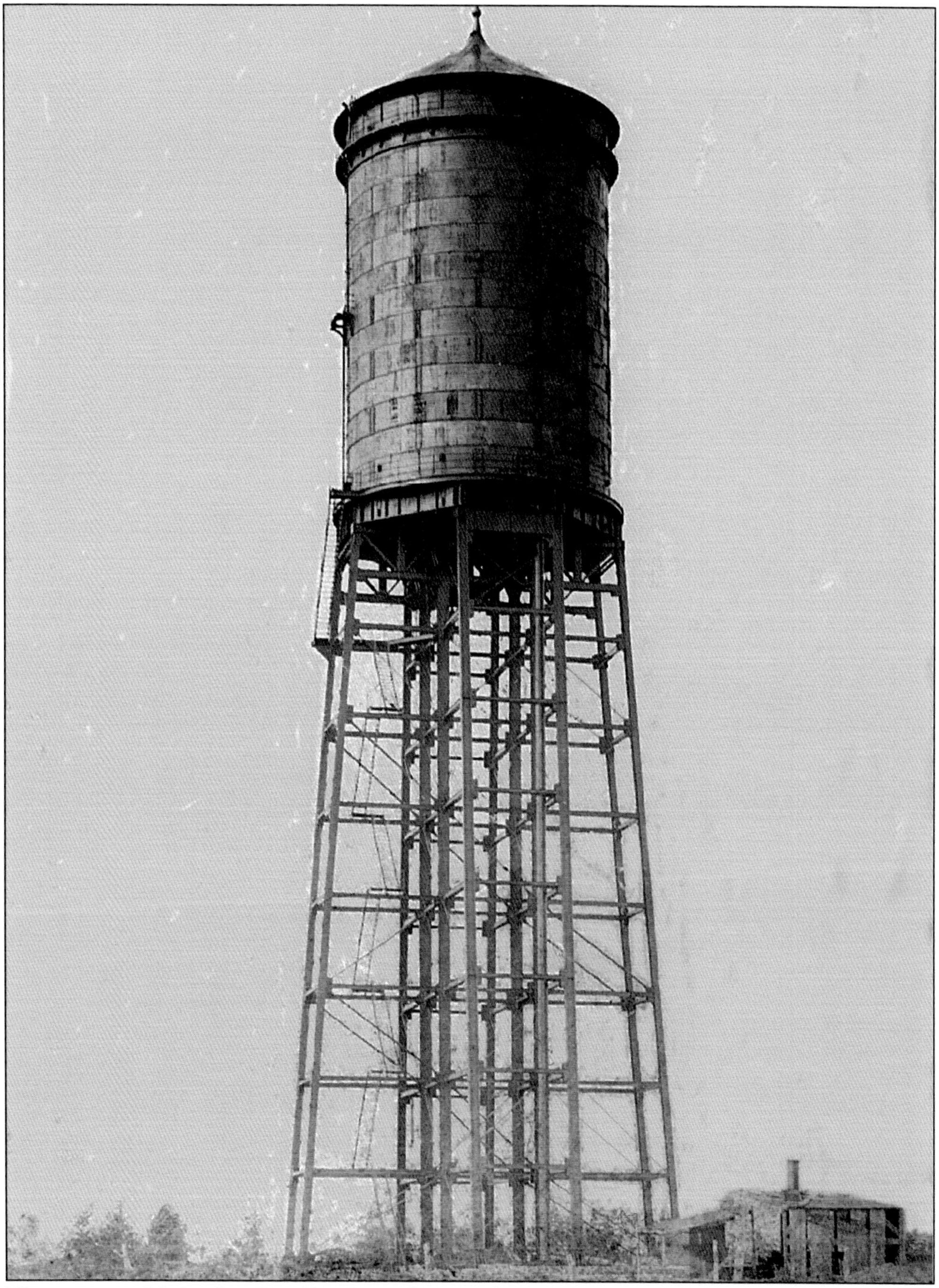

The most notable landmark in East Providence is the standpipe that rises over the Kent Heights landscape. It belongs to the East Providence water department and provides a gravity feed for water to reach the south end of the city. It was built in 1894 on farm land leased from Alfred J. Kent. The previous tank burst earlier that year and flooded the neighborhood with 800,000 gallons of water. The tank is due to be replaced again and the familiar landmark will be replaced by a modern structure.

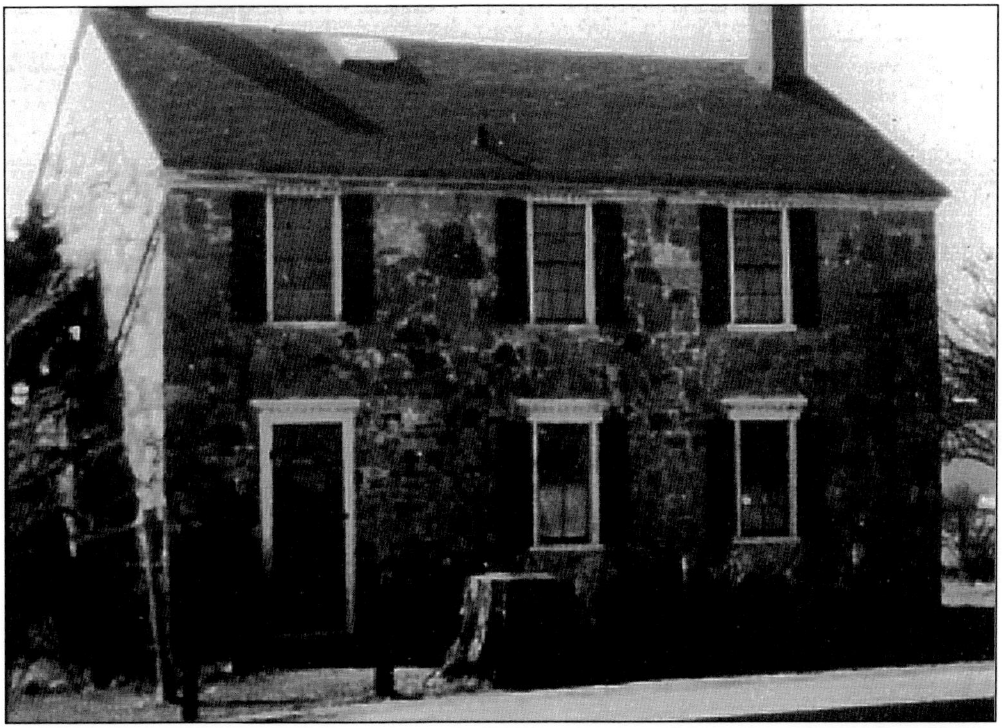

This stone house was built by the Armington family *c.* 1810 at the corner of Pawtucket Avenue and the Wampanoag Trail. This area at the intersection is still called Armington's Corners. The beautiful house and accompanying barn were torn down in the 1960s to make way for a gas station and convenience store.

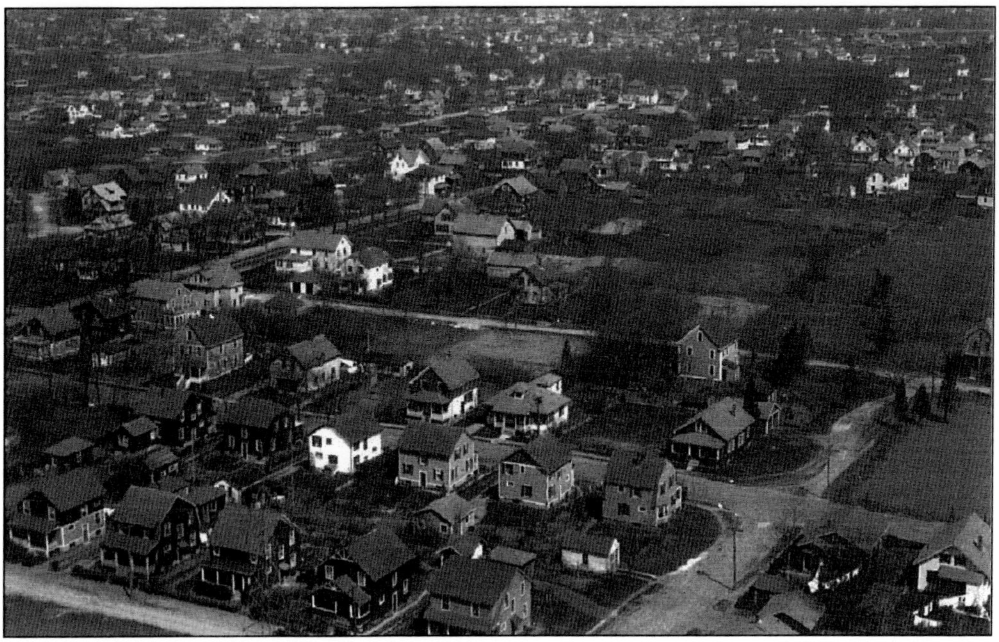

This view from the top of the Kent Heights water tower looks northwest across Kent Heights and Watchemoket to the Seekonk River.

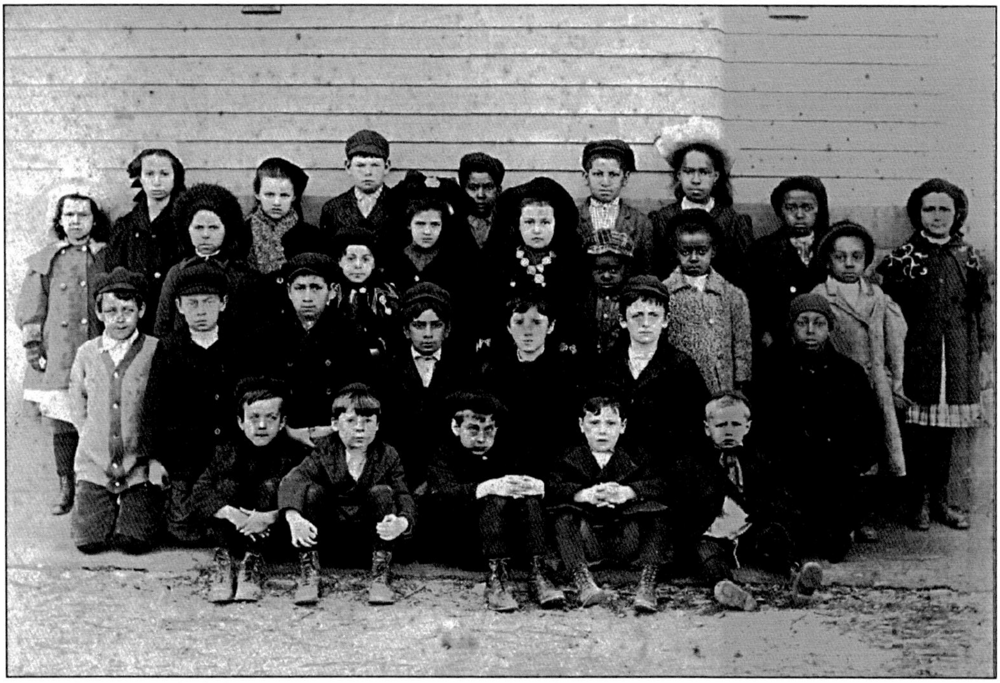

This class attended the Armington's Corners School on the corner of Vincent and Pawtucket Avenue. The one-room school was built *c.* 1869 and was formerly known as PS No. 5. Later the children called it Miss Pagny's School in honor of a teacher who taught there for many years.

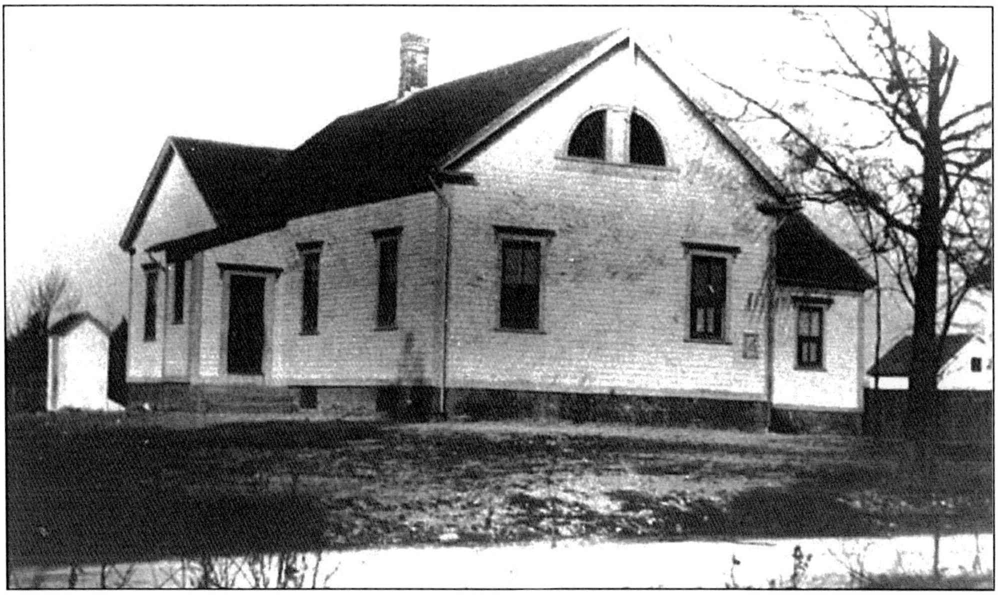

PS No. 4 was a one-room school built quickly in 1862 when the town first became East Providence. It was located just north of Warren Avenue on Pawtucket Avenue. Known as the Leonard's Corners School, it was located where the Rte. 195 expressway today passes under Pawtucket Avenue.

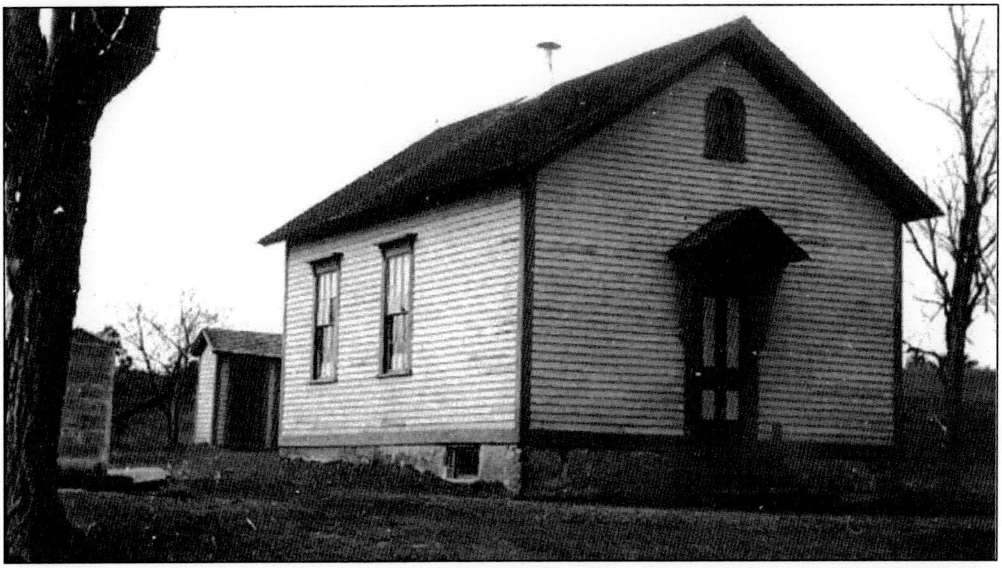

The one-room Runnins River School was built c. 1862 on the Wampanoag Trail near the Runnins River. This school and river originally were called Rhulin River, but because people had difficulty pronouncing it, the name evolved into Runnins.

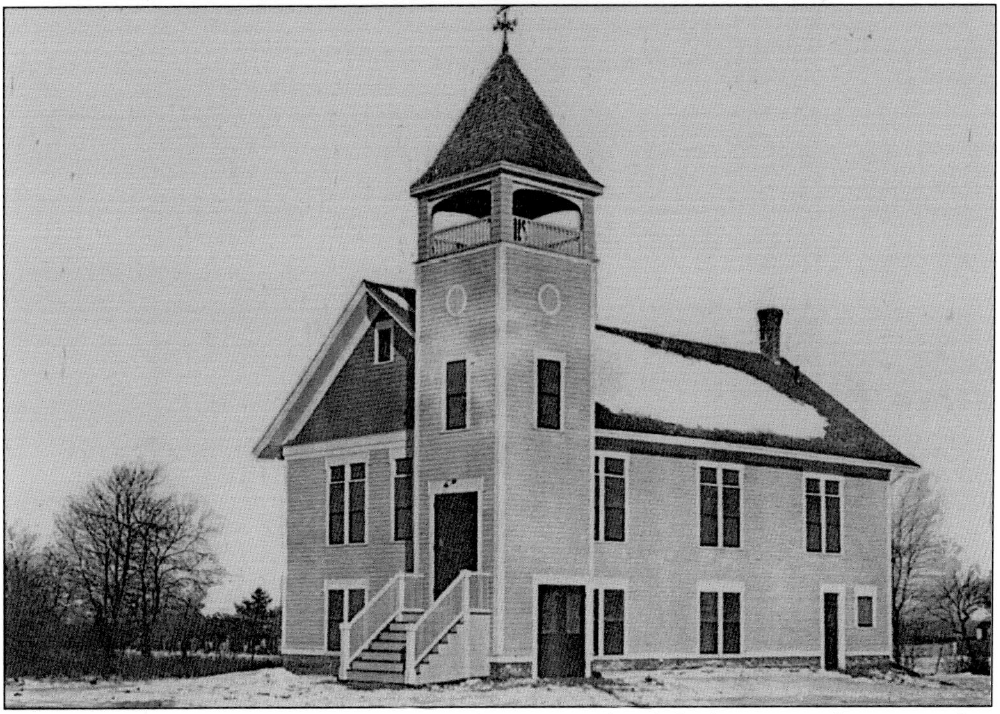

In the later part of the nineteenth century the Haven Church had an outreach program that met in the Armington's Corners School. Later the group grew and met by 1890 in the Roger Williams Grange. In 1899 the members organized the Congregational Society of Armington's Corners. In 1905 A.J. Kent gave a gift of land and a small church was completed on the site on Hazard Avenue in 1912. It was named the Hope Congregational Church. It is no longer a church building.

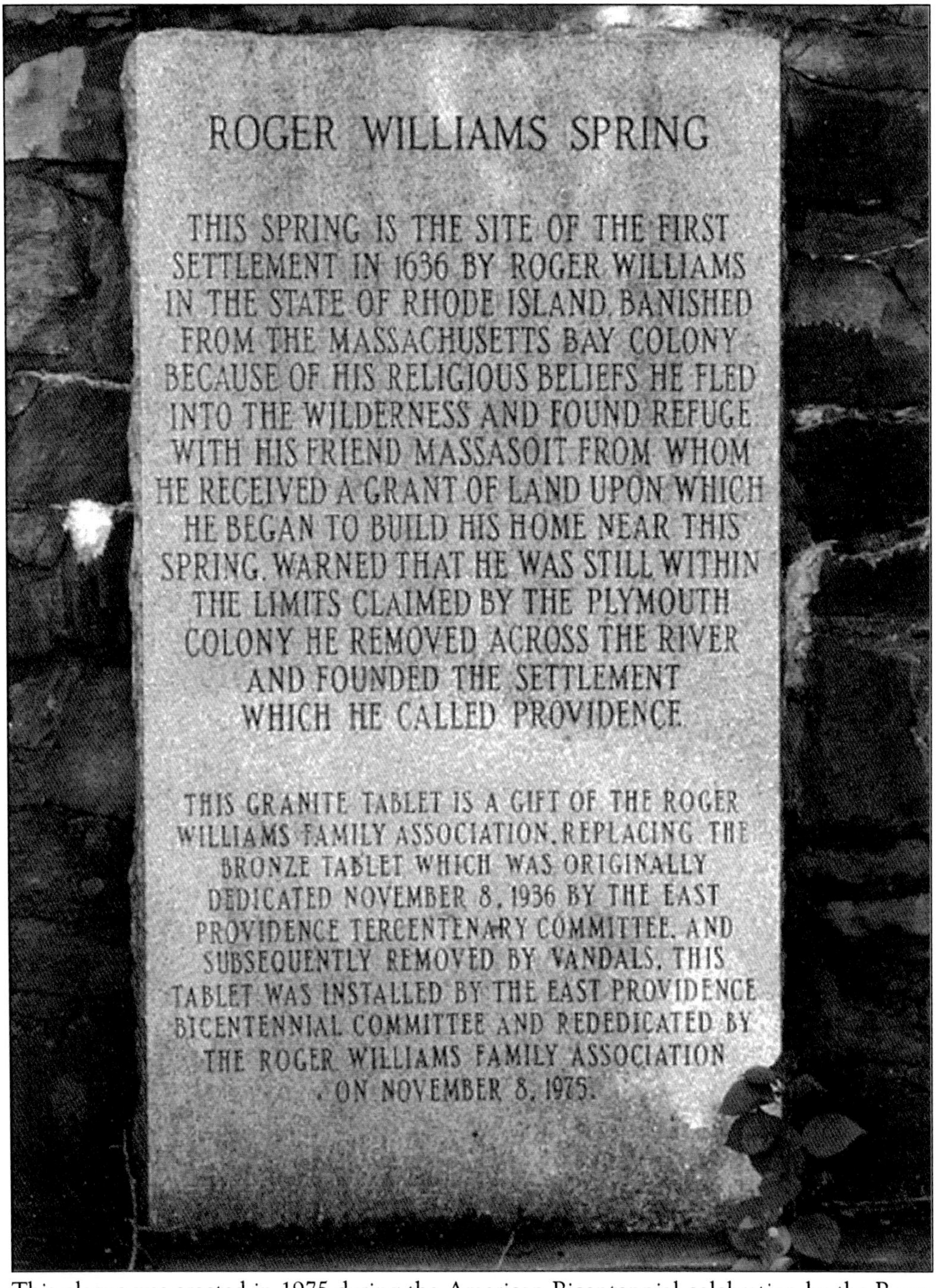

This plaque was erected in 1975 during the American Bicentennial celebration by the Roger Williams Association. It commemorates the site at the spring where Roger Williams first settled after being run out of the Massachusetts Bay Colony in 1636. After a few months on the shores of Seekonk Cove, now known as Omega Pond, he was forced to move across the Seekonk River where he founded Providence and Rhode Island. This site is on the right side of Roger Williams Avenue going north through Phillipsdale.

Three

Rumford

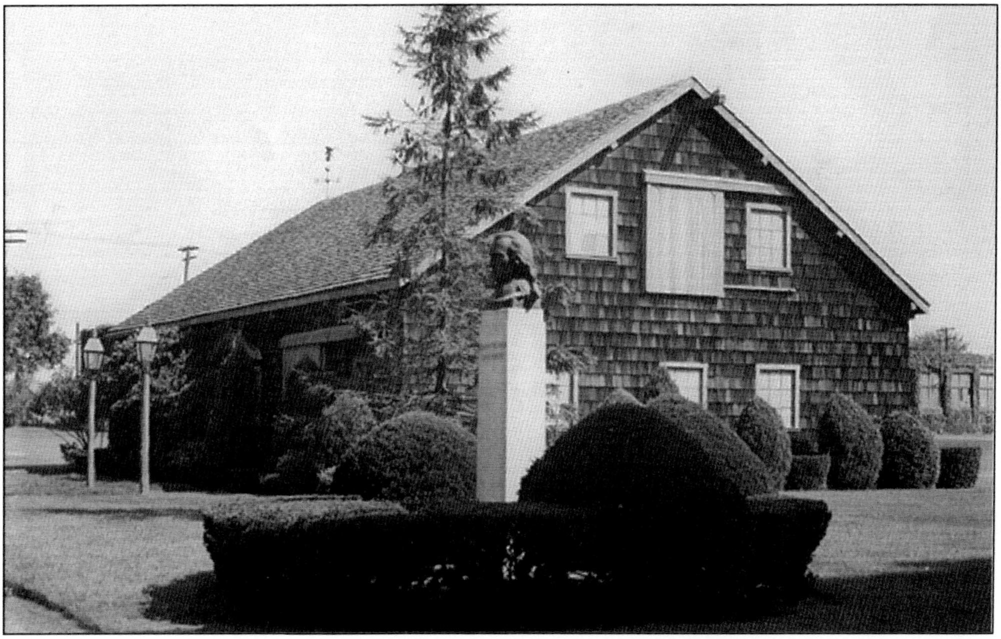

The northern part of the town of East Providence was farmland from the time the first fifty-eight Weymouth settlers under the Reverend Samuel Newman moved into the area in 1643. The land was purchased by John Brown and Edward Winslow from the Wampanoag Indians in 1641. The houses of the settlement were built in a circular formation that became known as the Ring of the Green. It was originally called Rehoboth by Reverend Newman, but in 1812 the name was changed to Seekonk. In 1862 Rhode Island absorbed the eastern side of the Seekonk River and this area was named East Providence.

In 1858, George Wilson, a Providence businessman, and Eben Horsford, a chemist, bought about 400 acres in the northern section of town, which at the time was still farmland. Soon the building above was built as a chemical factory to make baking powder for cooking. This was the beginning of the northern part of town's transition to industry. The Rumford Chemical Works rapidly expanded and eventually had its own post office, which gave the name of Rumford to the village. The company moved to Indiana in 1965, but the old factory remains, as does the village name of Rumford.

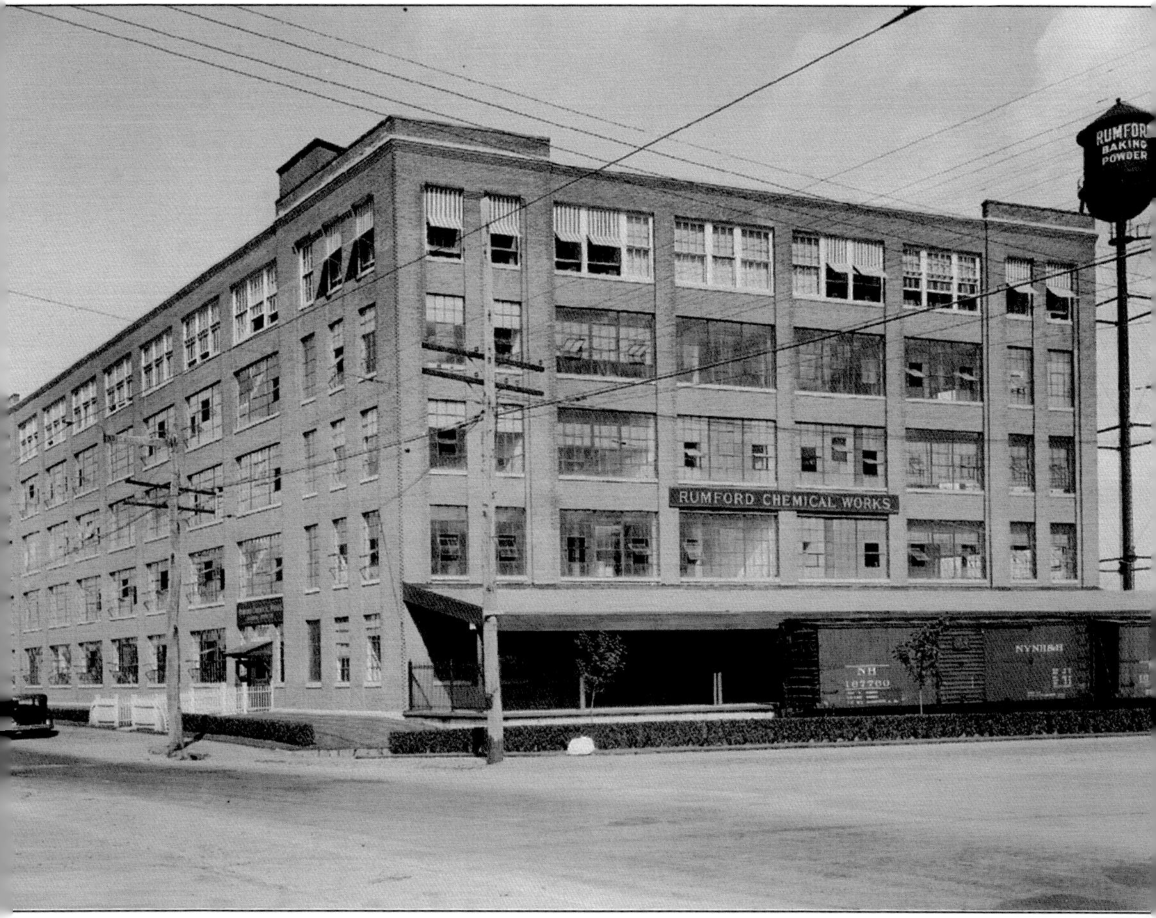

Building 31 of the Rumford Chemical Works was built in 1930–31 on the corner of Greenwood Avenue and Newman Avenue. The ingredients for baking powder were delivered in barrels to the fifth floor. The powder was mixed, canned, labeled, and boxed, moving down each floor before reaching the first-floor loading platform, where it was loaded onto trains. The powder was shipped all over the world from Europe across America to the Orient. At one time the Rumford Company was the largest chemical plant in America and made many other chemical products besides baking powder.

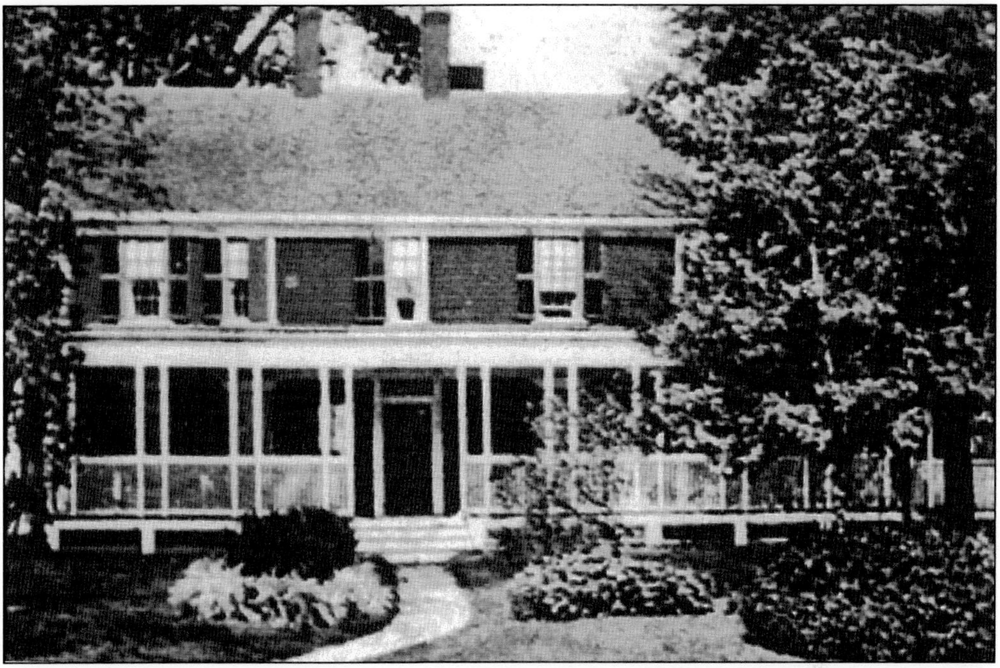

George Wilson bought this house *c.* 1860 on Hoyt Avenue shortly after opening the baking powder plant. The house was built on the foundation of a house that was on the Ring of the Green when King Philip, chief of the Wampanoag Tribe, burned all the settlement houses in 1675. This house is standing at the core of what is today the Wannamoisett Country Club.

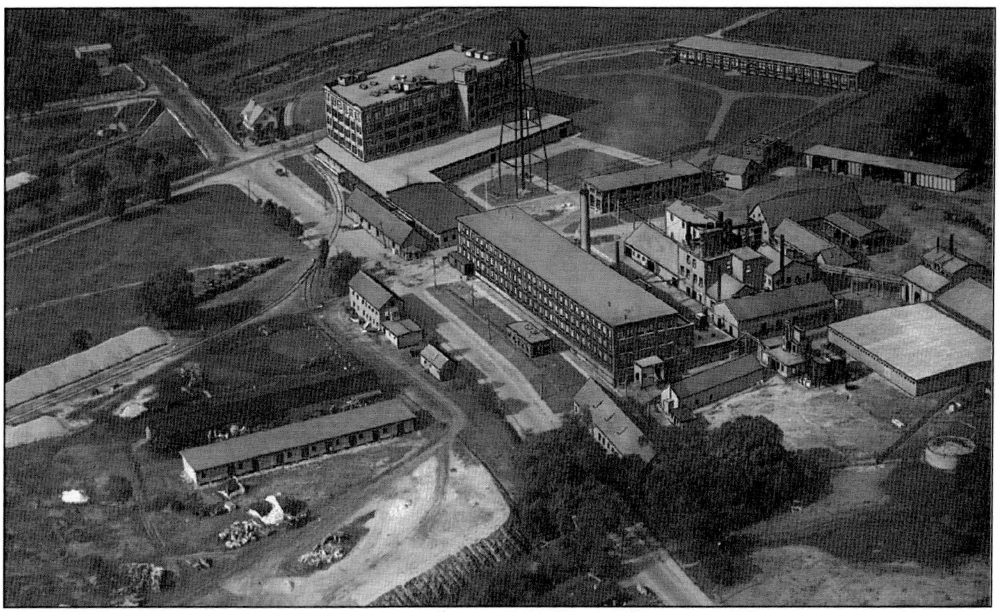

The chemical lab is the building at the top right of this *c.* 1931 aerial view of the Rumford plant.

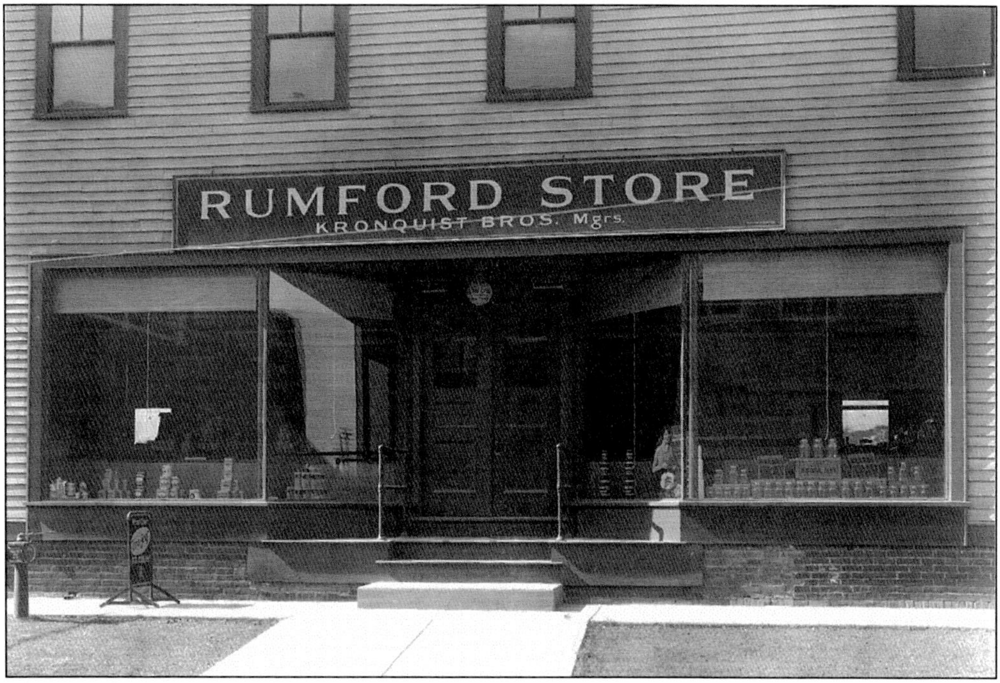

The Rumford store was the company store for plant employees. The Rumford Company ran a large farm on part of its acreage, and vegetables and meats from its cattle, among sundry other items, were sold here. For a few years the second floor housed the corporate offices of the company. The building is still standing on Greenwood Avenue.

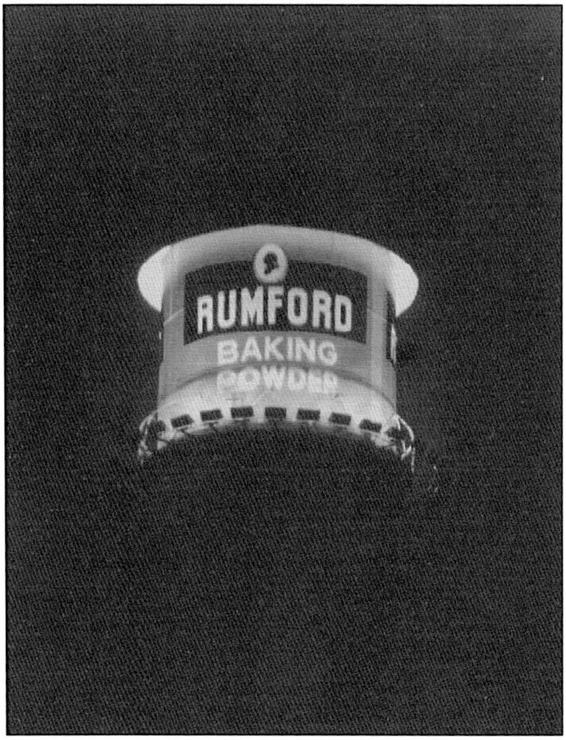

The most famous landmark in Rumford was the water tower built in the shape of a baking powder tin and painted in red, white, and black with the Rumford logo. It was dismantled in 1965.

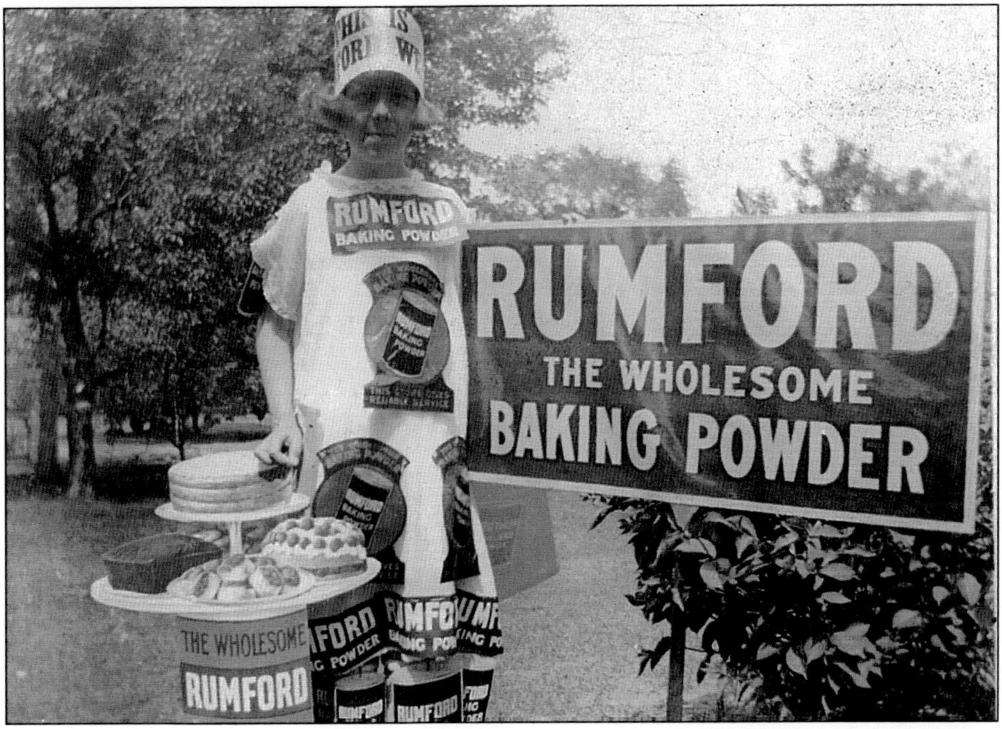

Helen (Holter) Smith is dressed as Little Miss Rumford Baking Powder in 1926. She lived across the street from the factory on Elm Street.

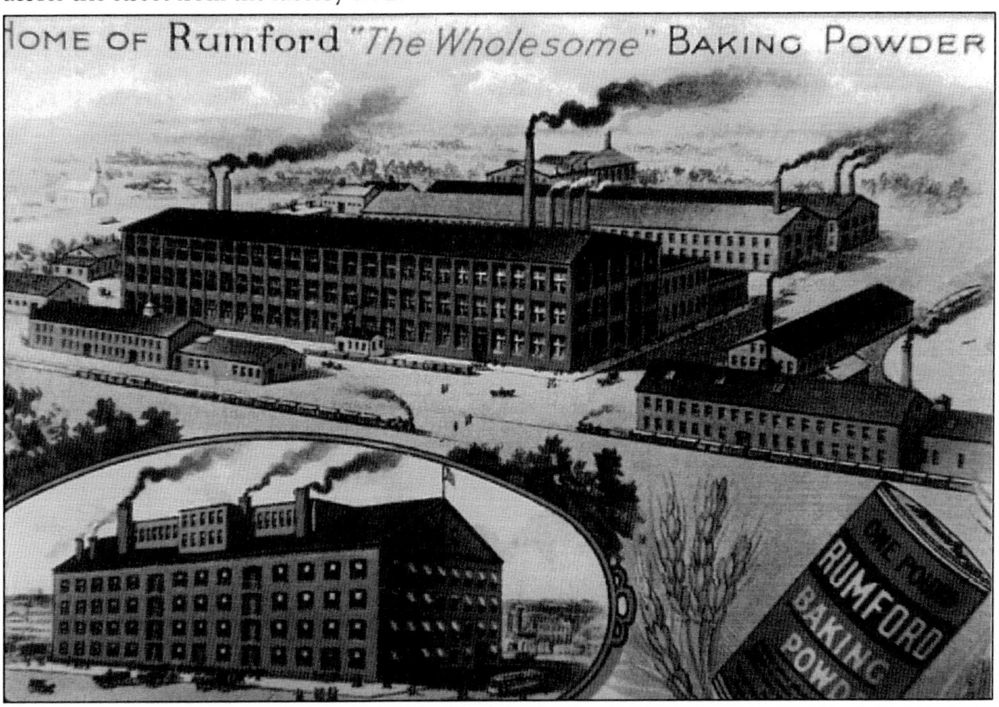

This postcard showing many views of the Rumford Chemical Company is one of many cards, booklets, and advertisements that the company distributed over the years.

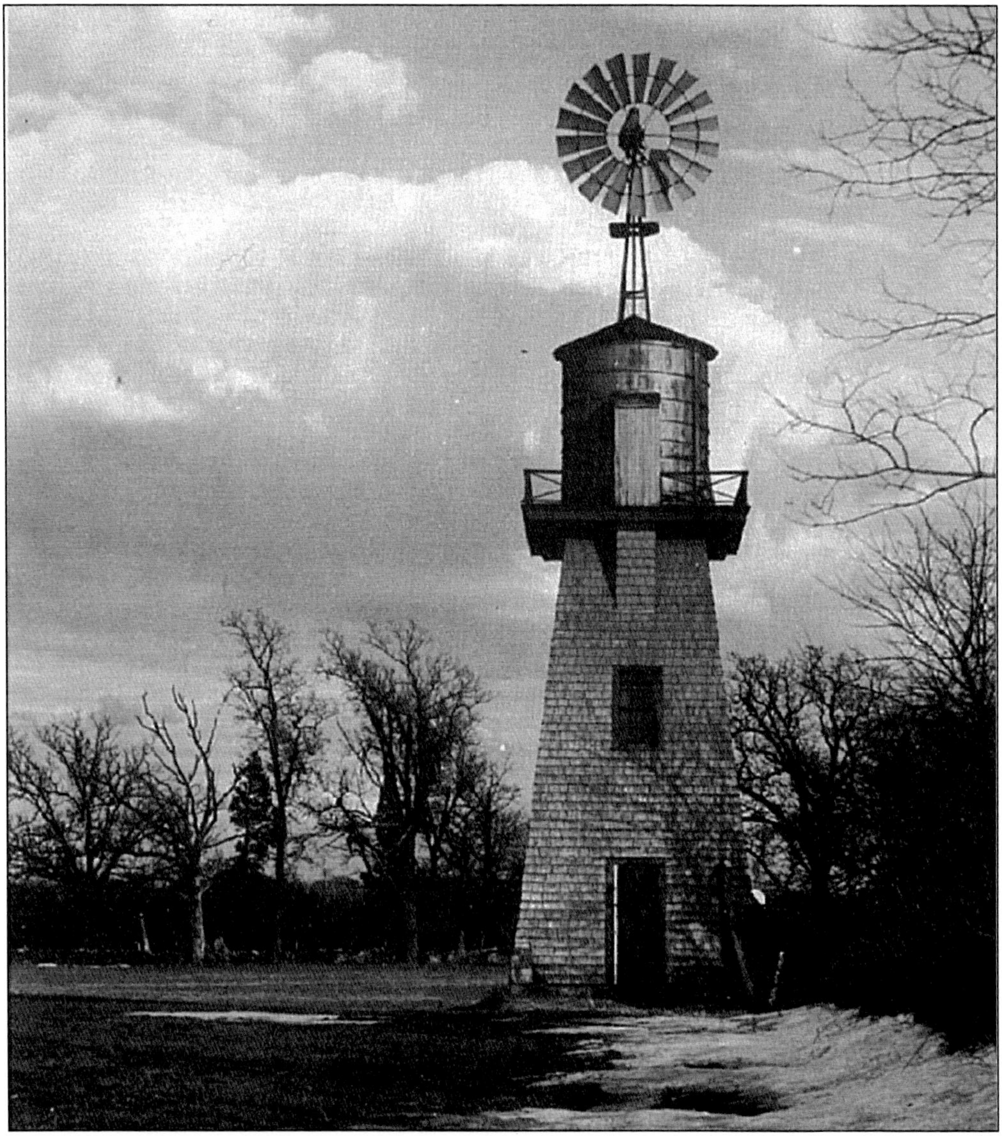

The Bridgham Farm Windmill is a notable landmark in the Rumford area. The Bridgham Farm sat between the Ten Mile River and Pleasant Street, which was one side of the Ring of the Green. The Bridgham family owned the farm for some two hundred years. The windmill, built c. 1862, is being restored by its new owner.

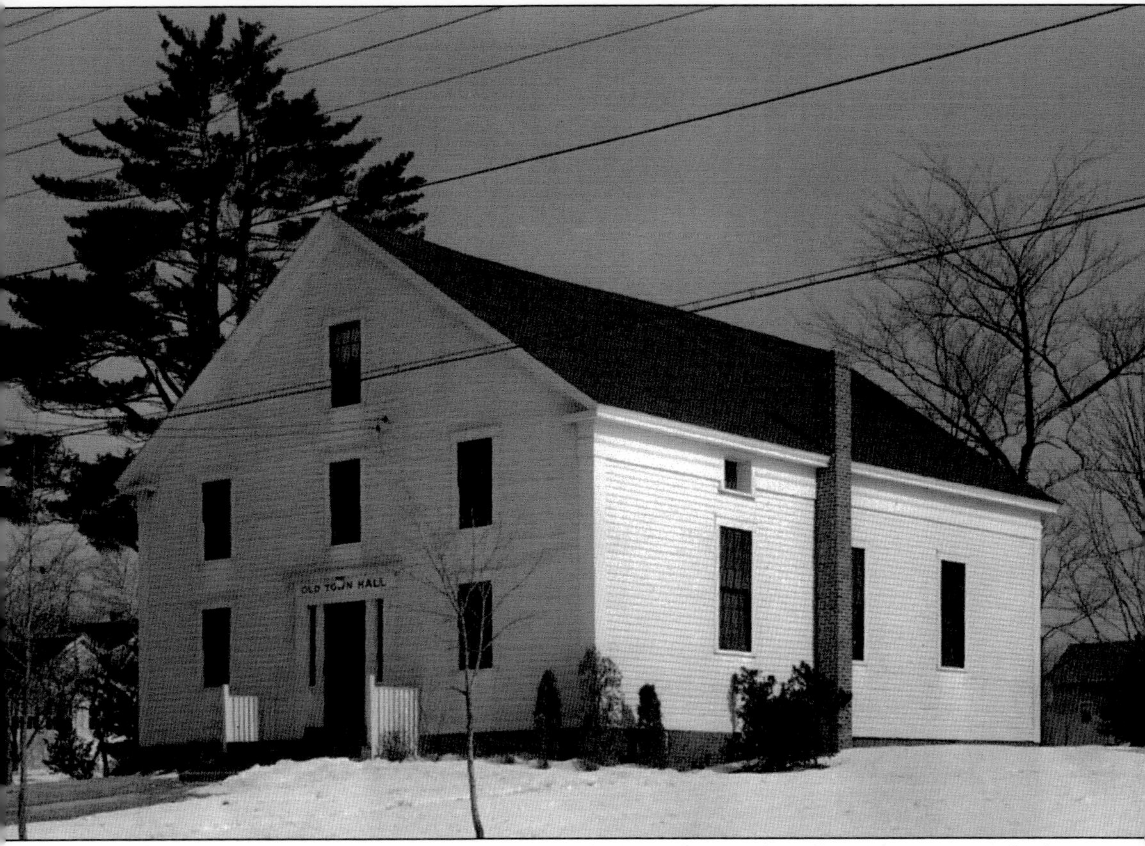

The old Seekonk Town Hall on the corner of Pawtucket and Miller Avenues was built c. 1812 when the town name was changed from Rehoboth. It was built from timbers used in the third Newman Meeting House. Until 1812, town government was conducted in the Newman Meeting House, where religious services were also held. In 1812 it was decided to have a regular town hall and the church decided to build a formal church building. In 1862 the name changed to the East Providence Town Hall when the town joined Rhode Island. It was actively used until the early 1880s, when a branch office was opened in Watchemoket. In 1889, a new town hall on Taunton Avenue was built. In the 1960s the historic old town hall was torn down, and recently the land on which it stood was made into a parking lot.

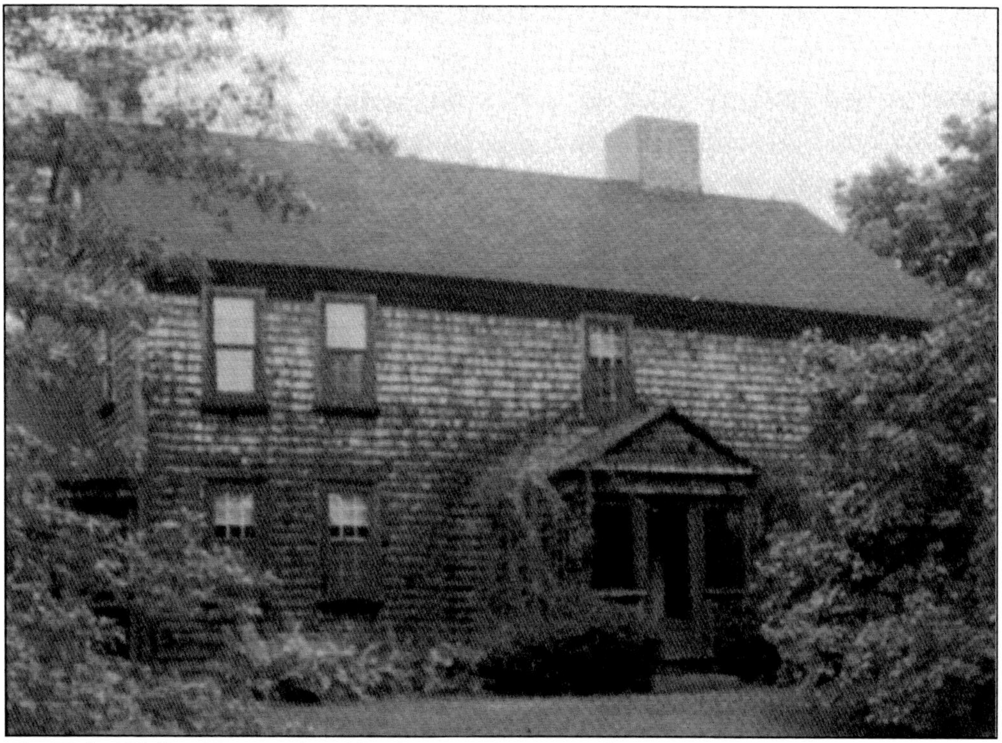

The Philip Walker House is the oldest house in East Providence. It was first built on the outskirts of the Ring in 1643, but it burned in 1675 and was rebuilt *c.* 1678. The house is listed on the National Register of Historic Places.

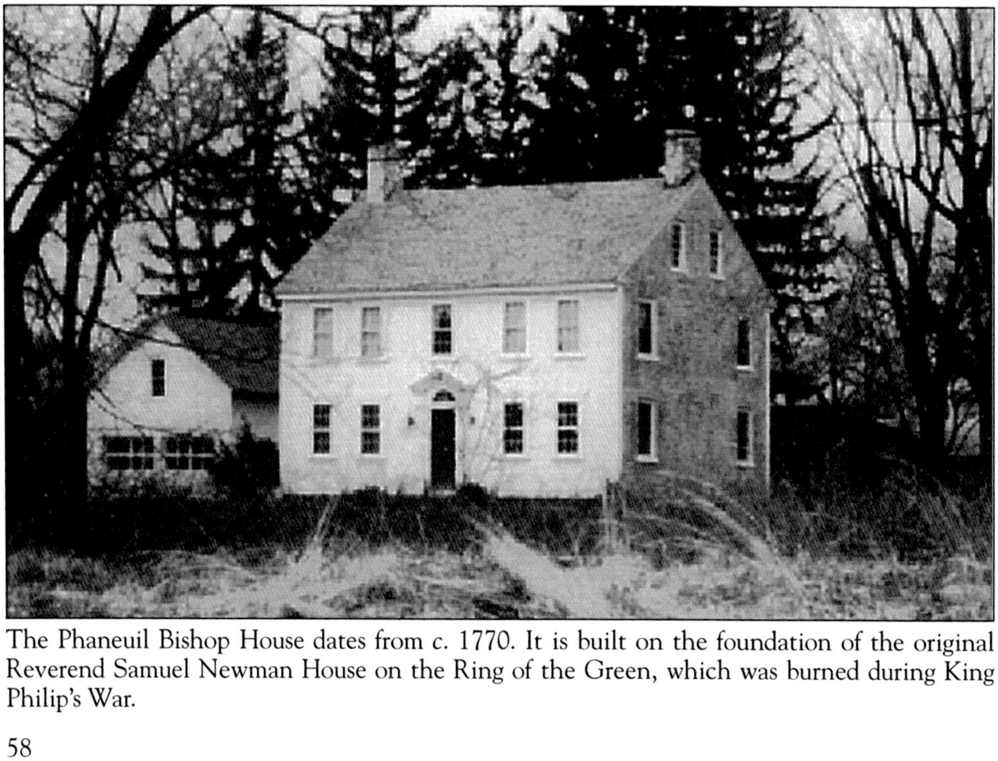

The Phaneuil Bishop House dates from *c.* 1770. It is built on the foundation of the original Reverend Samuel Newman House on the Ring of the Green, which was burned during King Philip's War.

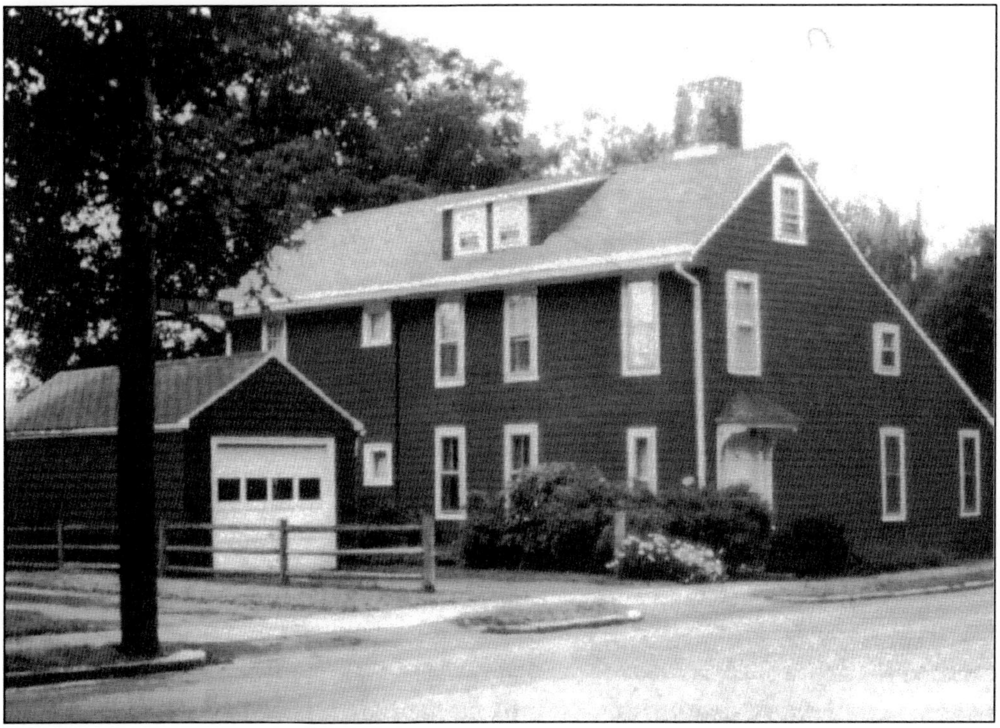

The Nathaniel Daggett House was built before 1708 on Roger Williams Avenue at the foot of Newman Avenue hill, which later became Wilson Avenue. Daggett was the son of John Daggett Jr., who is said to have built the Daggett House in Slater Park in Pawtucket. Daggett ran a shipping business behind this house on Omega Pond, then known as Seekonk Cove.

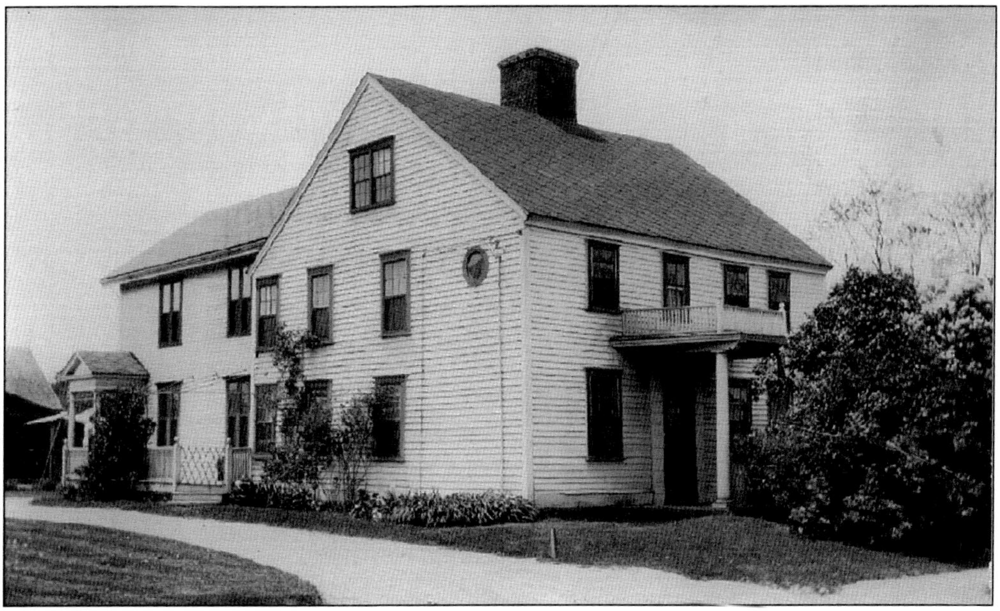

King Philip sat in a chair that was taken from the original Abell House, which stood on the Ring of the Green at this site. Built in 1643, it burned in 1675. This second Abell House was built on the old foundation *c.* 1750. The rear addition was built *c.* 1880.

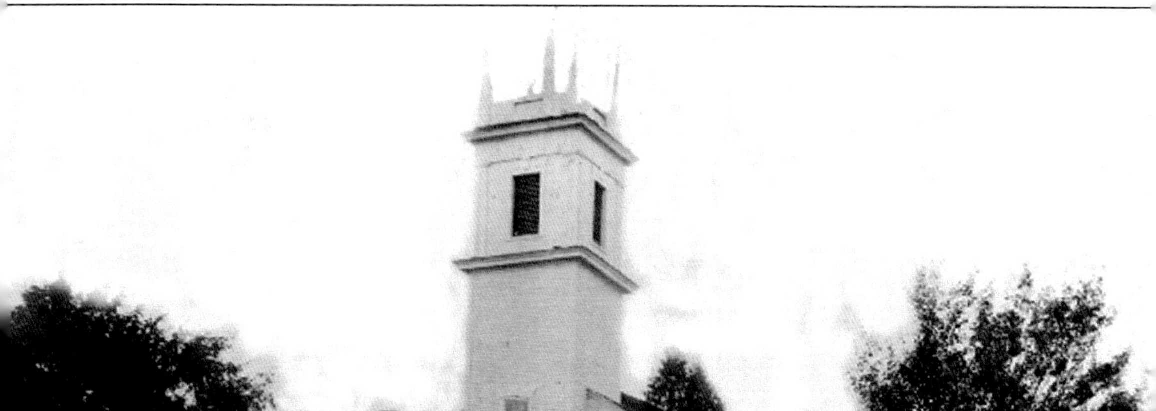

The Newman Congregational Church was built c. 1810 and redesigned in 1890 when the church was raised onto a foundation. The two side doors were removed and a portico was built over the front door. The congregation was organized in 1643 by the Reverend Samuel Newman and the first Newman Meeting House, which served also as a meeting hall for village business, was built across the street from this church in the center of what was the Ring of the Green. There is a stone indicating that site on Newman Avenue across from the present church. When King Philip burned the first meetinghouse in 1675, a second and later a third were built. By 1810 a move was in the works to change the town name from Rehoboth to Seekonk, and a new town hall was planned to go on Pawtucket Avenue. The congregation could now have a full-fledged church building. The lumber from the third meetinghouse was used to build the new town hall in 1812.

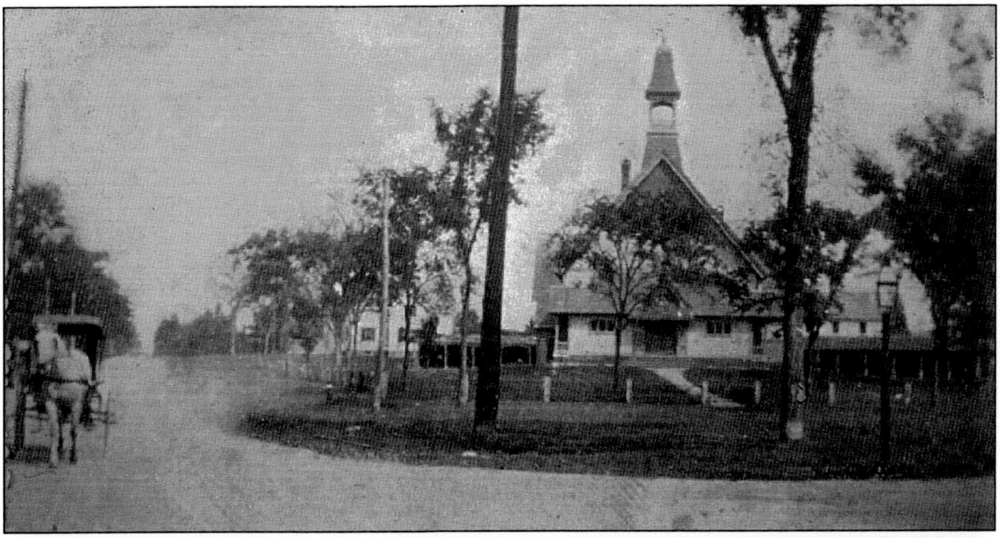

The First Baptist Church was built in 1897 on the site of the original church, which was built in 1790. The First Baptist still stands at the junction of Pawtucket Avenue (here a dirt road) and Pleasant Street. This scene was photographed *c.* 1890. Just visible over the carriage sheds at the right of the photograph is the old Rumford firebarn.

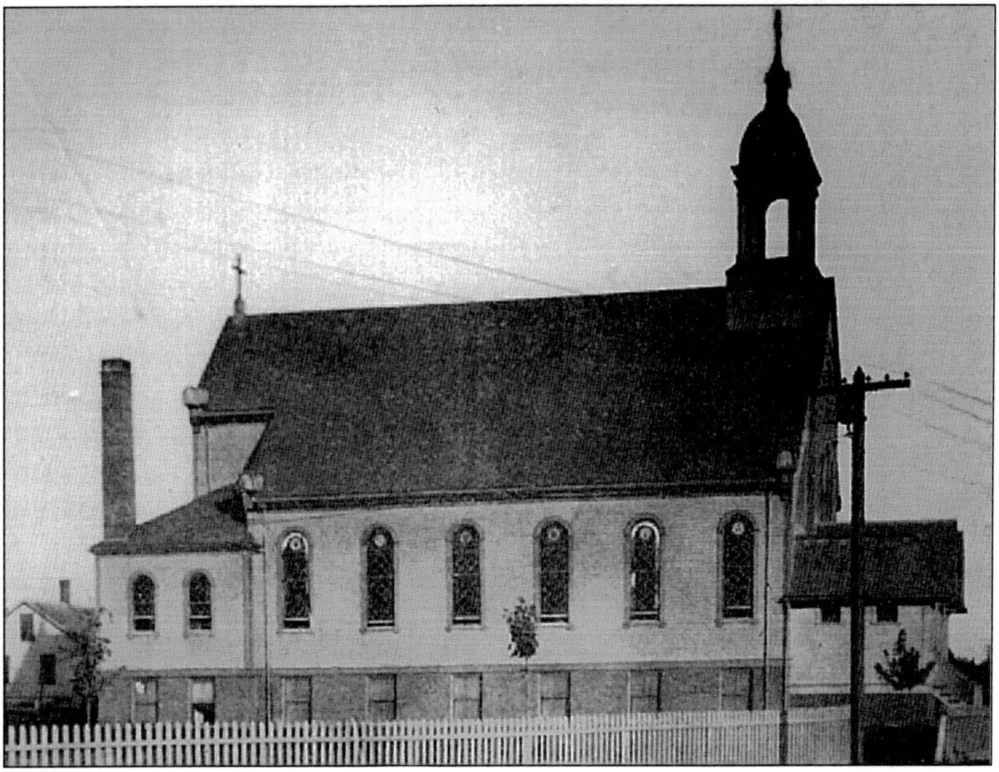

Bishop Matthew Harkins gave permission for a Catholic church to be built in the Rumford area in 1888. A meeting was held in the town hall to raise money for the new church. Ellery Wilson of the Rumford Chemical Works pledged $500 and donated a lot of land on which the first Saint Margaret's Church, pictured here, could be built.

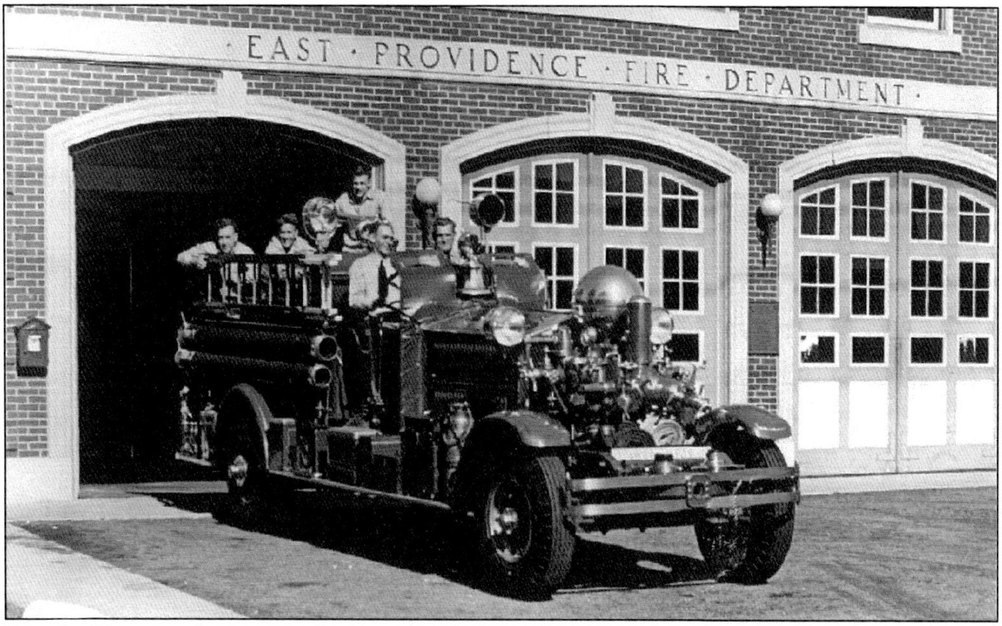

Rumford Engine Company No. 3 replaced the volunteer fire companies on Pleasant Street, the Rumford Company and the Phillipsdale Volunteers. This building is located on Newman Avenue across from the former Rumford Chemical Works. The photograph dates c. 1950.

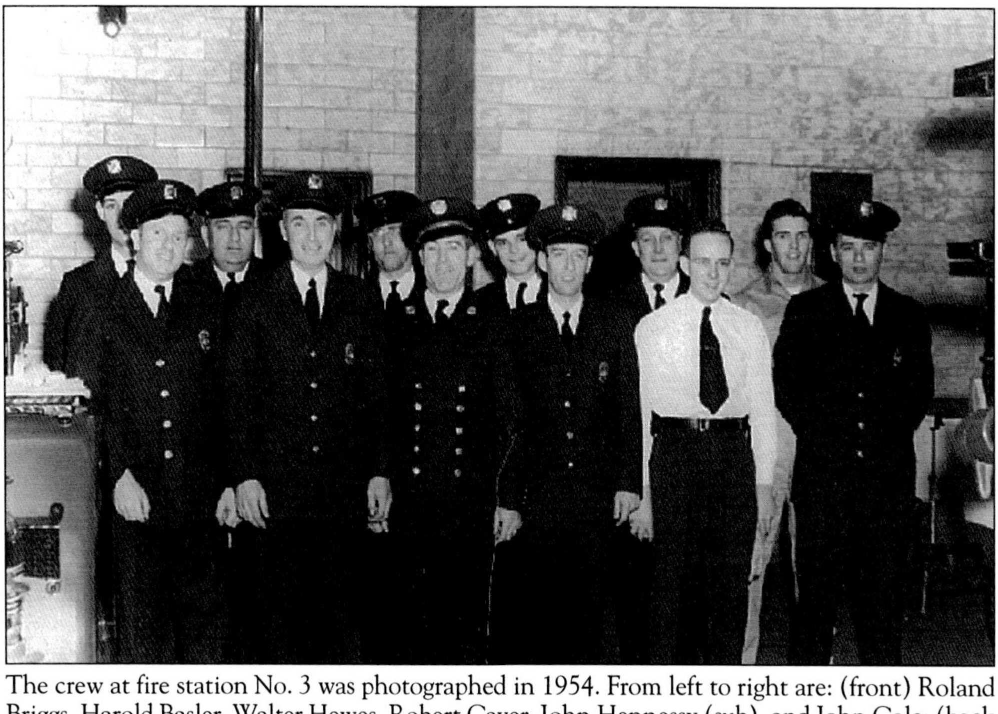

The crew at fire station No. 3 was photographed in 1954. From left to right are: (front) Roland Briggs, Harold Basler, Walter Hewes, Robert Cayer, John Hennessy (sub), and John Cole; (back row) Joe Lawrence, Harold Unsworth, Norm Gladding, Roger Cronin, Martin Norman, and Vincent Poland.

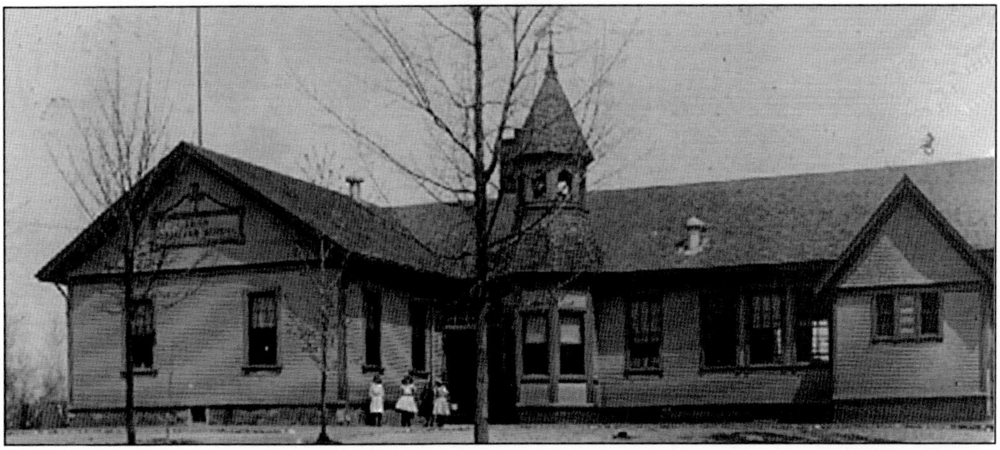

The Union Primary School was originally built as a two-room school in 1874. Later additions were built in 1900, 1904, and the 1960s. No longer a school, it is the East Providence Community Center and is on Pawtucket Avenue. The school bell is in the foyer of the Francis School on Bourne Avenue.

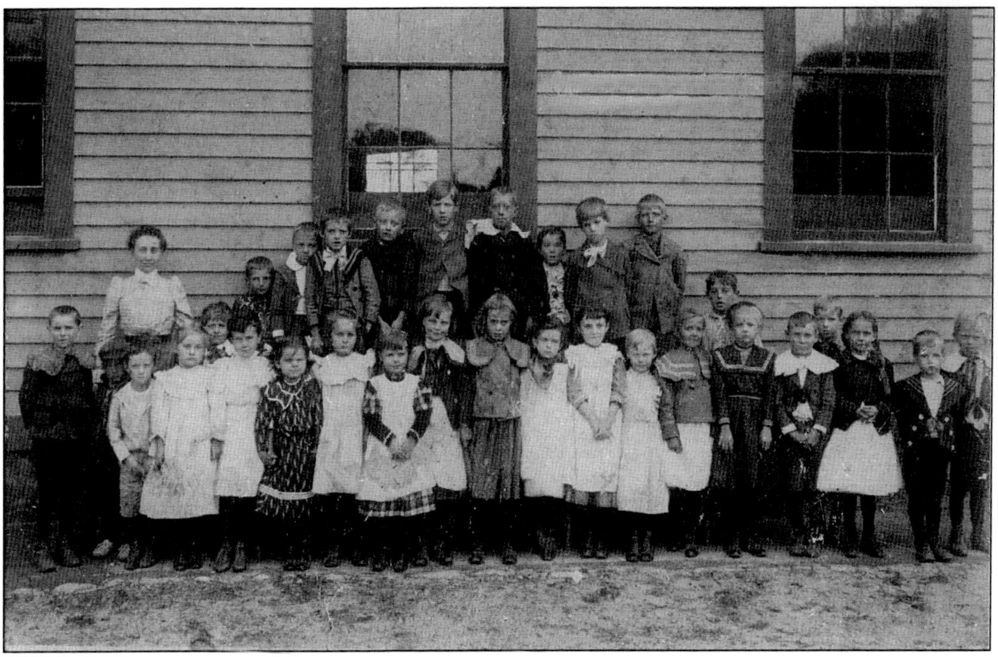

The teacher of the Union Primary Class of 1898 was Miss Moe. The students are, from left to right: (front row) Charles Carlson, Sidney Sharp, John Hall, Martha Nelson, ? Radigan, Edith Burgess, Emily Hammarlund, Esther Rich, Mary Pisber, Alice Anderson, Anne Hall, Helma Anderson, Selma Sandbeck, unidentified, Hattie Sharpe, Paul Dunbar, and Joseph Johnson; (back row) Elmer Linberg, William Sharpe, Victor Sharpe, Robert Dunbar, ? Johnson, ? Nelson, Sven Swenson, and Steve Hopkins.

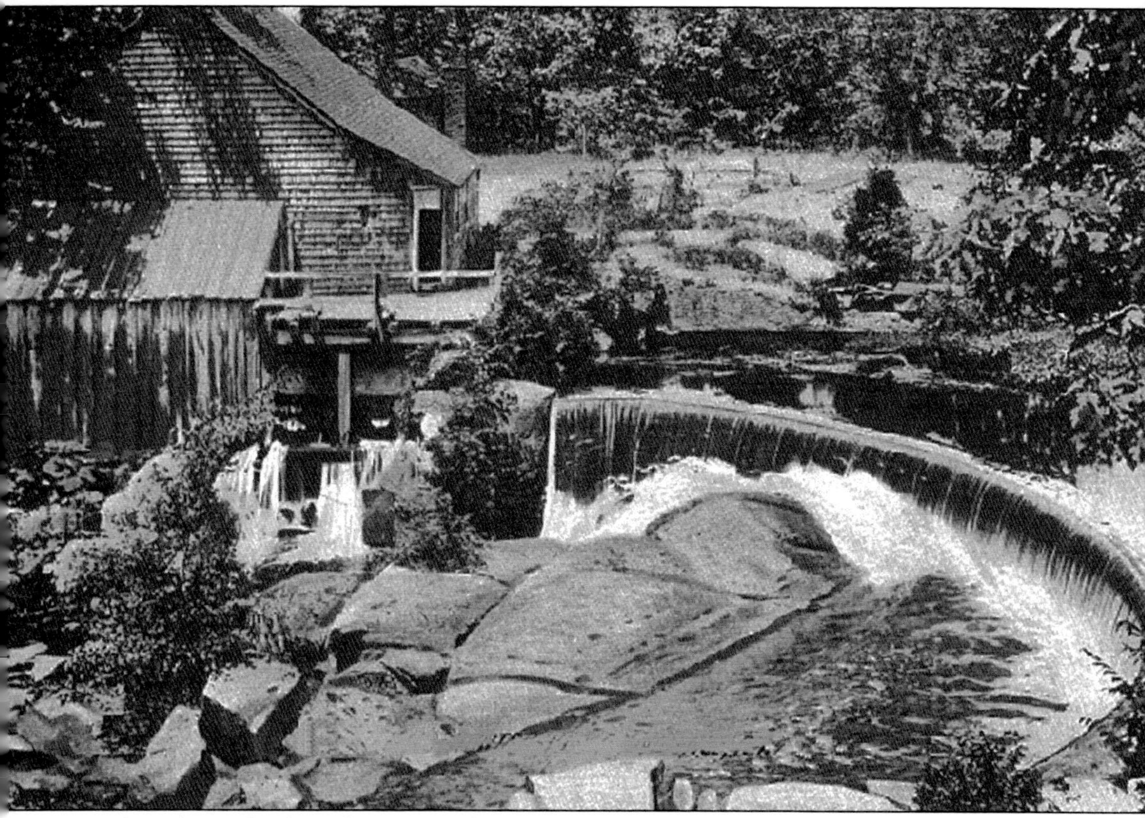

When the Seekonk settlement was being planned, the first buildings erected were the sawmill and gristmill on the upper part of the Ten Mile River. Across from the John Hunt House today are the remains of a natural dam and the remaining foundation of the original gristmill built there by Stephen Paine, one of the original fifty-eight settlers. The first mill was built in 1643 and was burned in 1675 during King Philip's War. This second one was rebuilt soon after and remained standing until the 1890s, when the Rumford Chemical Works tore it down. In 1878 the Rumford Company had purchased much of the surrounding area, which had become known as Hunt's Mills, to serve as a water source for its factory. The natural dam is to the left of the picture and the man-made dam to the right was built in the late nineteenth century. This postcard picture became a kind of logo for the Hunt's Mills area over the years.

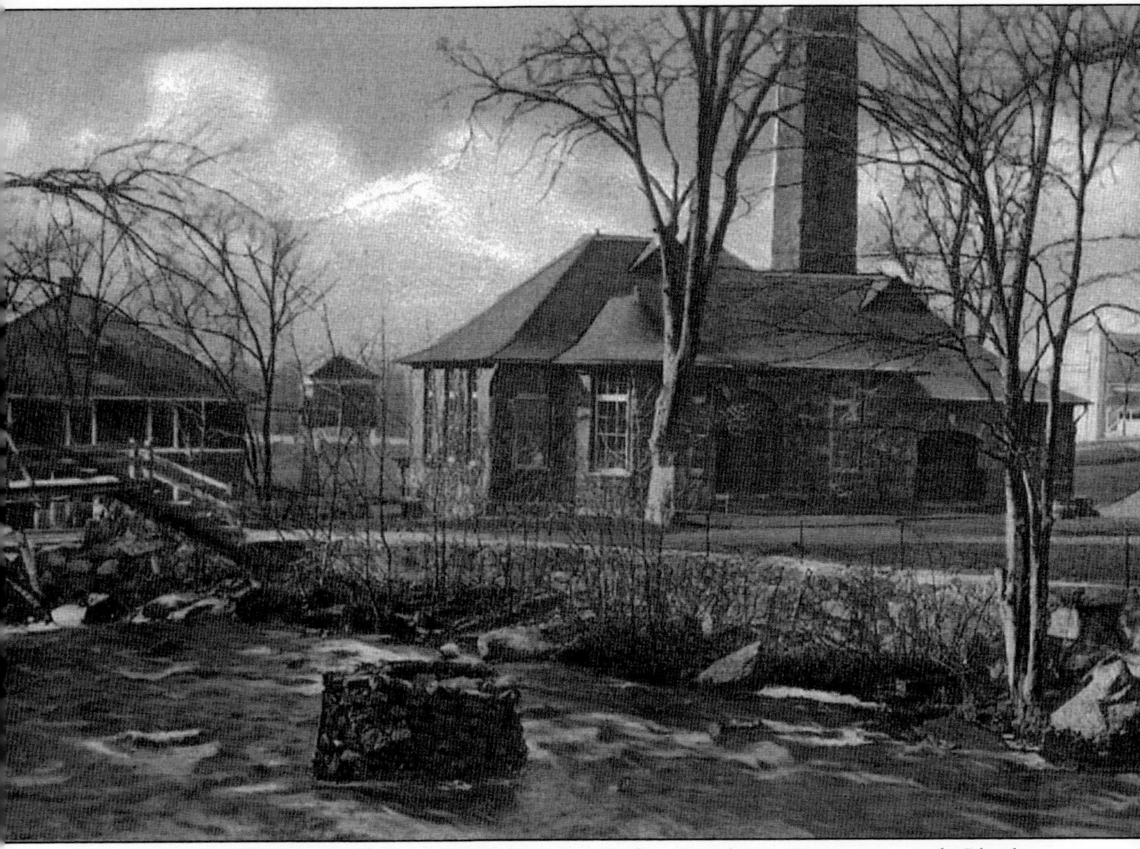

In *c.* 1894 the Rumford Chemical Works, the Sayles Finishing Company, and Glenlyon Bleachery joined forces to build a water company at the old mill site on the Ten Mile River. The pump house pictured here was built on the site of an old fulling mill. The turbine within provided power to pump water to the Kent Heights water tower. Several auxiliary buildings were also built to aerate and purify the water. Power from the pump house generated enough electricity to power an amusement park, which was built soon after 1895 at the site. At first the company was the privately owned East Providence Water Company. The Town of East Providence bought the operation in 1928 and ran it until the City of East Providence tied into the Scituate Reservoir supply in the late 1960s.

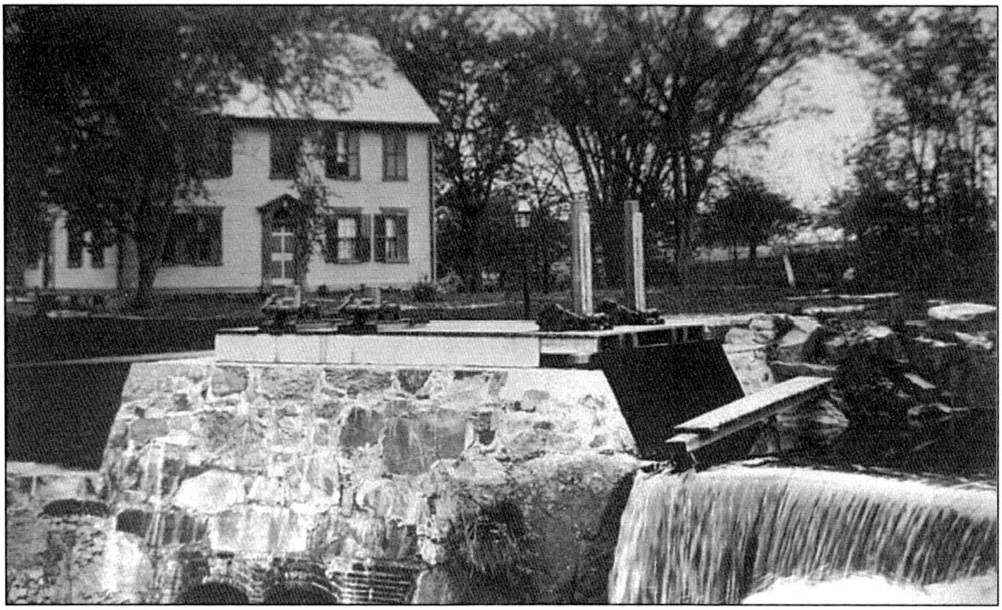

One of the first things that the Rumford Chemical Works did after buying the Hunt's Mills area was to take down the old gristmill. The foundation is in the foreground. The John Hunt House was built *c.* 1790 by John Hunt Jr. in the Federal-Georgian style. This house has been the headquarters of the East Providence Historical Society since 1988 and is owned by the City of East Providence.

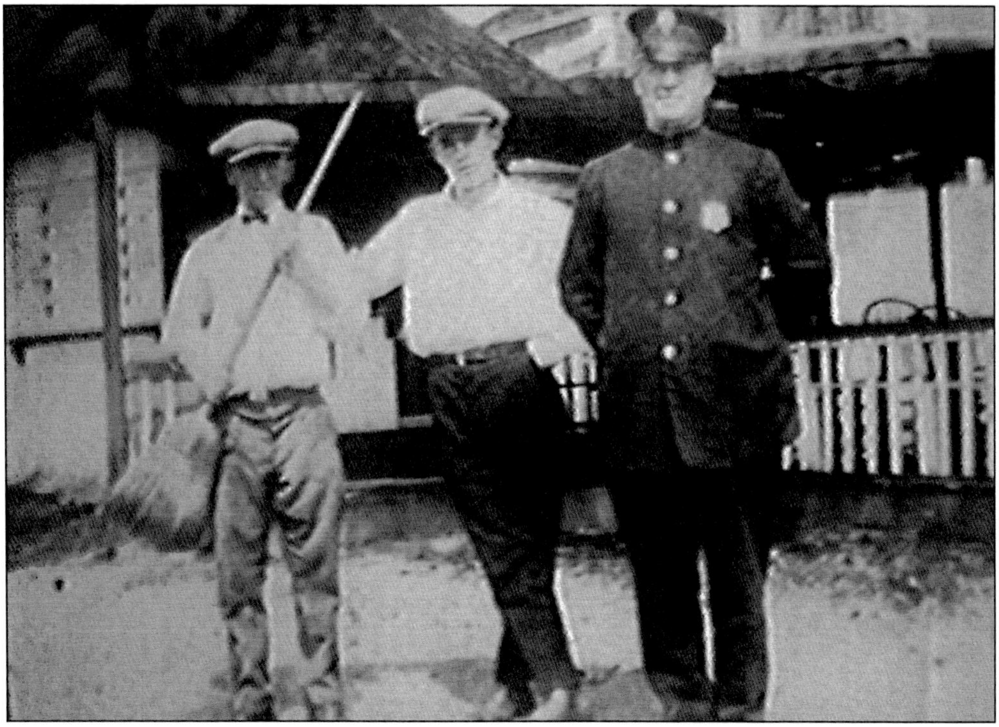

At the entrance to the Hunt's Mills area was a small variety store. A policeman patrolled the area on foot and is here pictured with one of the Rix boys and Jin Trainor (with the broom).

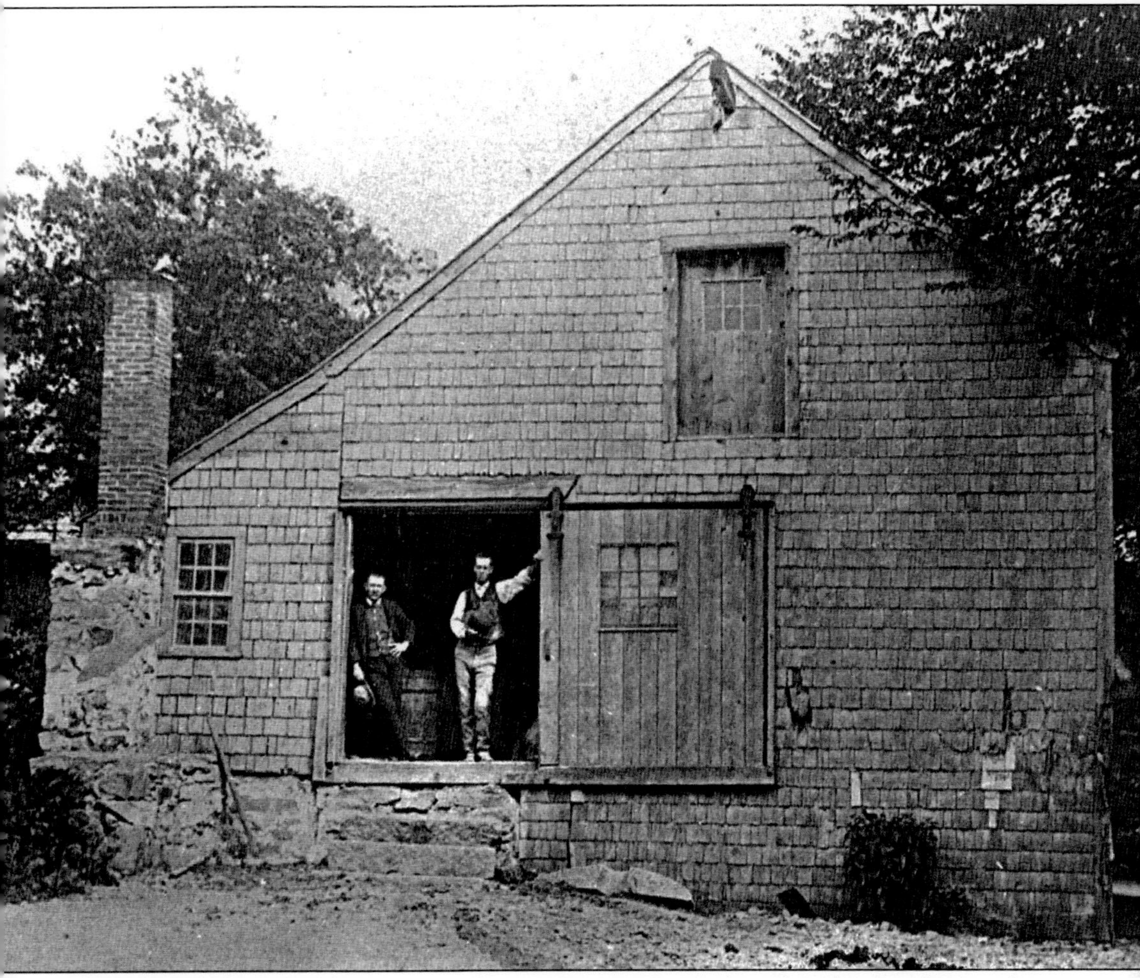

This gristmill at Hunt's Mills was just about to be torn down when this photograph was taken. Payne built a total of four mills in this area. There was a sawmill, dye mill, and fulling mill along with housing for the mill owner. John Hunt Sr. bought the four mills and surrounding farm from his father-in-law, Henry Sweeting, in 1712. His son continued on, building the John Hunt House and adding a satinet mill. The Hunt family continued running the mills until 1866. In 1878 the Rumford Chemical Works bought the area. It seems apparent that the Rumford Company used the building for some purpose until it was razed. The steps below the two gentlemen are still in place along with the foundation, and are directly across from the Hunt House Museum. The City of East Providence owns the Hunt's Mills area today.

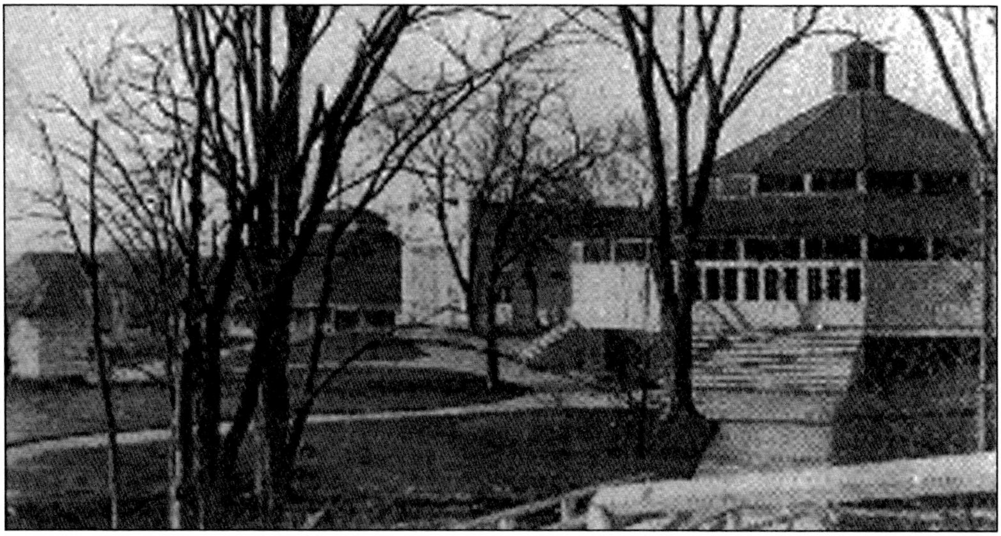

The Rumford Chemical Works, Glenlyon Print Works, and the Sayles Finishing Company opened an amusement park around the water company c. 1900 to provide entertainment for their employees and their families in summer. Its fame soon spread and the park became known as Hunt's Mills Park.

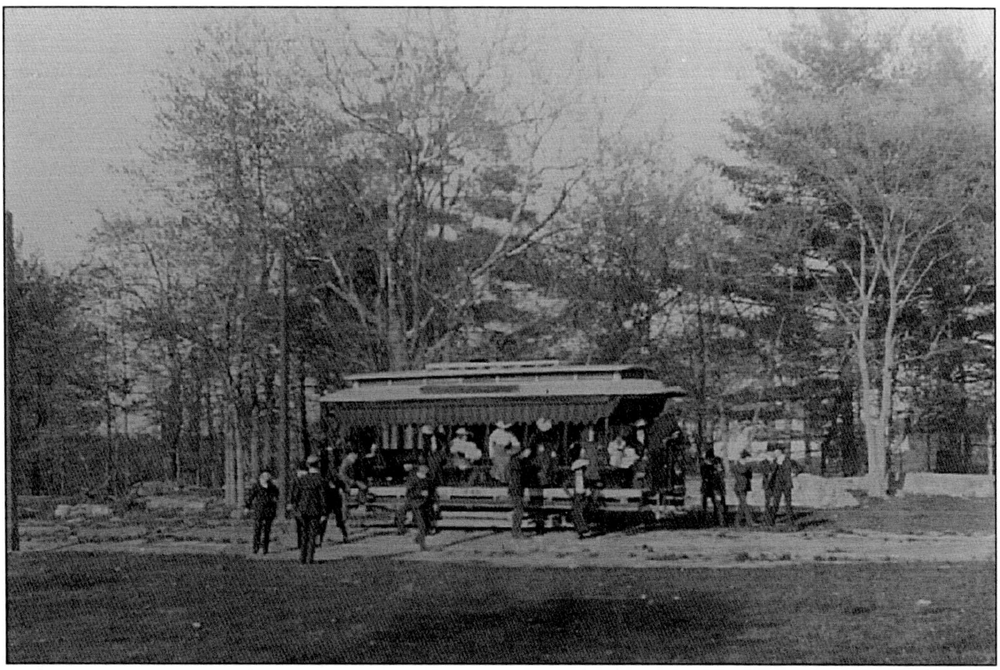

The trolleys crossed a trestle across the Ten Mile River to the park and returned to Providence the same way.

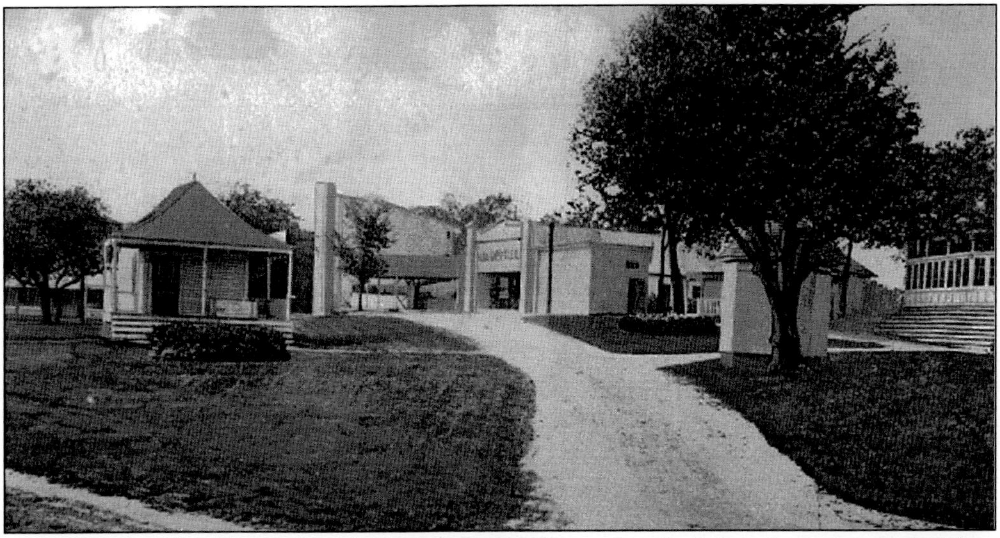

Hunt's Mills Park had a midway behind the pump house. On the left is the only park building still standing today. It was the park manager's office.

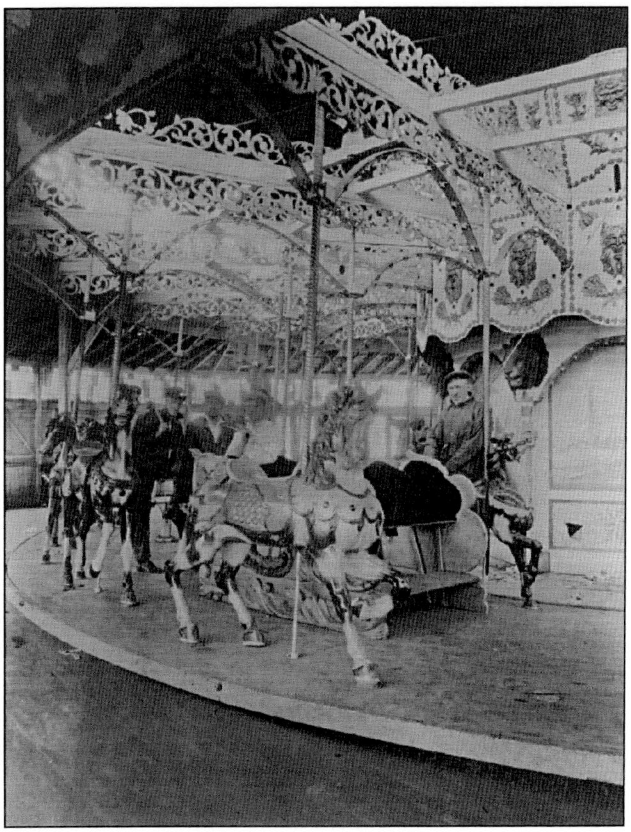

This is an extremely rare view of the interior of the Hunt's Mills carousel.

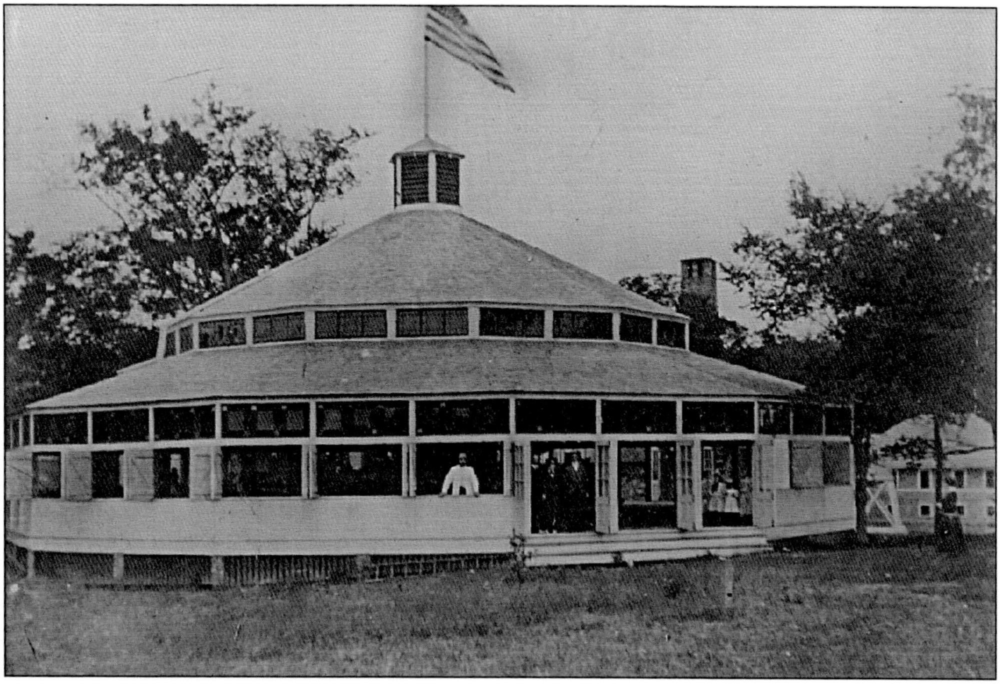

The carousel at Hunt's Mills Park is shown here *c.* 1910. The chimney of the pump house appears to the right of the roof. After the park closed in 1925, the merry-go-round was traded for a boxcar and $1,200 by Edward Fay, who had been operating it. It was moved to Atlantic Beach in Misquamicut, where it ran until the 1938 hurricane destroyed it.

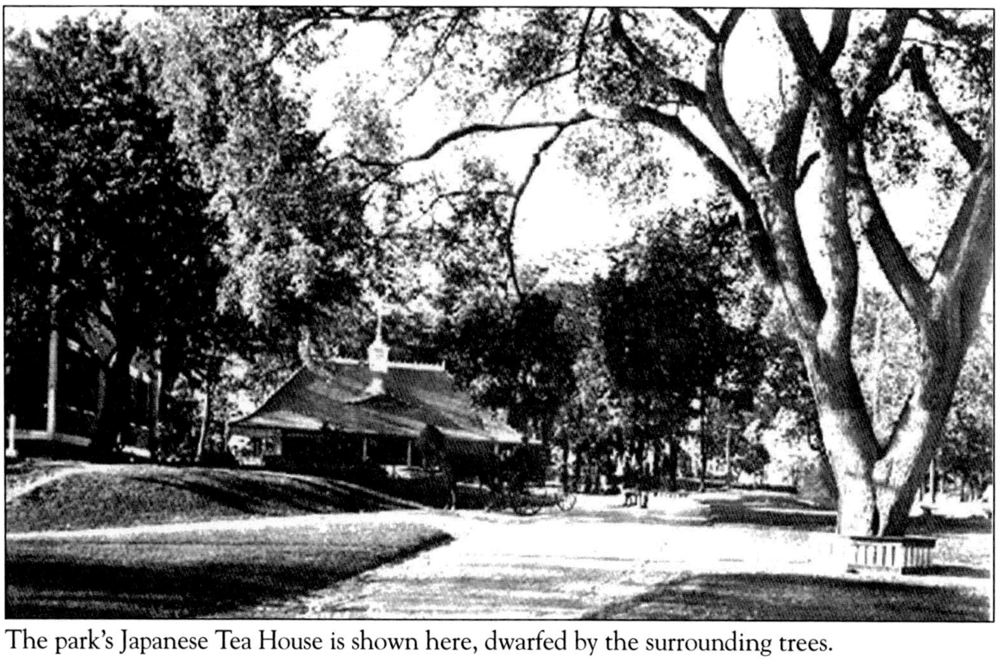

The park's Japanese Tea House is shown here, dwarfed by the surrounding trees.

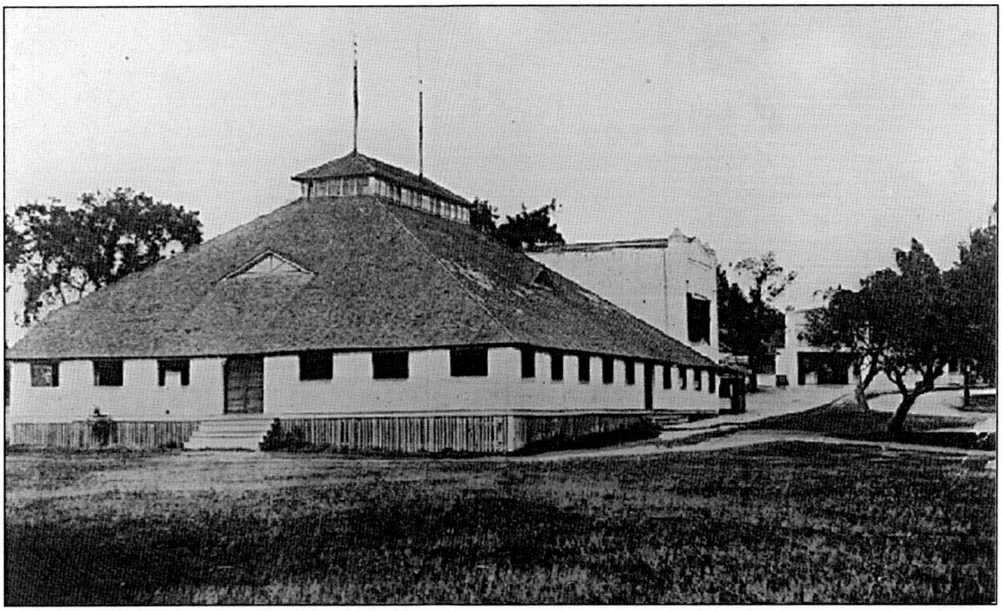

The Hunt's Mills Dance Hall was a popular place to go in northern East Providence. People traveled here from all corners of Rhode Island. When the dance hall burned down in 1925, it marked the end of Hunt's Mills as an amusement park.

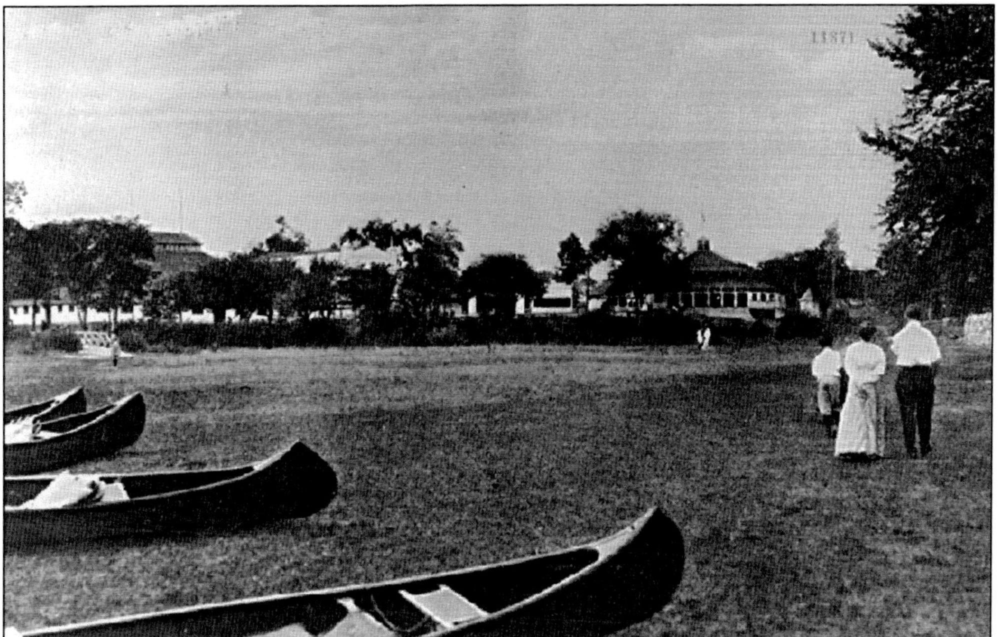

Canoeing on the Ten Mile River was a favorite weekend pastime. A couple could paddle up the river, park the canoe on the lawn, and dance the evening away or ride the merry-go-round.

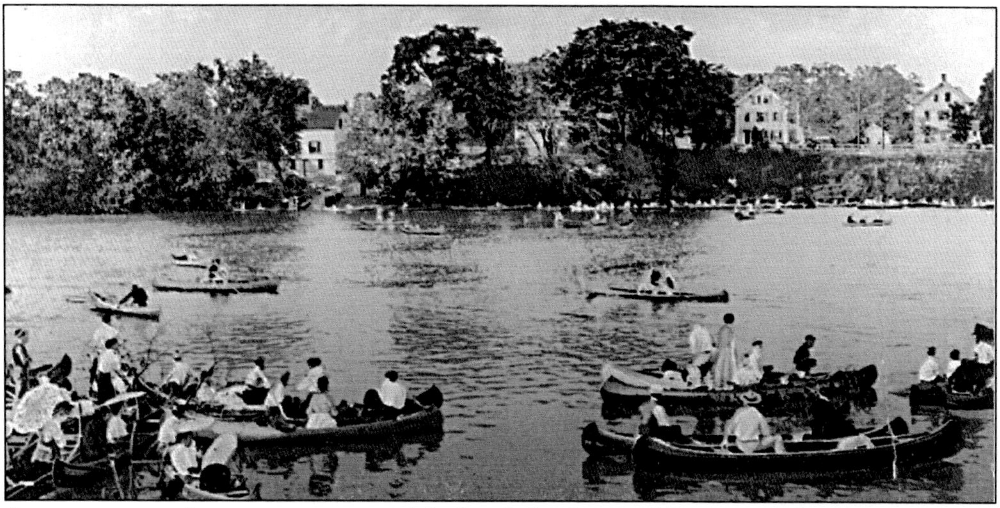

As many as two dozen private canoe clubs lined the shores of Omega Pond and the Ten Mile River. The pastime ended in the 1920s when the river and pond were lined with factories and the waters became polluted. The pond is Seekonk Cove, where Roger Williams first settled.

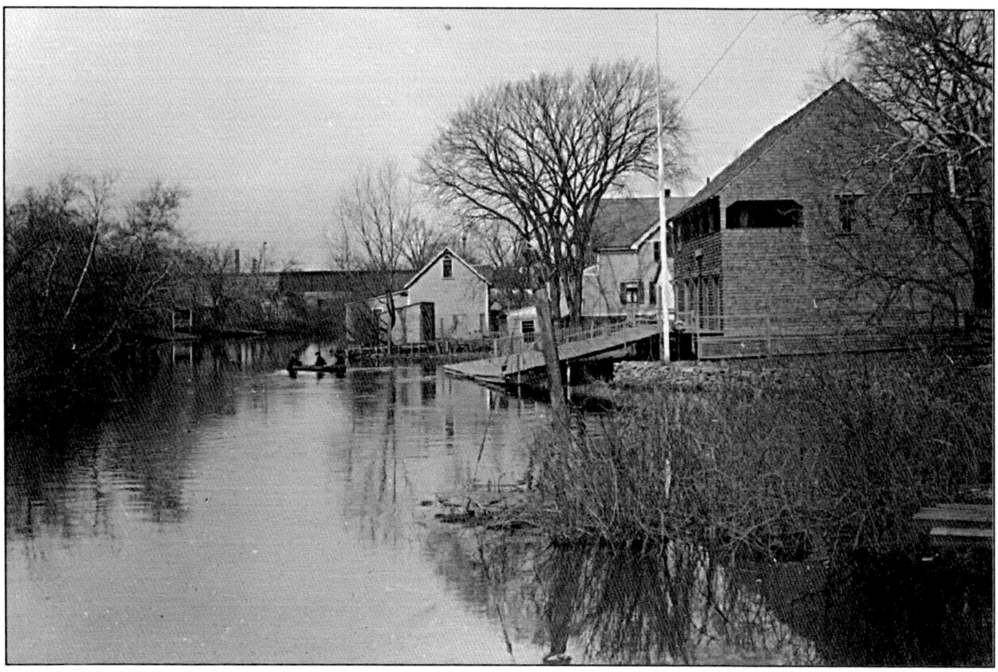

This view of the Ten Mile River is as it turns to enter Omega Pond just before the railroad trestle that crosses Roger Williams Avenue. The photographer was standing where the Sunshine Creamery parking lot is today.

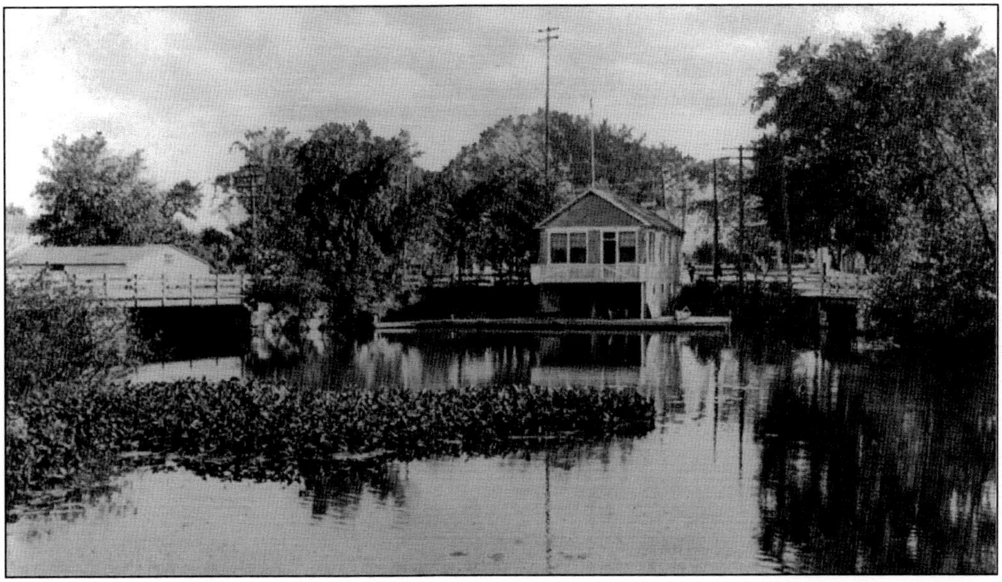

The canoe house above stood at the junction of North Broadway (on the left) and Roger Williams Avenue (to the right), and directly in front of the Agawam Hunt Club. The intersection became known locally as the "Boat House."

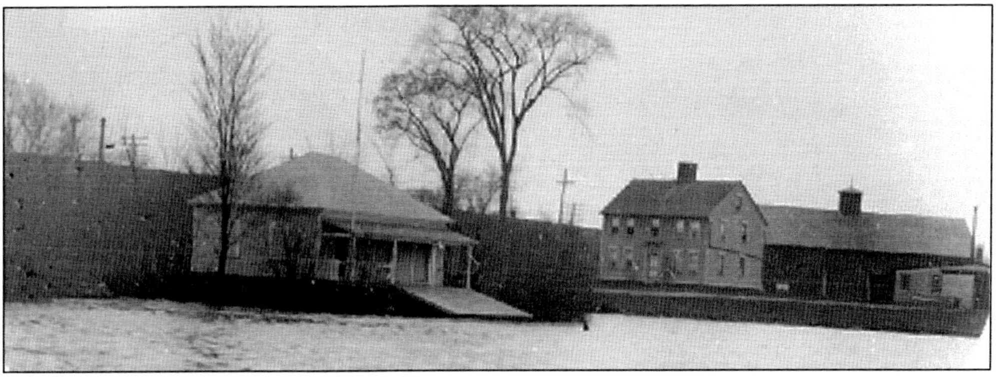

This canoe house on Omega Pond lay below the railroad tracks that crossed Roger Williams Avenue.

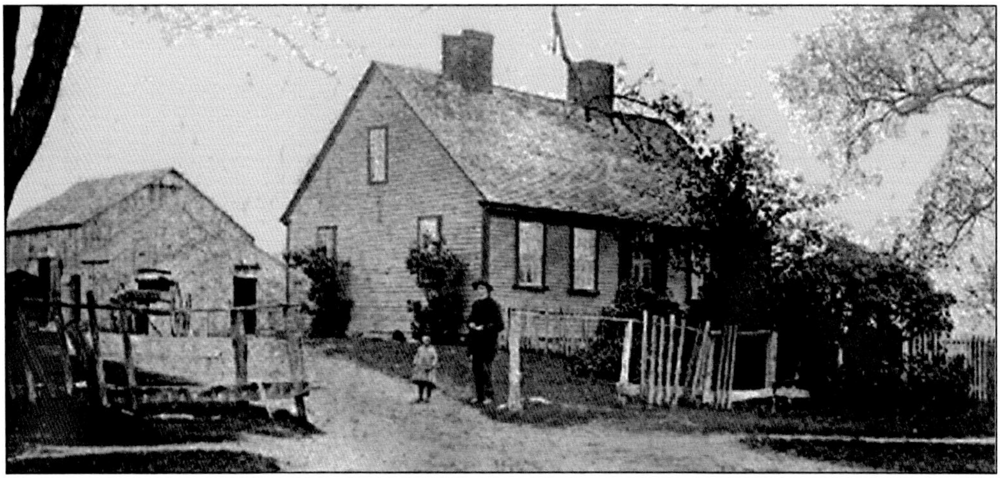

This photograph of the McManus House at 331 Newport Avenue was taken in 1865. The house belonged to James E. McManus. It had a barn and was probably built *c.* 1765. In 1865 Newport Avenue was a dirt road.

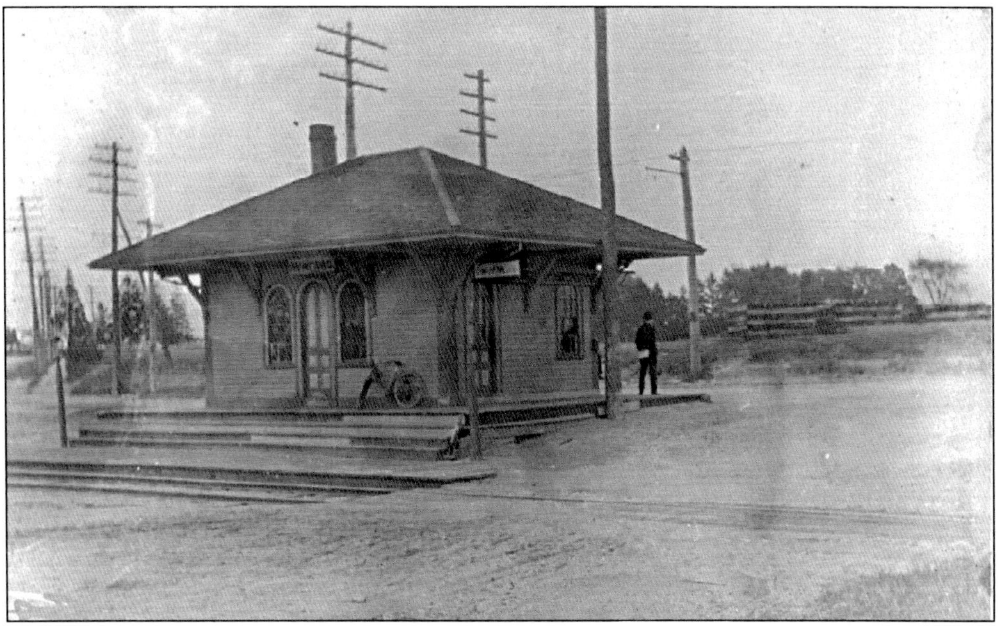

The old Rumford Depot stood right beside the tracks at the Greenwood Avenue crossing. Postmaster Britton ran the Rumford Post Office in the same building. It was razed in 1912 when the new Rumford Post Office and the railroad bridge were built. Trains stopped here on their way to Boston as early as 1835.

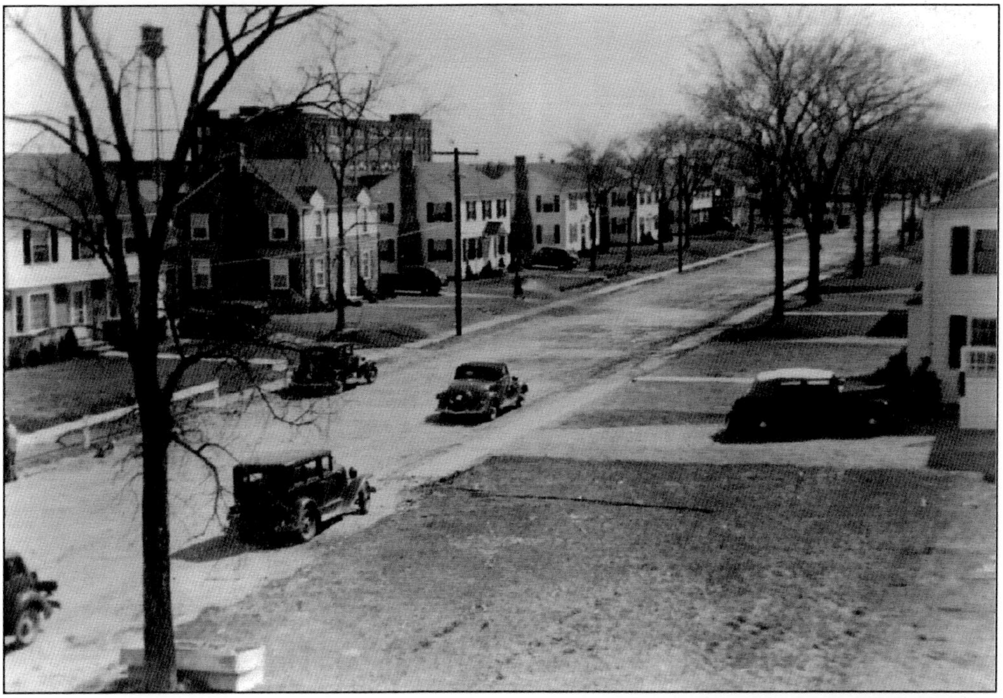

Whenever the Rumford Company ran low on money, another few acres of land would be sold off and platted. Don Avenue, named for a chemist at the baking powder plant, was developed in the early 1930s. Even though it abutted a railroad track, it was considered an upscale development at the time.

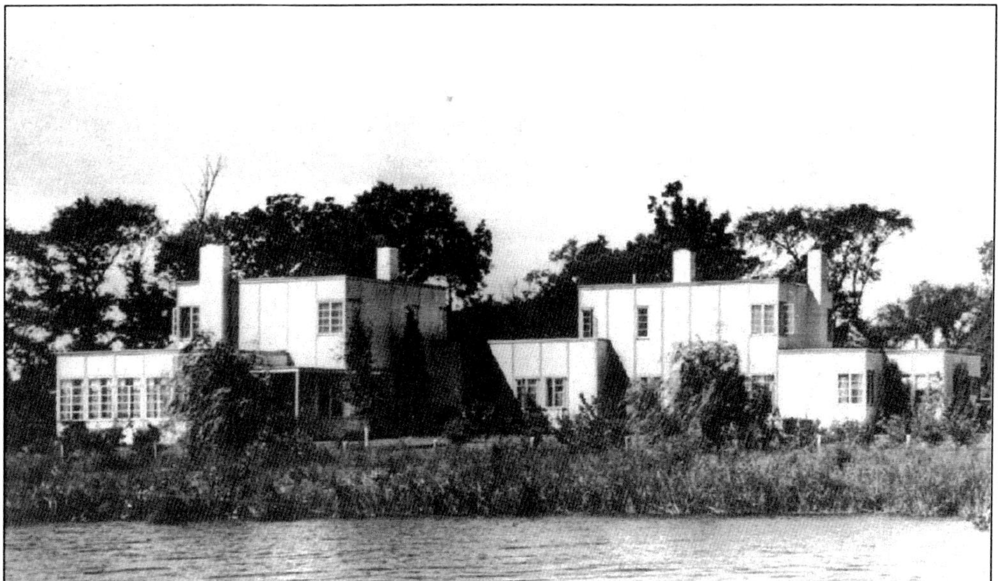

The Monsarrat Houses built *c.* 1936 just off Newman Avenue abutting the reservoir were considered experimental housing when designed by the General Housing Corporation. The two houses were connected and made of interchangeable panel construction.

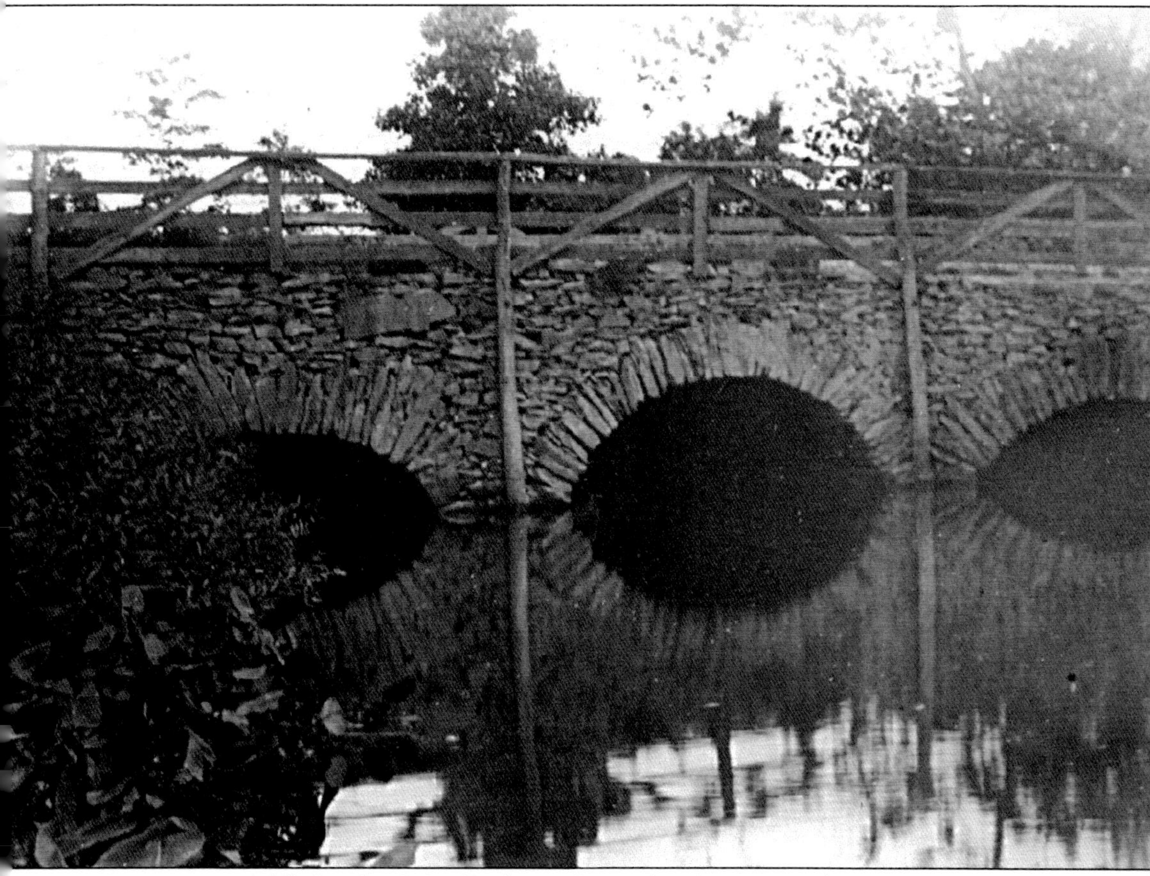

Canoes were paddled under Cole's Bridge on Pawtucket Avenue on their way up the Ten Mile River to Hunt's Mills. The bridge has been replaced.

Four

Phillipsdale

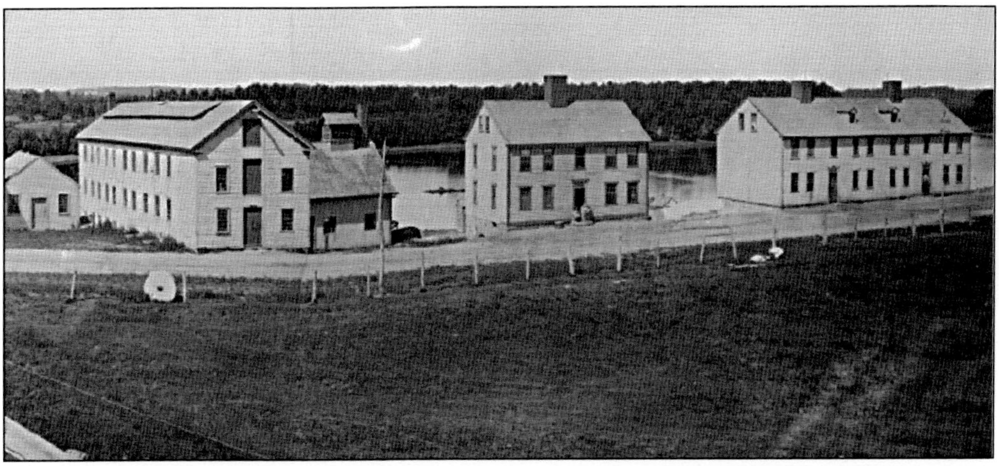

The Providence and Worcester Railroad laid track through the Rumford area while it was still called Seekonk in 1835. A spur laid in 1870 to Omega Pond along with docking facilities on the pond did much to attract factories into the area. The Omega Mill (shown here), also known as the Clyde, was built at the time of the American Revolution, and for a time cannonballs were made here. It was also used during the War of 1812 and to make ammunition during World War I. The mill on the left burned in 1976, but the millhouse at the far right still stands. This mill was followed by the Rumford Chemical Works, American Electrical, the Richmond Paper Company, the Glenlyon Print and Dye Company, the Sayles Finishing Company, and Bird & Son. This strip of land in Rumford along the pond and river became heavily industrial and became known as Phillipsdale. It was named after Eugene Phillips, who had founded American Electrical.

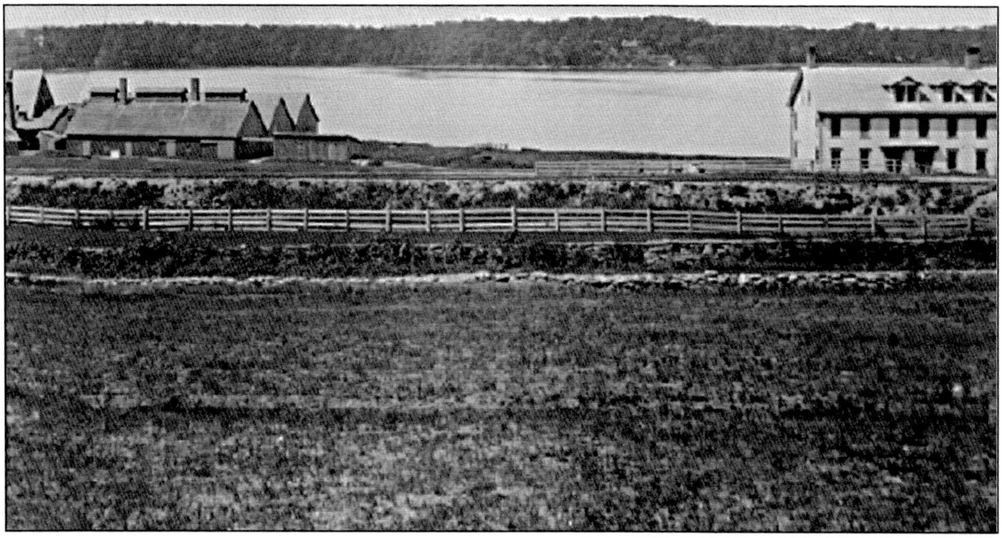

The Riverside works above are the site of American Electrical, later called the Washburn Wire Company.

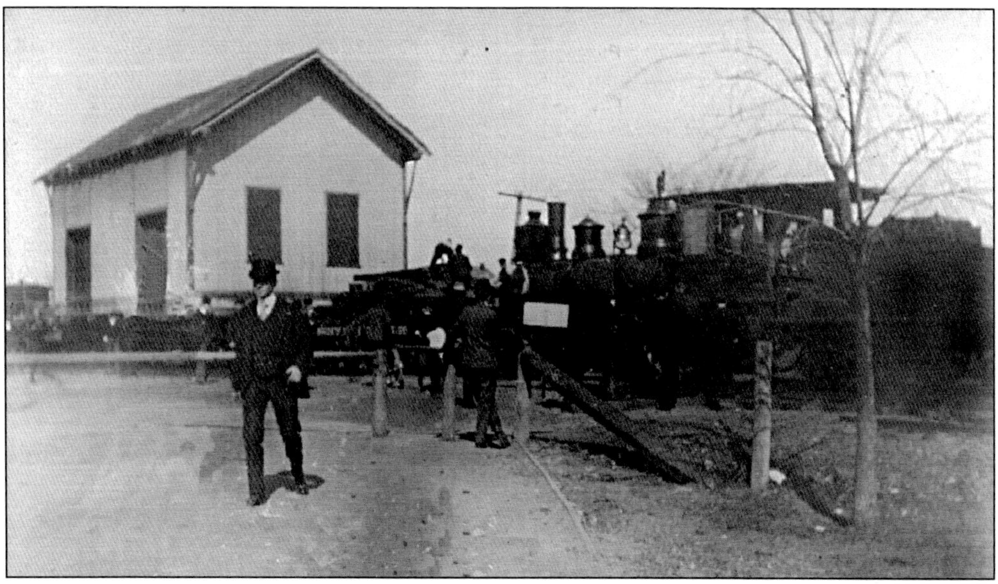

The Phillipsdale railroad station was located at the lower end of Bourne Avenue. This photograph was taken *c.* 1890.

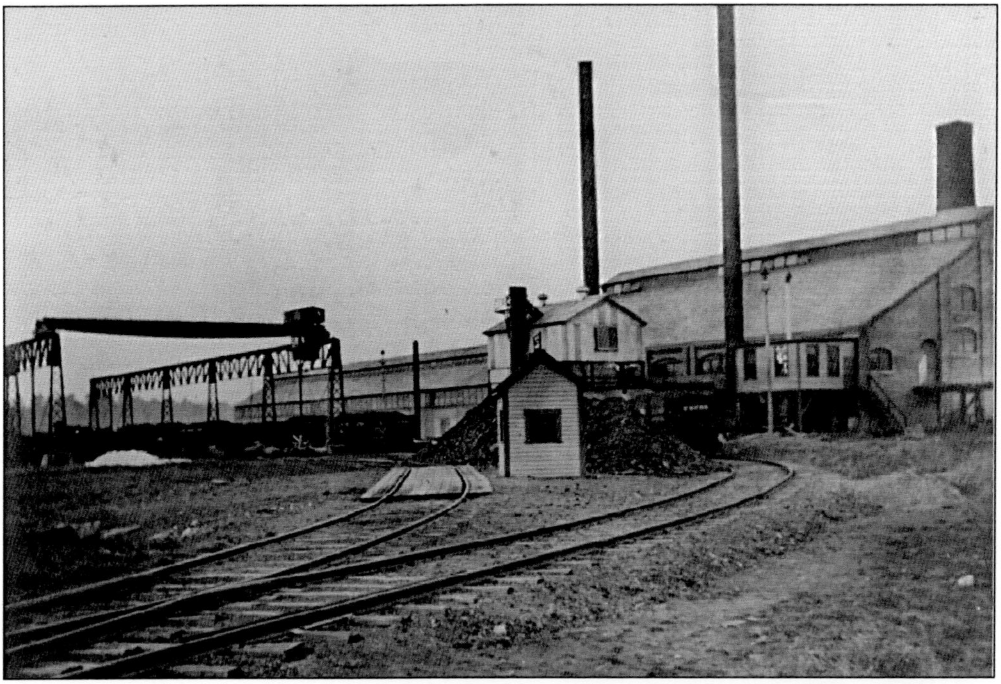

This photograph of the railroad yard at the Washburn Wire Company was taken *c.* 1900.

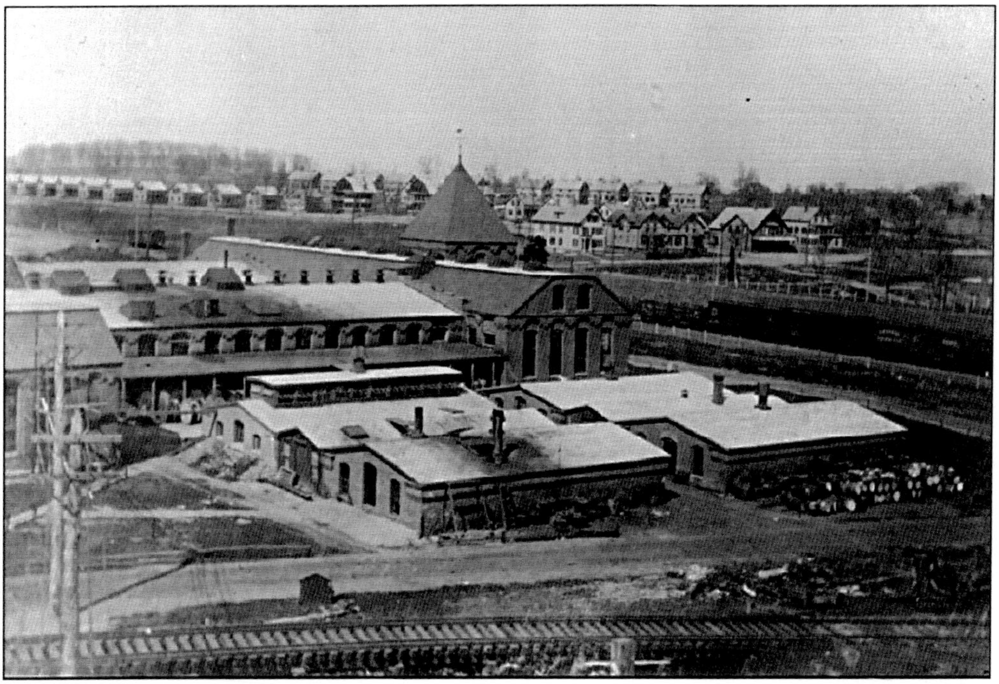

Taken in 1900, this picture of the Washburn Wire Company shows the row of mill houses built by Eugene Phillips for his employees. The houses are still standing today on Roger Williams Avenue. A few of those houses on Ruth Avenue above Roger Williams appear in the center top area of the photograph.

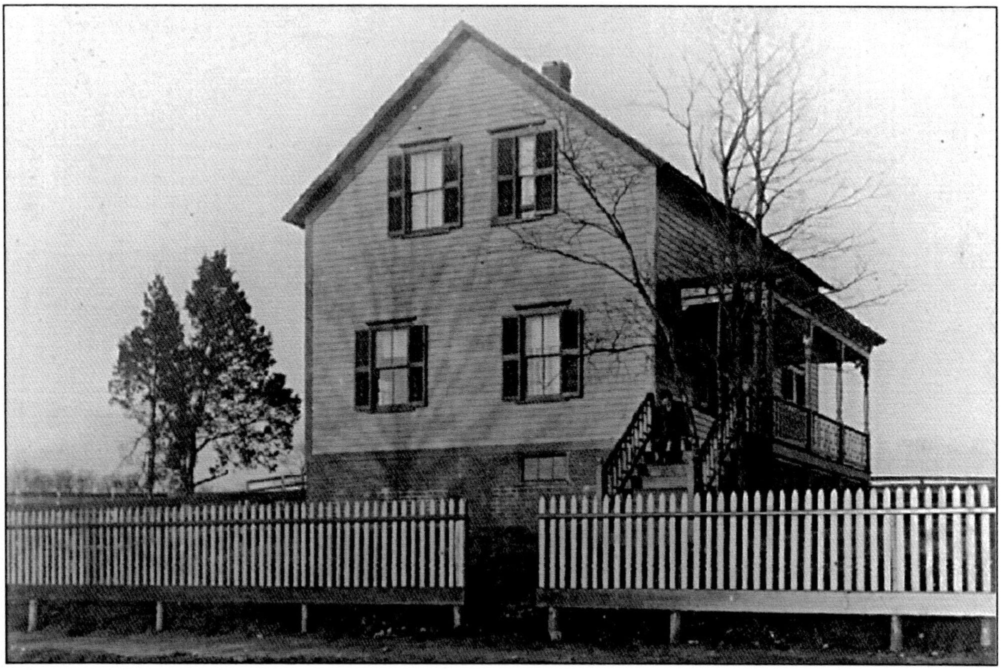

This Washburn worker's house is one of those single family mill houses on Roger Williams Avenue. Those on Ruth Avenue were two-family houses.

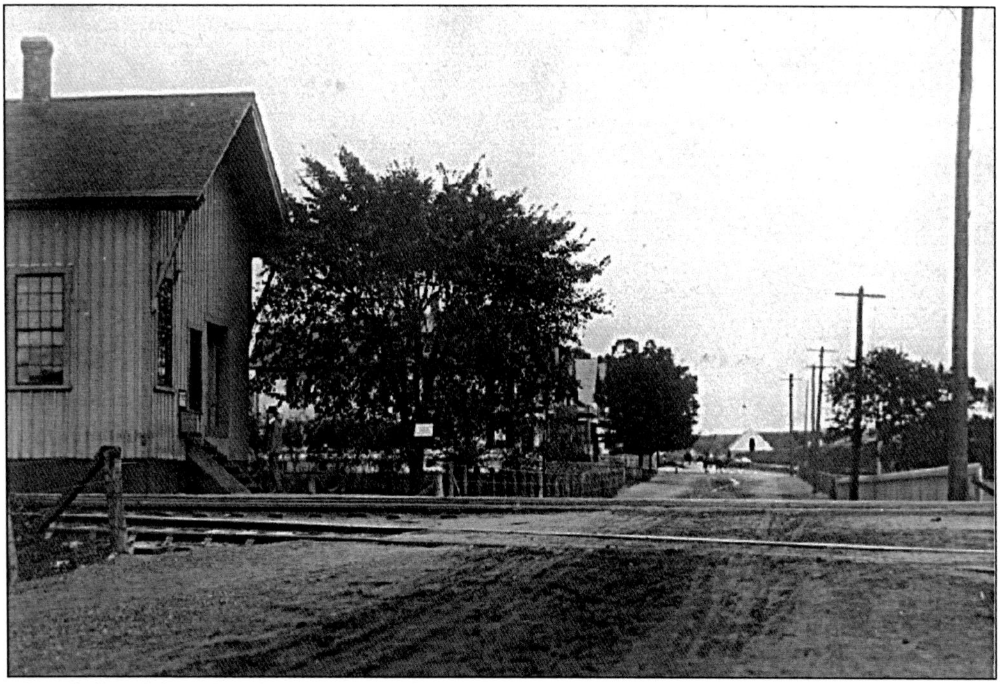

The Phillipsdale railroad station was taken down only a few years ago. Bourne Avenue looking east was a dirt road in 1910.

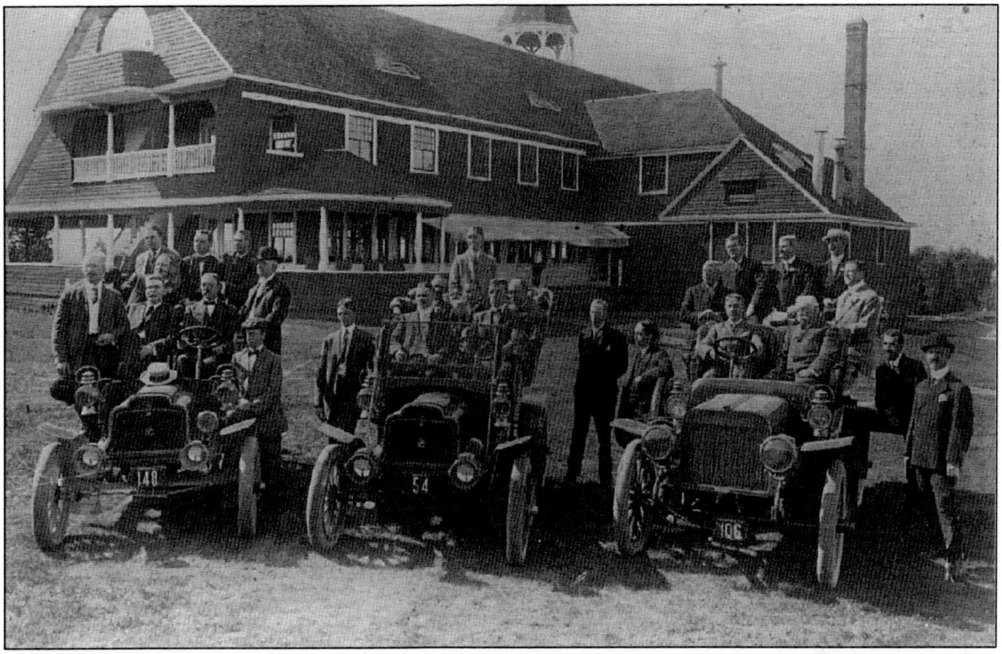

The Washburn Wire Company held its annual workers' family clambake at the Pomham Club in 1906. The club was famous for clambakes and was located in Riverside on Narragansett Bay.

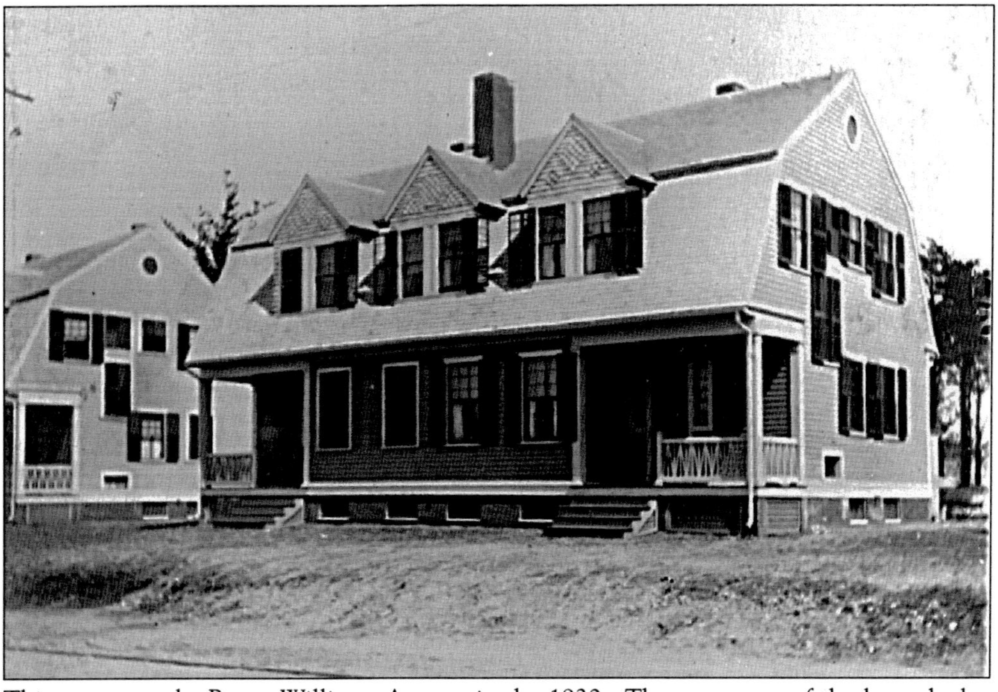

This appears to be Roger Williams Avenue in the 1930s. The occupants of the large duplex were the Macdougald family on the left side and the Farrell family on the right.

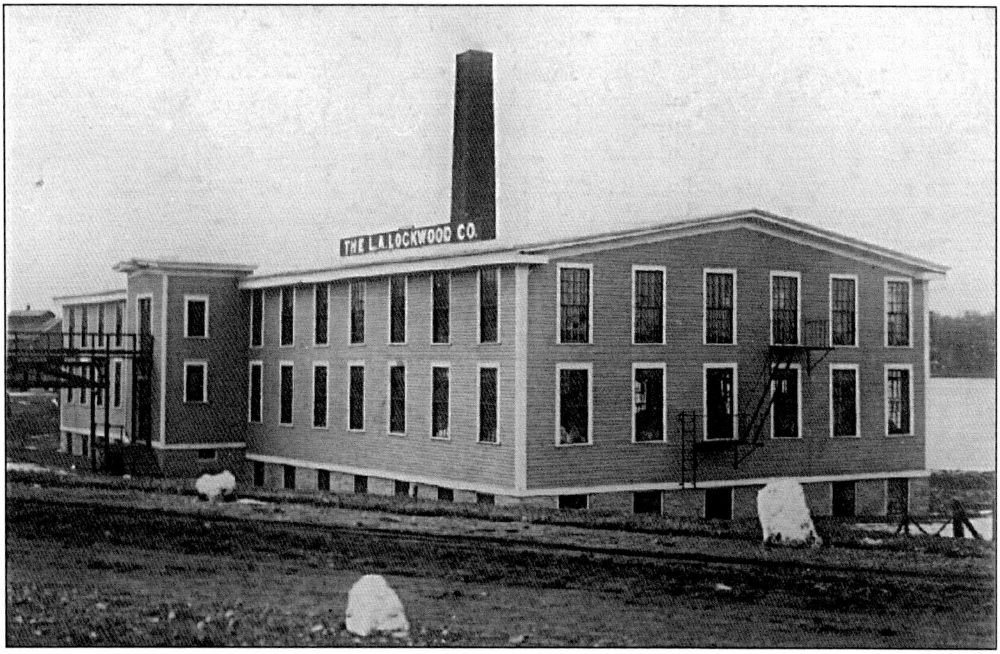

The L.A. Lockwood Company mill was located near the Omega Pond. The year was c. 1910.

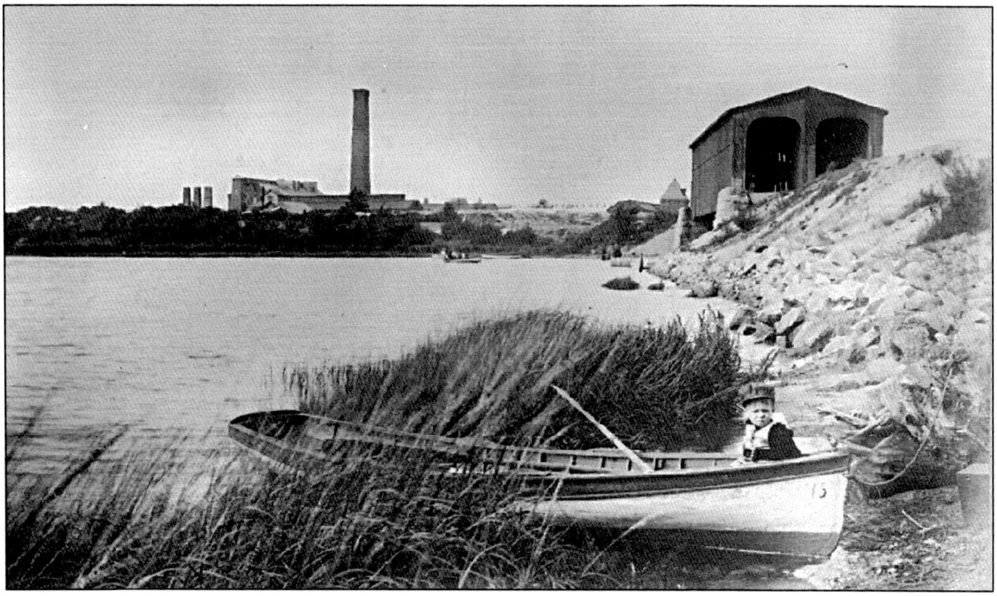

Whoever took this photograph of the little boy in the rowboat on Omega Pond recorded for posterity the old "Tin Bridge" and Washburn Wire Company in the distance as they appeared c. 1900.

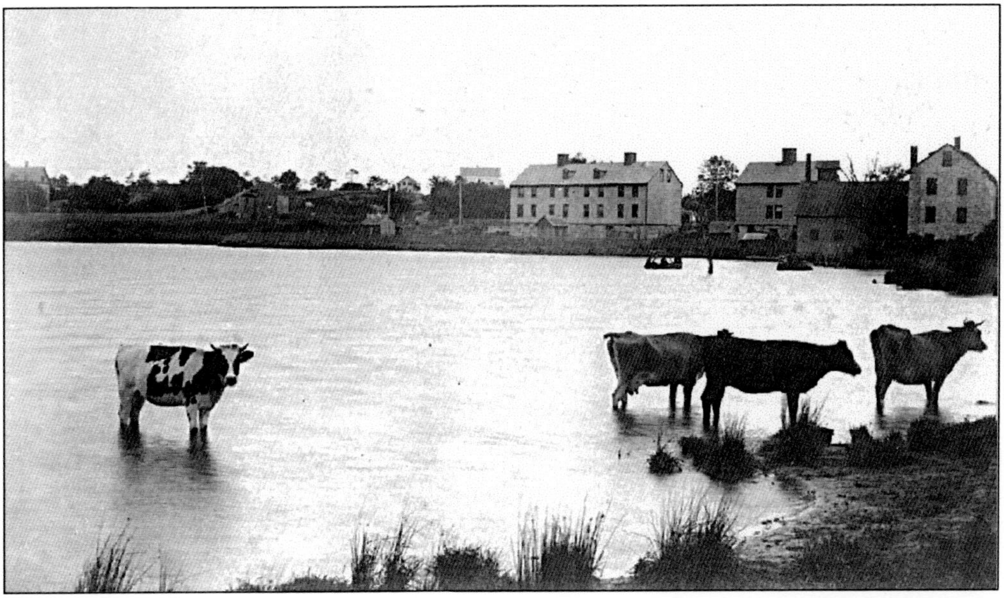

This rear view of the Omega Mills on Roger Williams Avenue taken *c.* 1890 indicates that some farming was still going on in the area. Farming here did not continue much beyond 1900.

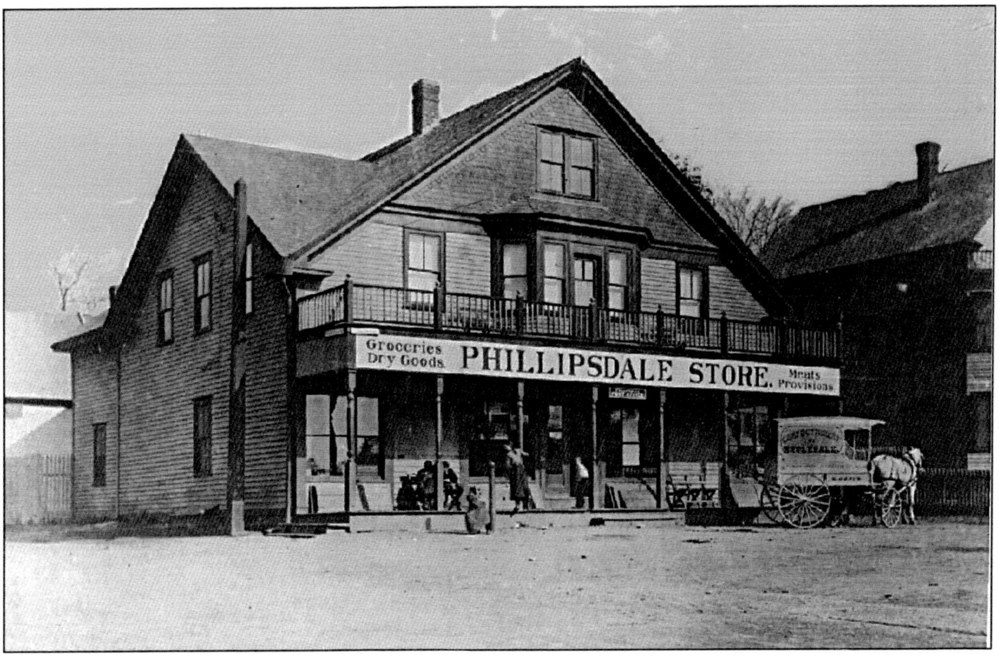

The Phillipsdale store was the company store serving Wire Company employees and their families. It also housed the Phillipsdale Post Office. Located at the corner of Roger Williams and Bourne Avenues, the building still stands as a reminder of a way of life long since gone. Almost all manufacturing in Phillipsdale has ceased.

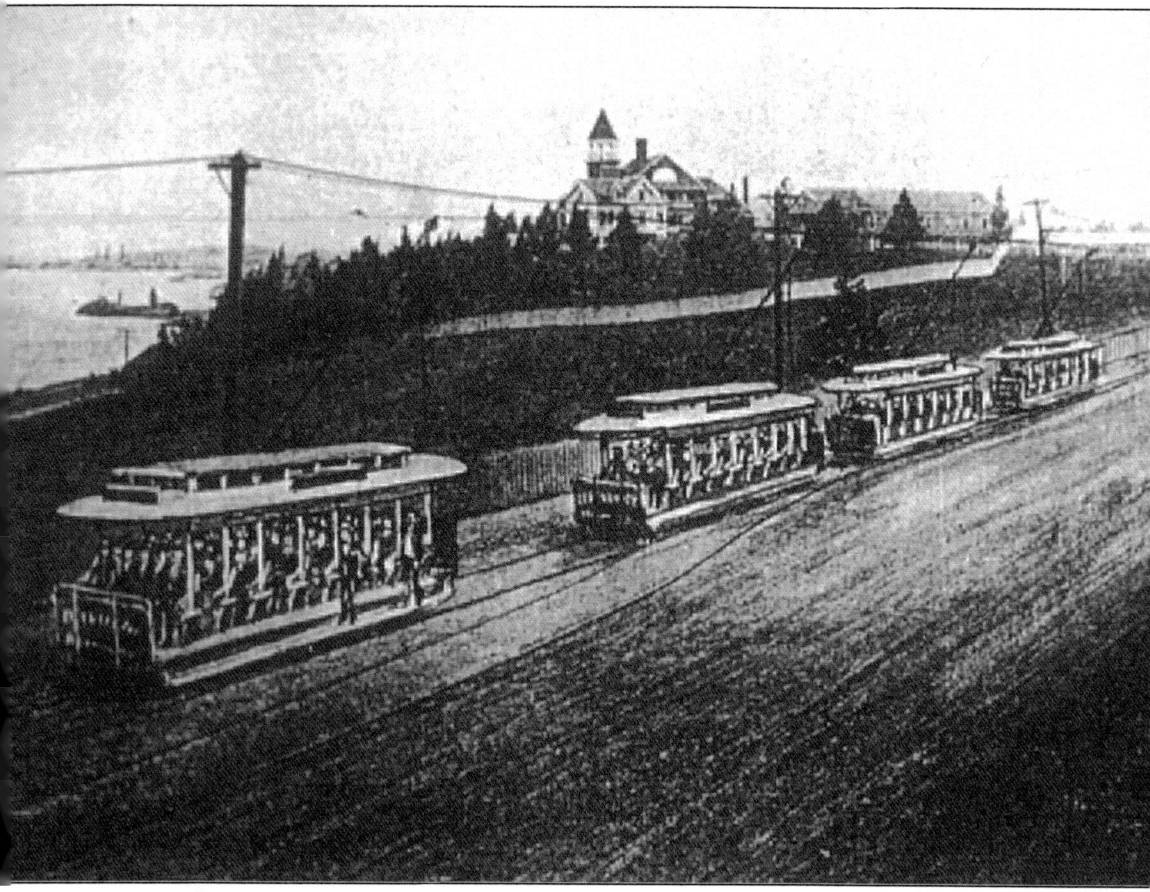

Open trolley cars were used in the summer to provide cool rides to East Providence. Not only would people be seated inside, but dozens of people would hang onto the sides of the car standing on a running board. The cars were a lot of fun to ride, but they could also be dangerous.

Five

Riverside

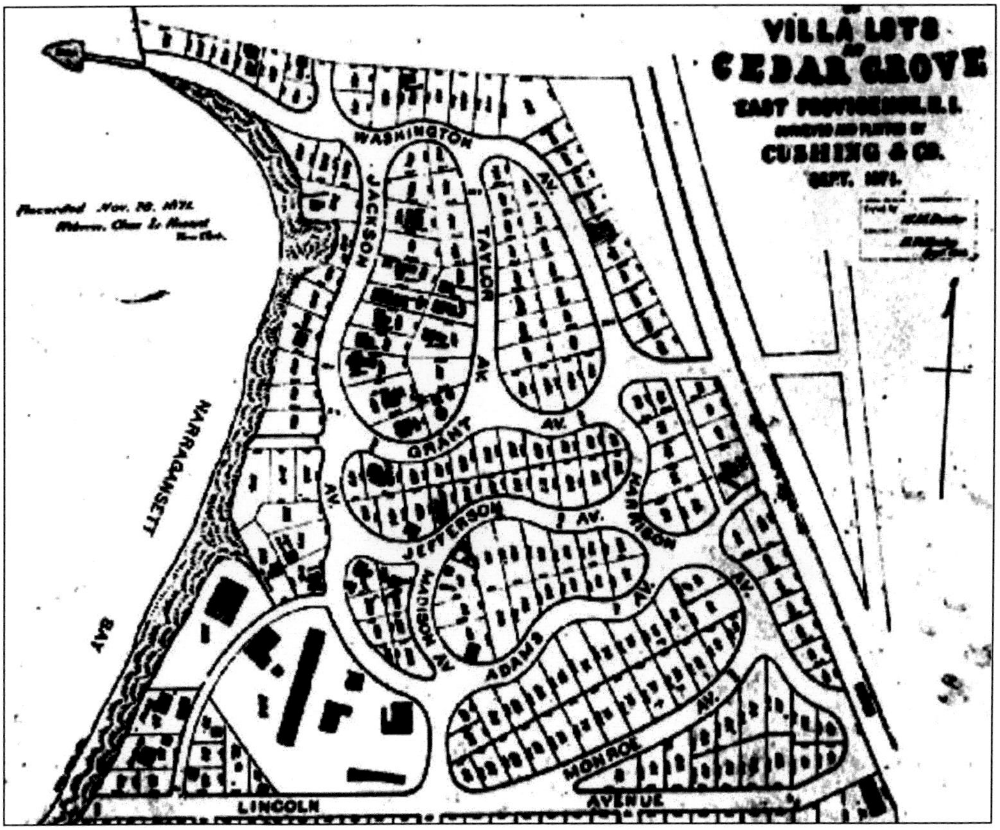

Riverside was known as Cedar Grove until 1878. Originally, the settlement in the southern end of Rehoboth was a farming and fishing area. In 1647 this part of town joined the Town of Swansea because it was too far away for citizens to attend town meetings in the Ring of the Green. The area rejoined Rehoboth in 1747, becoming Seekonk in 1812. By 1850, when the train depot was built in the square, the area was becoming desirable as the place to go in the summer for fishing and swimming. In 1871 Lysander Flagg bought the Medbury, Lewis, and Lawton Farms and platted a new neighborhood which became known as the Maze. All the streets were named for American presidents. The Maze lies between Bullocks Point Avenue and the Bay. The streets to the south of the Maze were platted in a grid and named for trees.

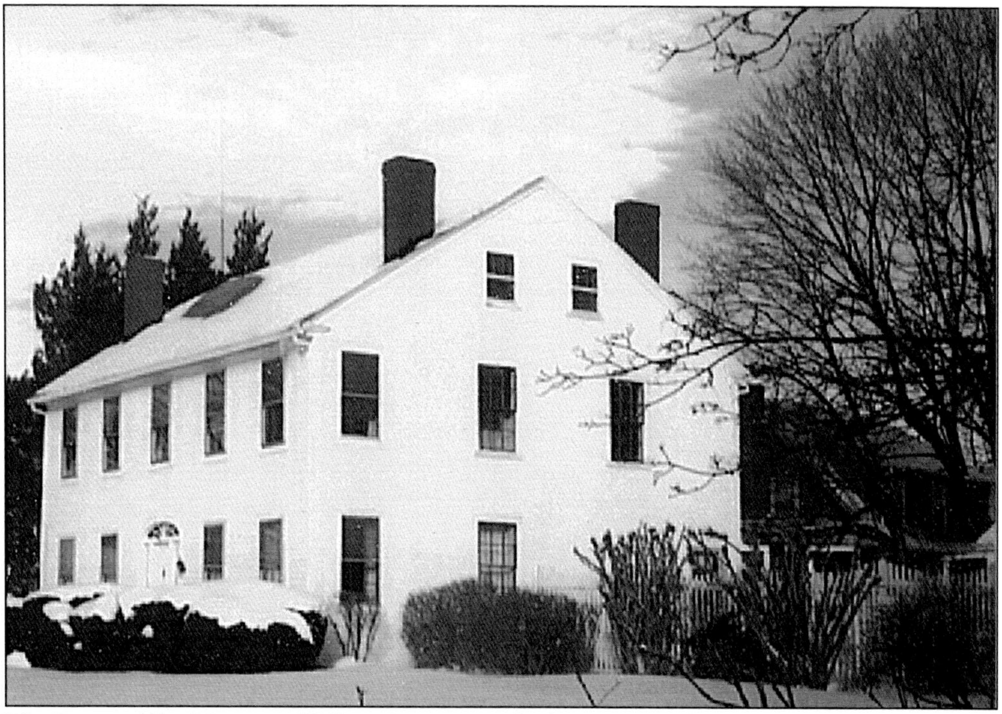

The Pearce Allin House on Willett Avenue was built *c.* 1805. Allin was a wealthy sea captain. It is now known as the Whitcomb Farm.

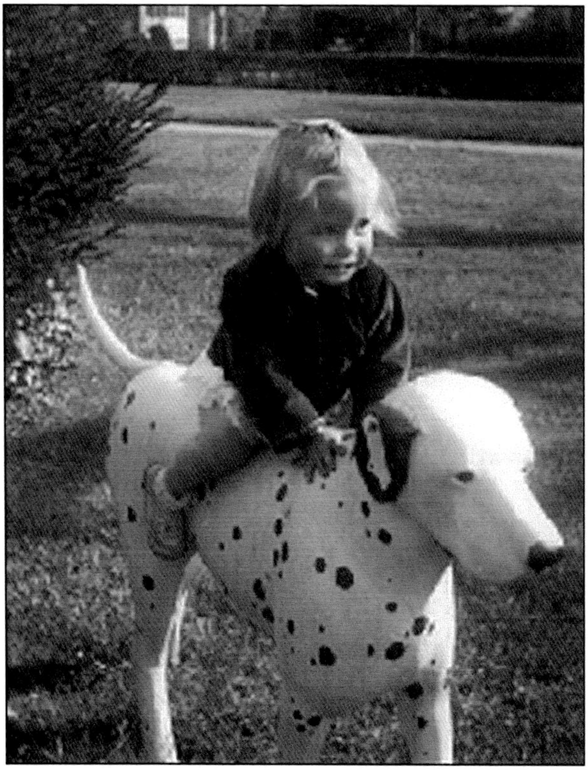

All children in the area remember the metal Whitcomb dog located in the Whitcomb Farm front yard.

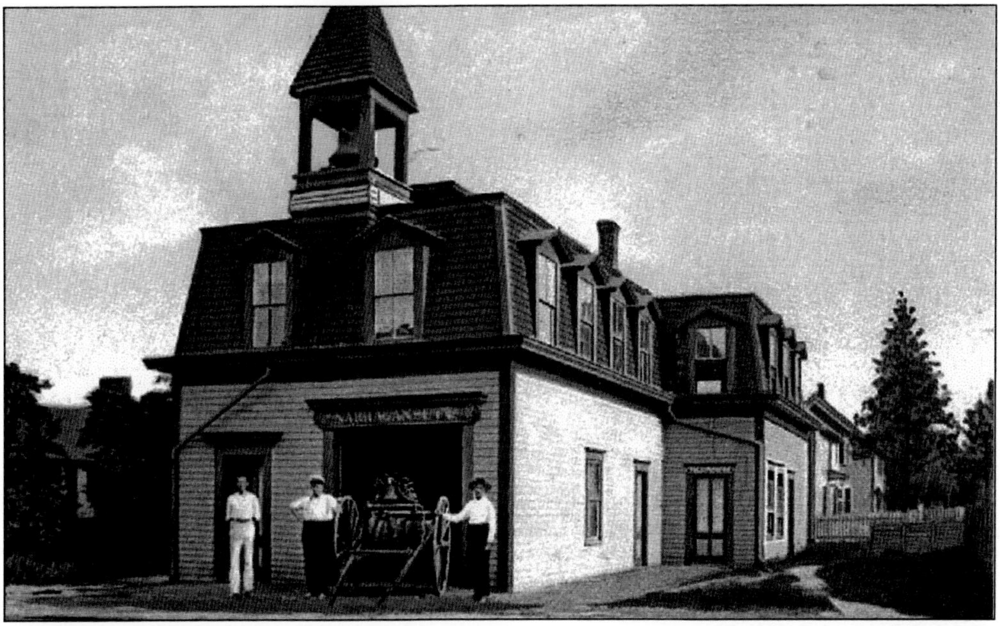

In 1878, as the population of Riverside increased and building expanded, it was necessary to form the Narragansett Engine Company No. 2. The fire apparatus was stored on George Paton's lot and the meetings of the volunteers were held in Winchester Hall in Riverside Square. This firehouse was built shortly after 1880 on Turner Avenue. It is still there, minus the belltower and the engine company.

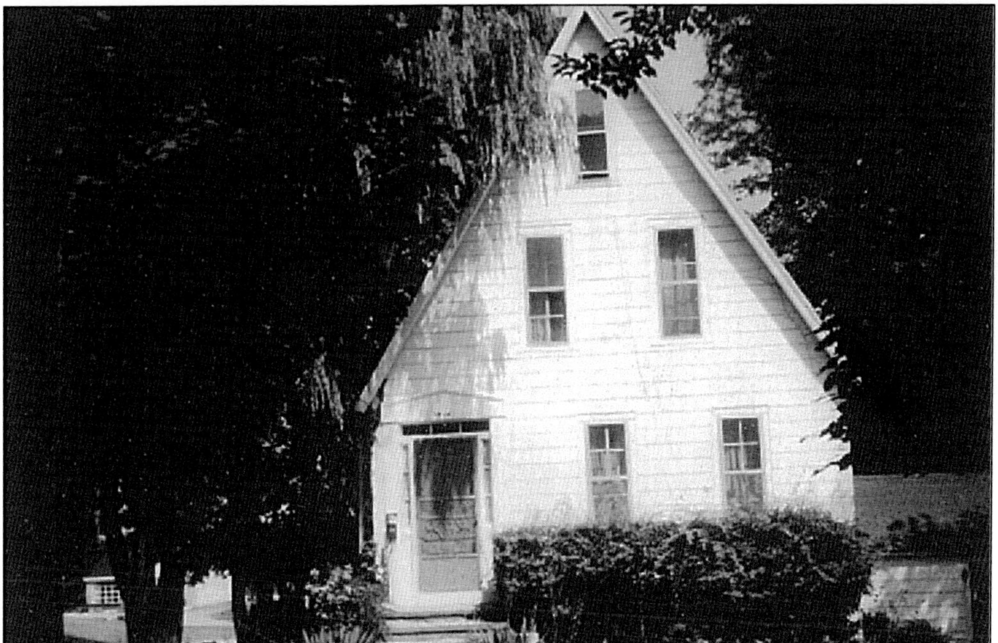

The Lightening Splitter House was built across the street from the Allin (Whitcomb) Farm for an Allin daughter *c.* 1840. There is a second lightening splitter-type house a few house lots farther east on Willett Avenue.

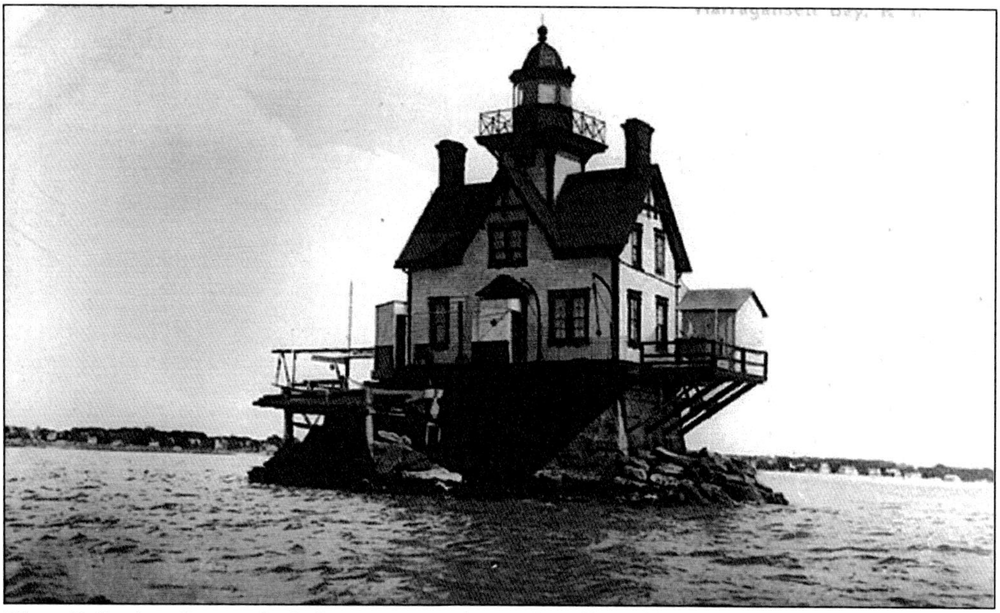

The Bullocks Point Lighthouse was located off Bullocks Point, also known as Narragansett Terrace.

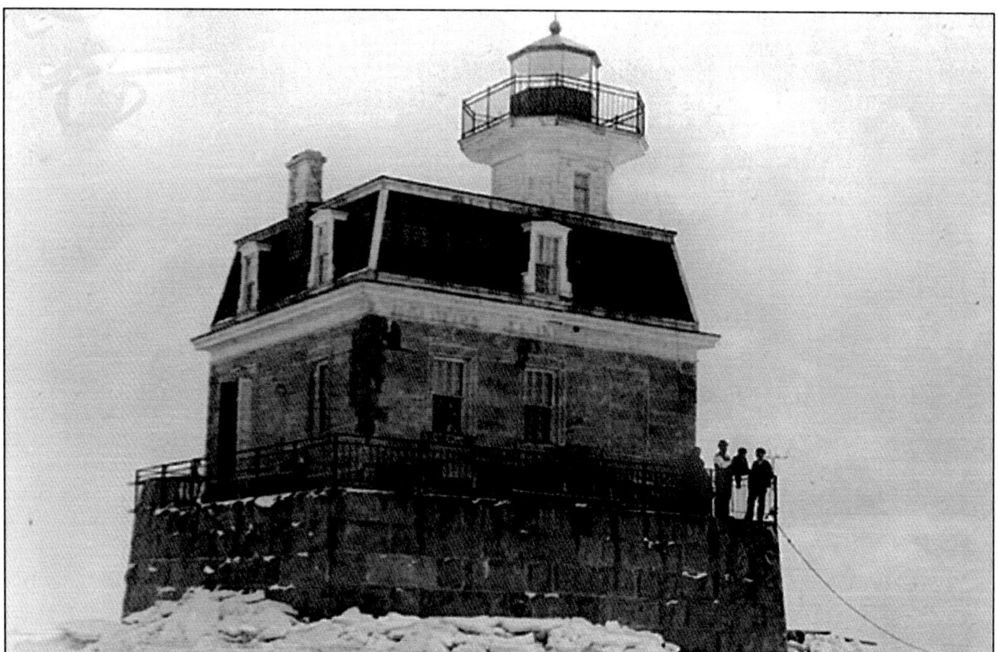

The Sabin Point Lighthouse was located off a point of land called Sabin's Point, which jutted out into Narragansett Bay.

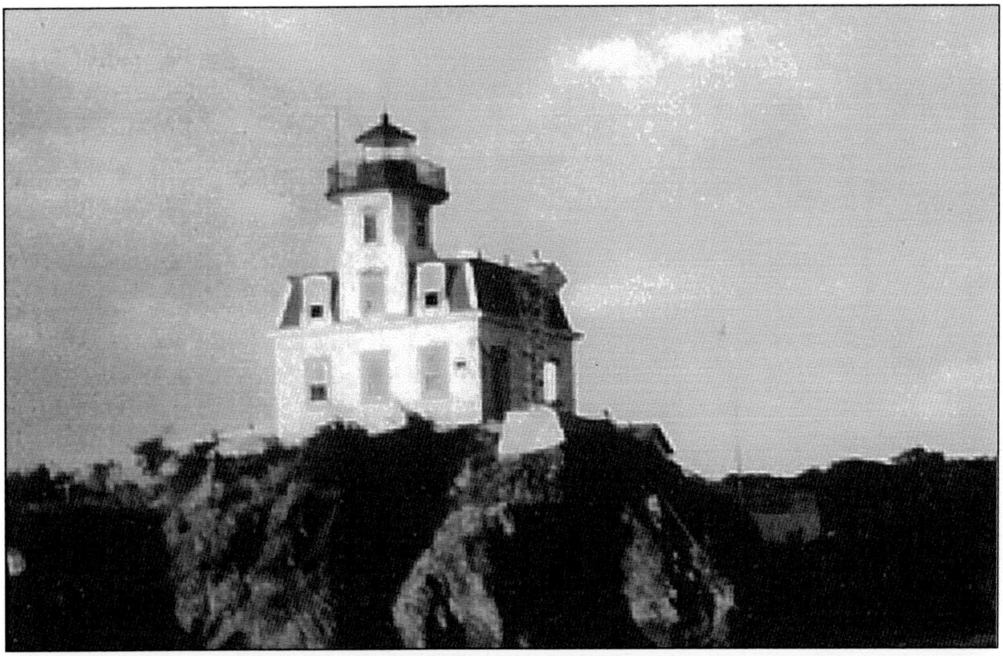

The U.S. Coast Guard manned the Pomham Lighthouse close to the shore of northern Riverside, where the Pomham Clambake House was once located and where the Stonegate Condominiums are today.

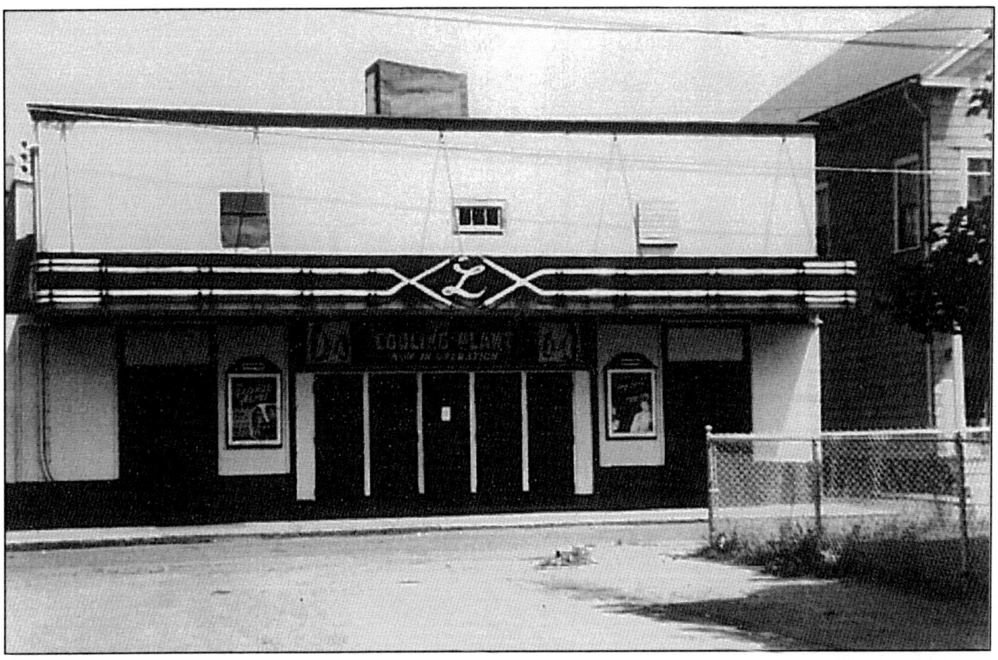

The Lyric Theater opened on Maple Avenue *c.* 1920 and was operated by Edith Chase, who ran silent movies that she accompanied on the piano. In 1928 sound (talking) movies began and the Lyric was the second theater in the state to have sound movies. Fay's in Providence was the first. Later the name was changed to the Gilbert Stuart. The building remains, but the theater is closed.

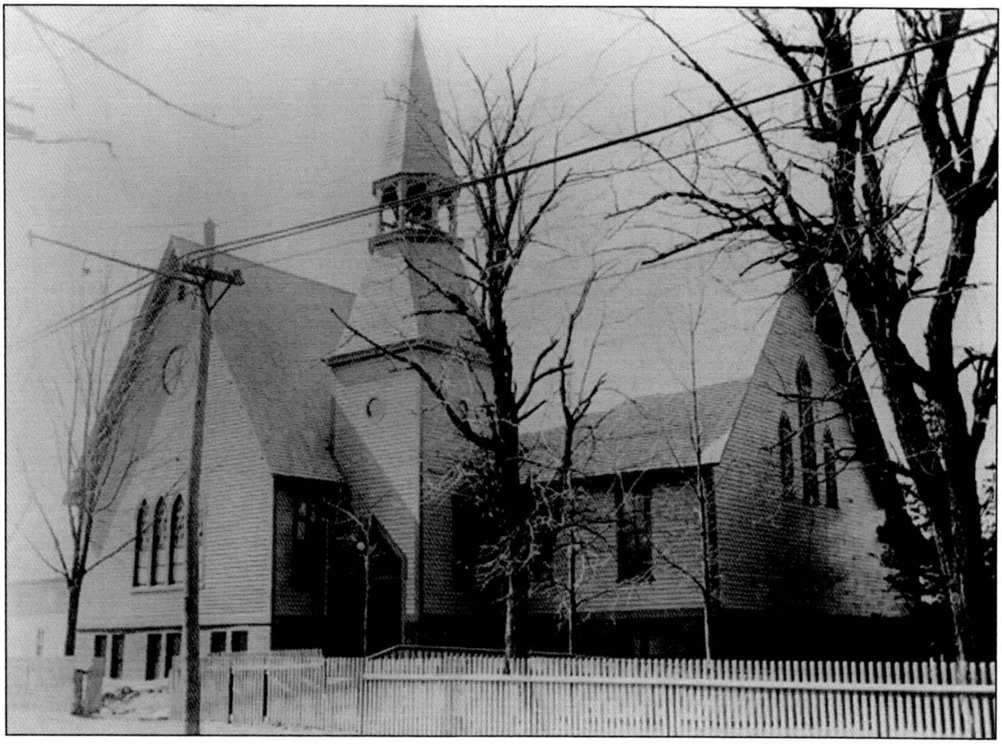

This first building of the Riverside Congregational Church on Bullocks Point Avenue was built in 1881. It was an outgrowth of the Riverside Congregational Episcopal Church built by Lysander Flagg and James Davis in 1872 on Narragansett Terrace and called the Union Chapel. It served summer residents of the Terrace. The Union Chapel building no longer exists.

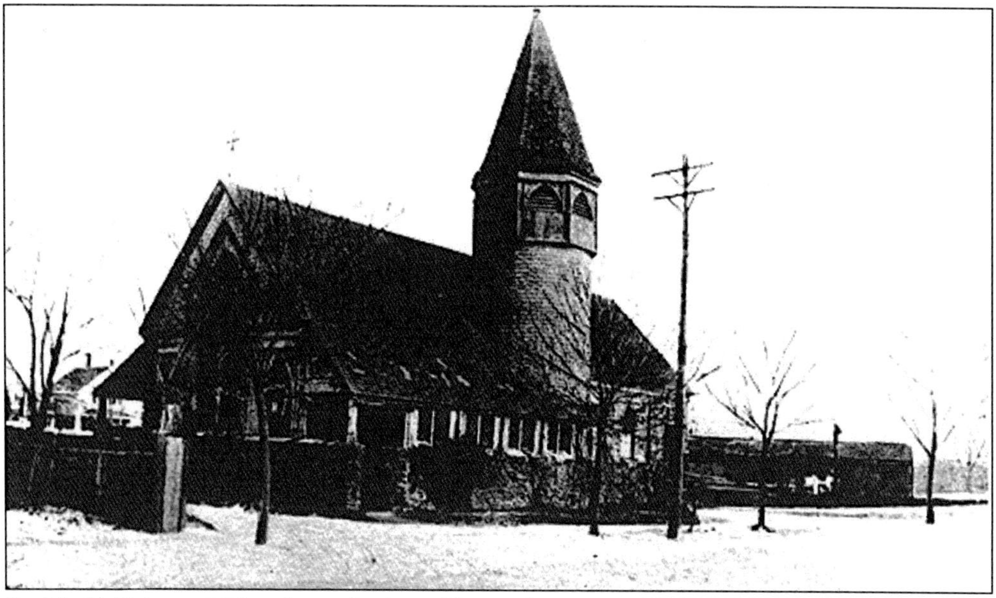

St. Mark's Episcopal Church was built on Turner Avenue in 1885 and it too was an outgrowth of the Union Chapel on the Terrace. A new church was built in 1956–57. In 1965 the church was damaged by fire and a newly restored church was opened in 1966.

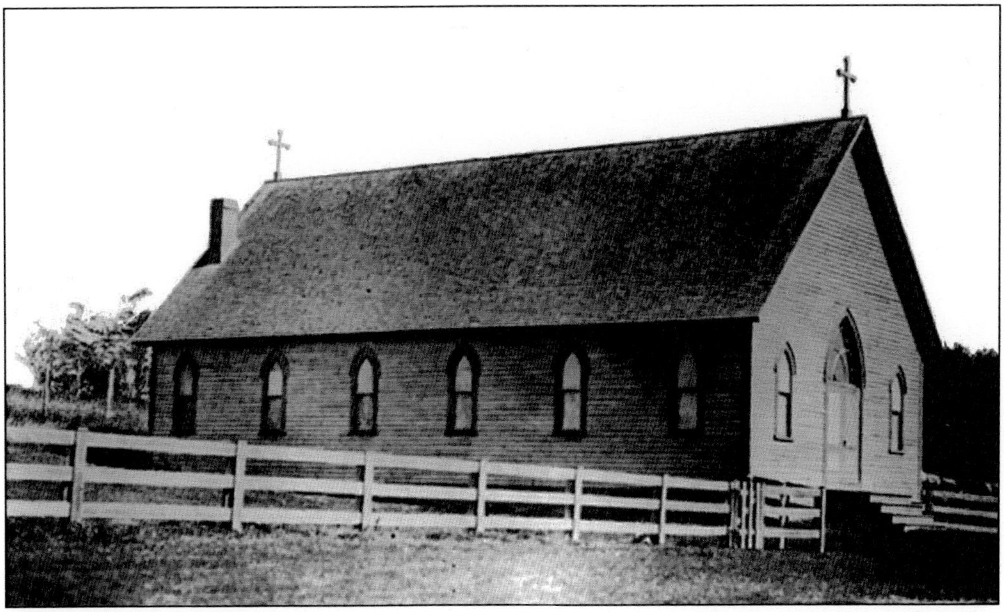

The first St. Brendan's church was built on Sprague Avenue in 1909. The building still stands, but the Gothic-style windows have been replaced.

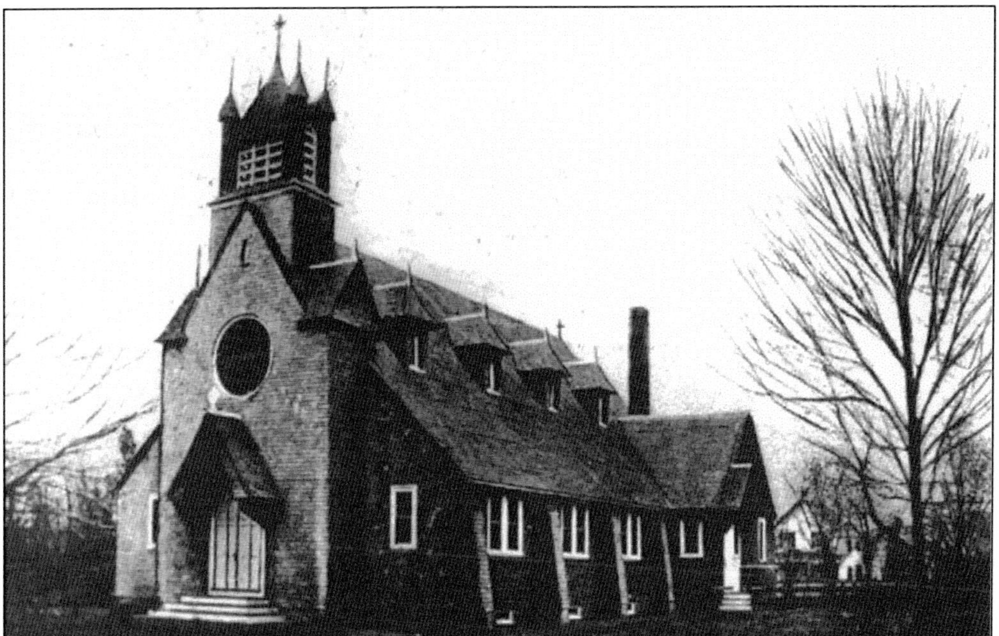

This "new" St. Brendan's was opened a few years later on Turner Avenue and is seen as it looked in 1915. It burned in 1957.

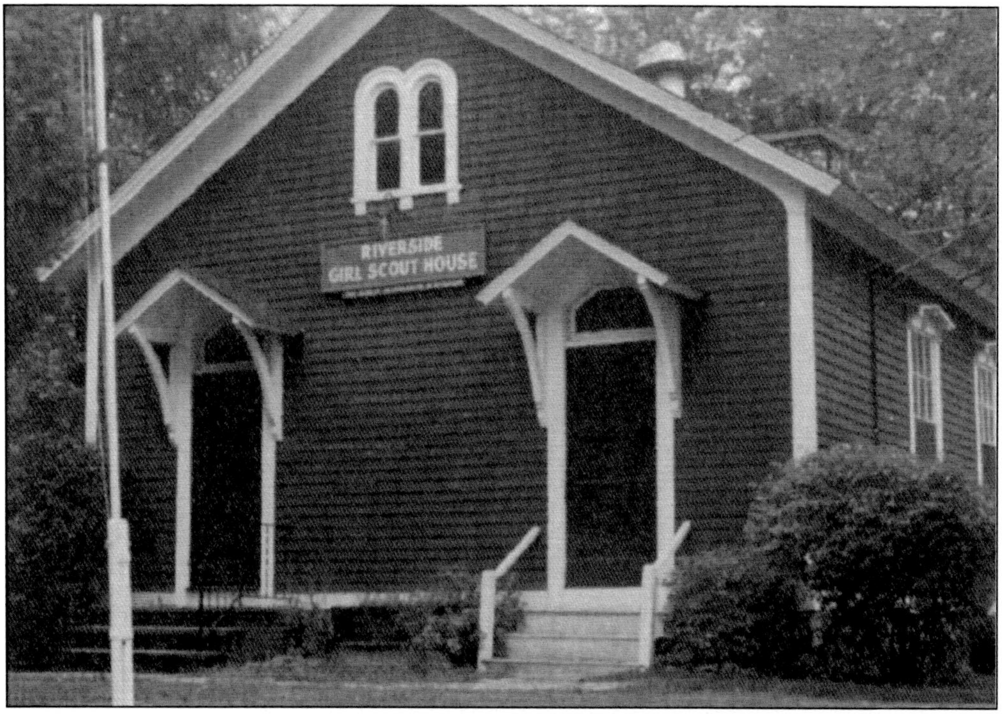

The Riverside Girl Scout House on Willett Avenue is actually the oldest school still standing in East Providence. It was built in 1869–70 and was called PS No. 6. It is owned by the city.

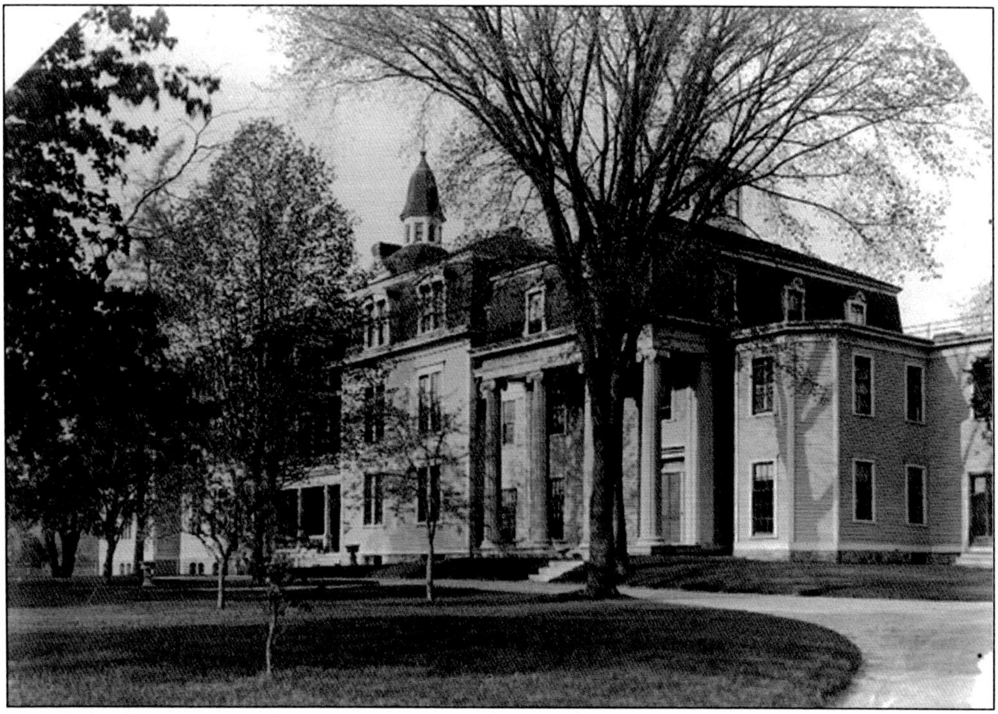

St. Mary's Bayview Academy started as a boarding school for girls in the late part of the nineteenth century. It is located on Pawtucket Avenue.

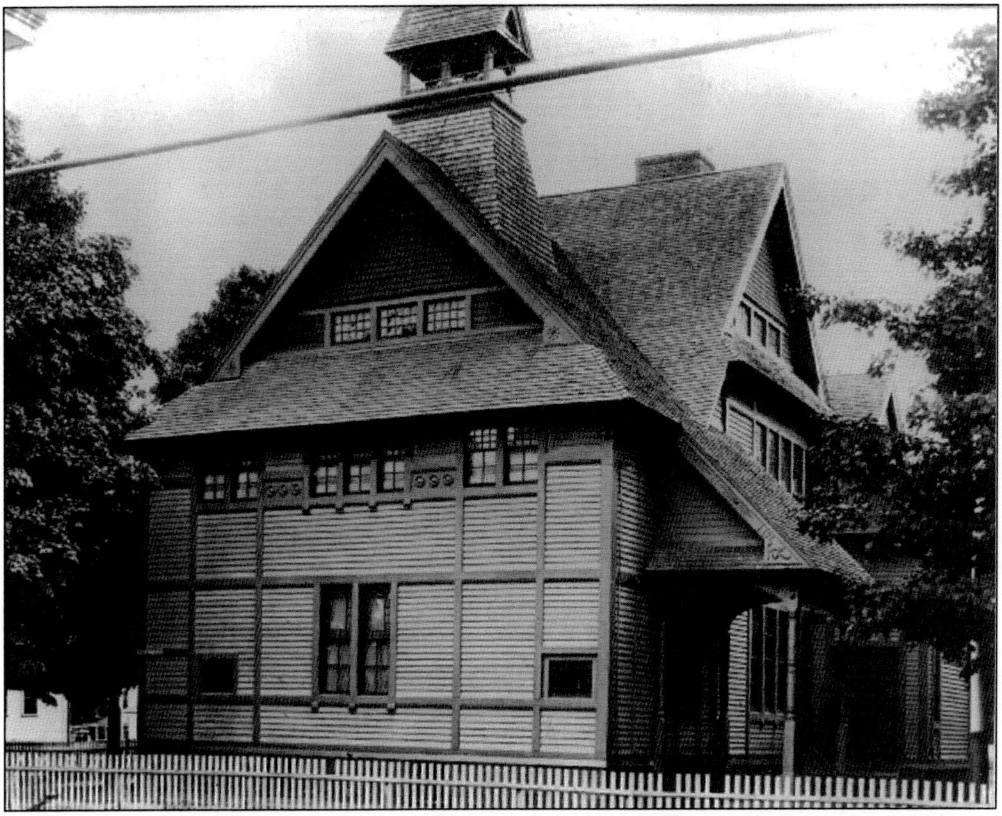

The Turner Avenue School was built on Turner Avenue in 1881 as a four-room school and an addition was built in 1893. It is no longer in existence. At one time it was used by St. Brendan's Parish for a parochial school.

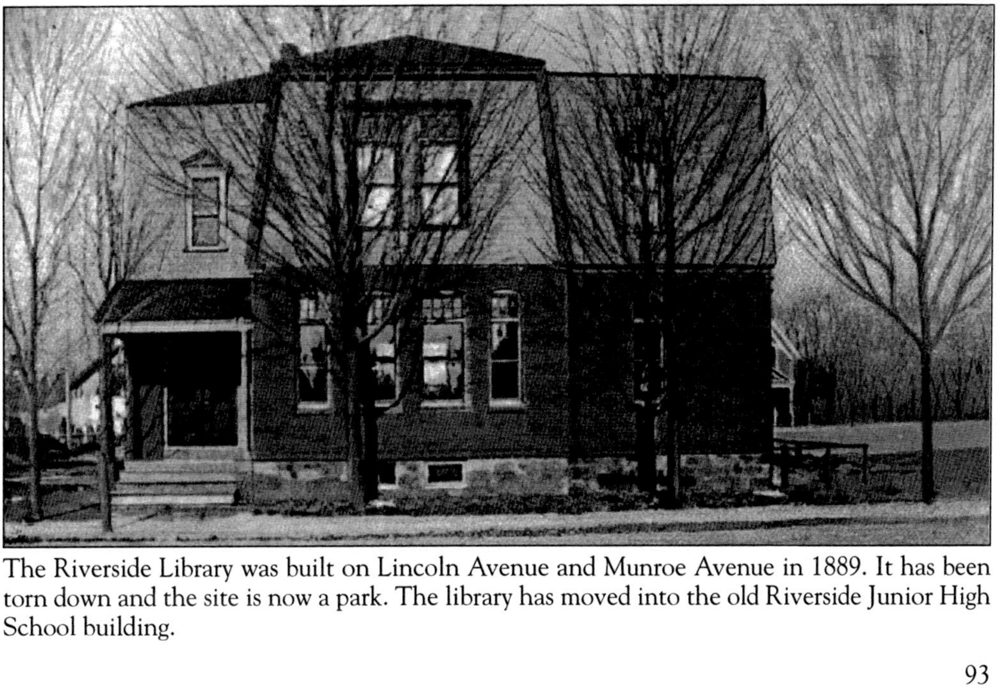

The Riverside Library was built on Lincoln Avenue and Munroe Avenue in 1889. It has been torn down and the site is now a park. The library has moved into the old Riverside Junior High School building.

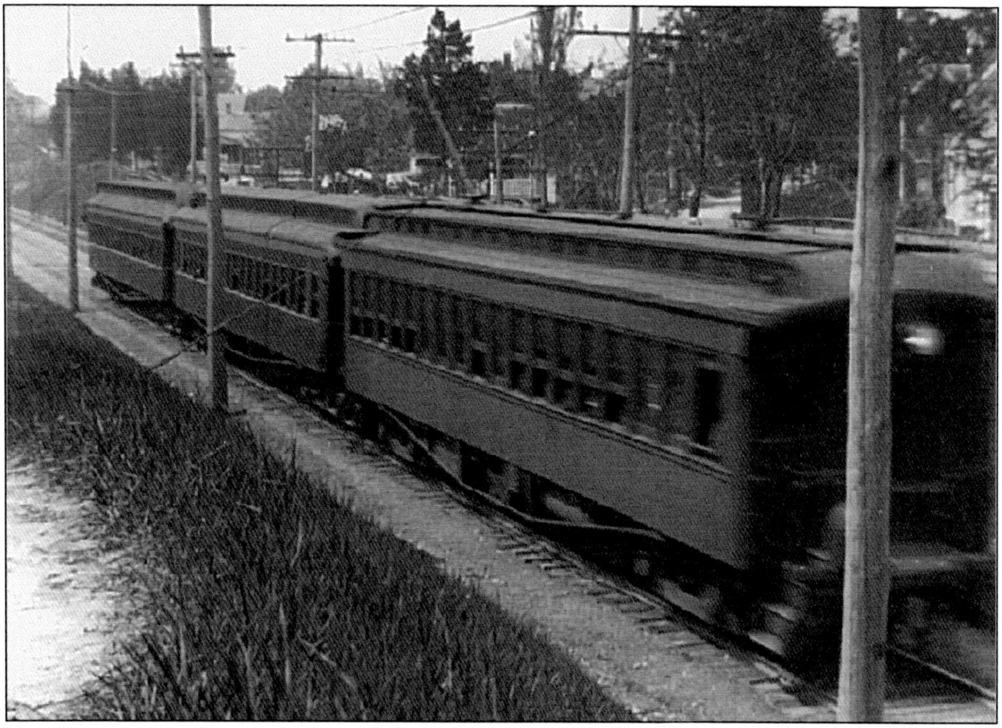

The three-car electric train passed from Providence through Riverside on its way to Barrington and Warren in 1932.

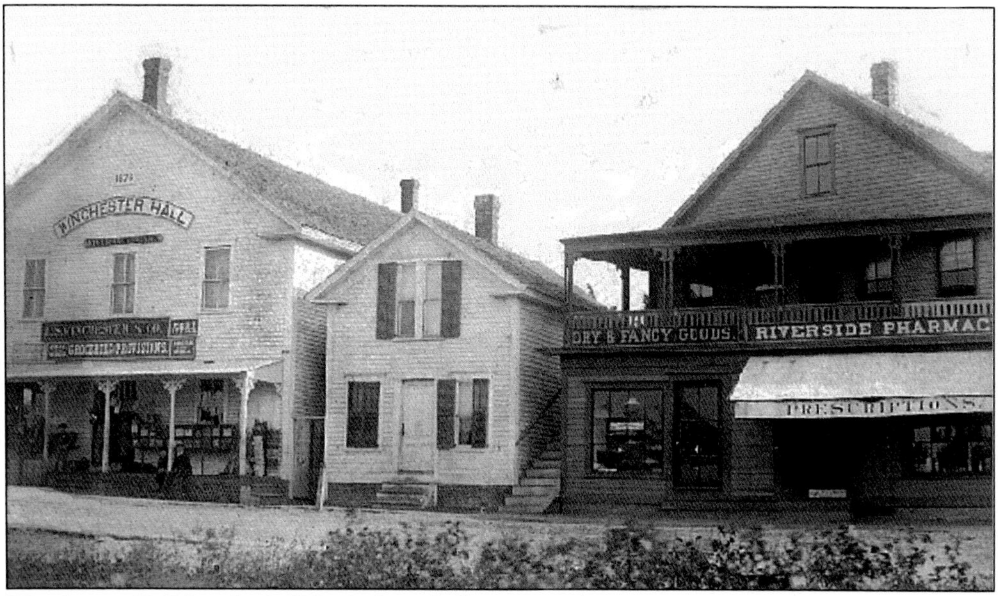

Winchester Hall (on the left) had a large hall upstairs where various groups held meetings while a store occupied the first floor. A dry goods store and pharmacy were in the building to the right. Many of such stores were clustered around Riverside Square to service the summer tourists who crowded the streets every summer. The street is Lincoln Avenue off the square.

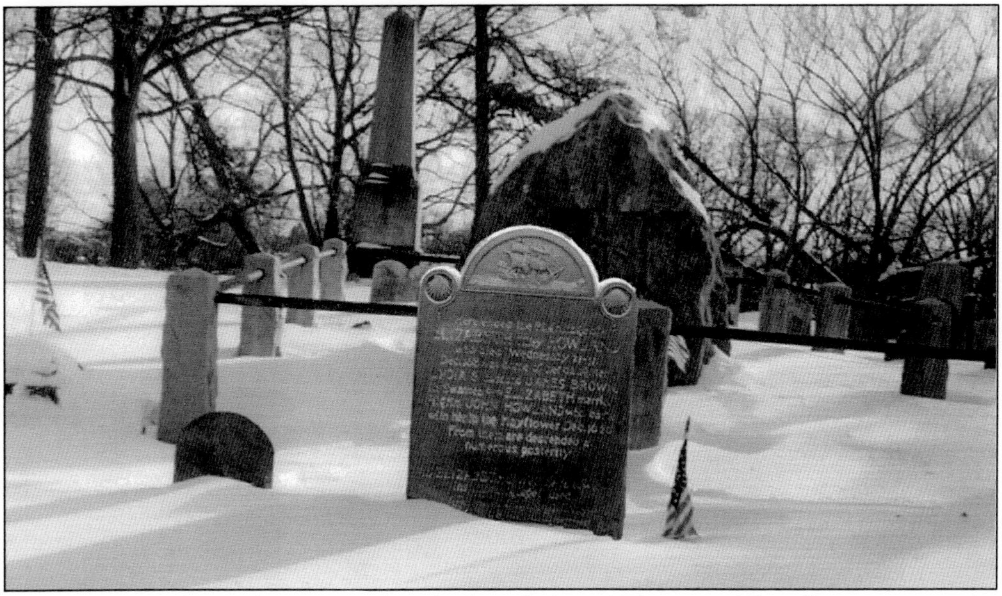

The historic Little Neck cemetery has the burial plot of Thomas Willett (large stone in the background), the first mayor of New York City, and Elizabeth Tilley Howland (in front). Elizabeth was a child passenger on the *Mayflower*. She died in 1687 when Riverside was Swansea in the Massachusetts Bay Colony.

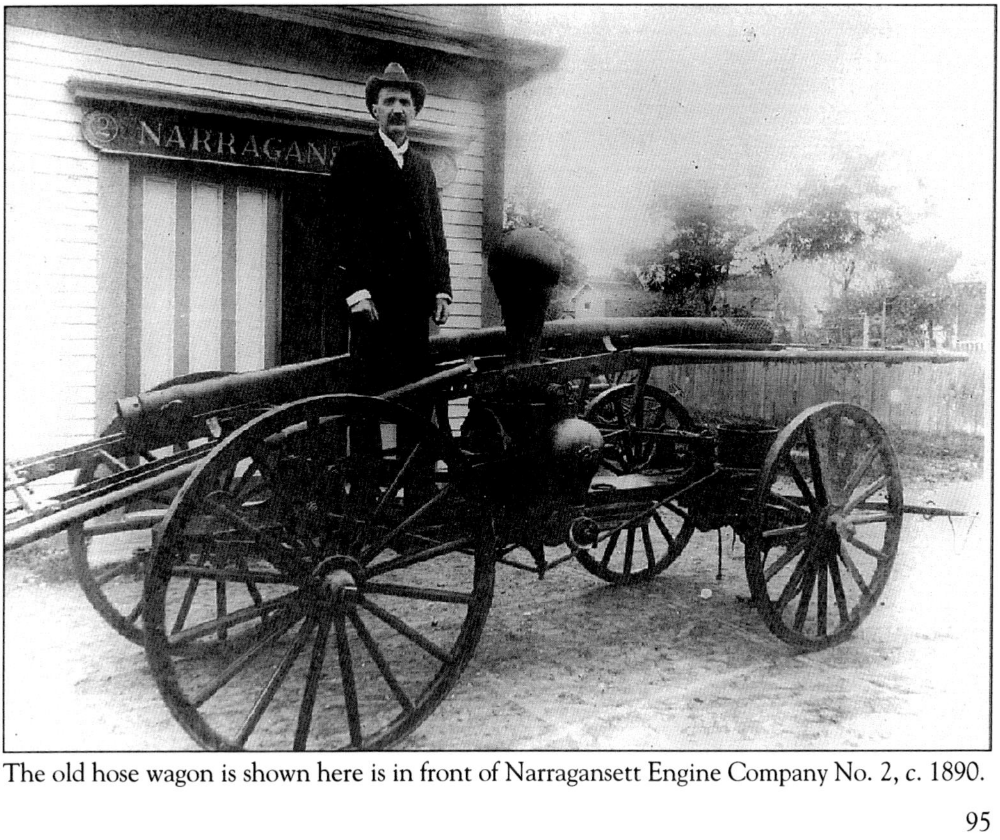

The old hose wagon is shown here is in front of Narragansett Engine Company No. 2, *c.* 1890.

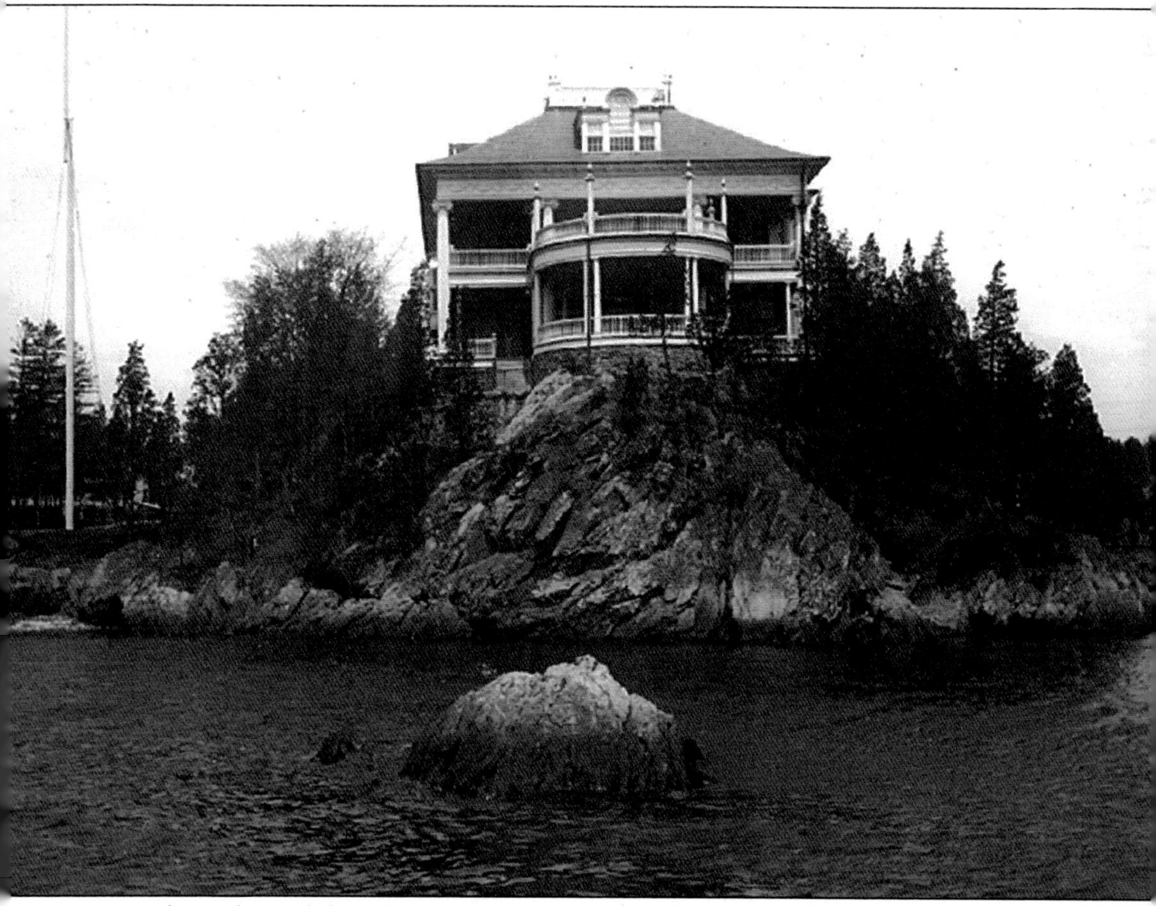

Several members of the Class of 1844 from Providence High School had two interests in common: sailing and seafood. They incorporated as the Squantum Association in 1872 and built the handsome Squantum Club and Clambake Building on the Bay (shown above) in a secluded area off the present Veteran's Memorial Parkway. It had an exclusive membership that was limited to males. It continues its operation today.

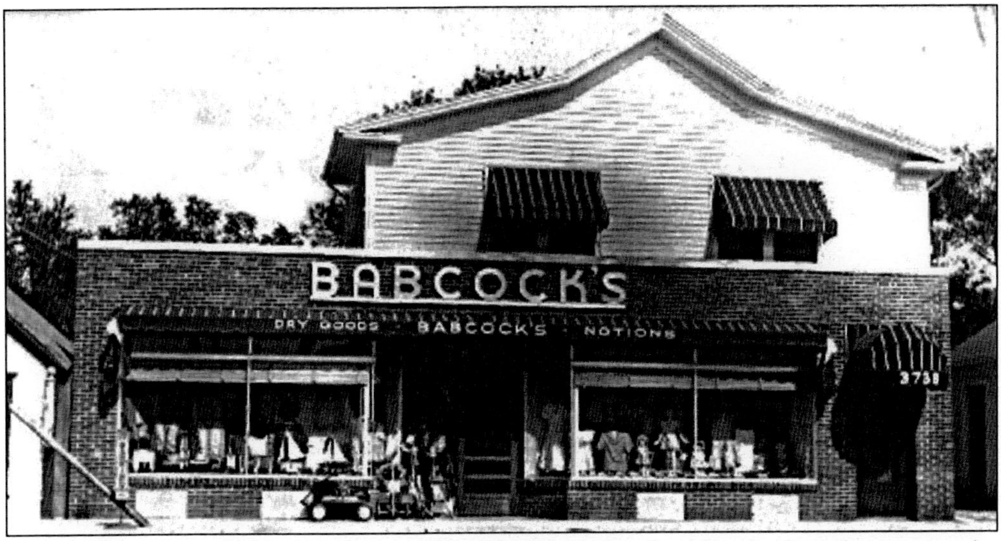

Arthur Babcock, a tumbler/acrobat, and Dorilda Tetreault, who played a French vamp on the Keith-Orpheum vaudeville circuit, made up "Babcock and Dolly." They married, and when they retired *c.* 1930 they moved to Riverside and opened Babcock's Variety Store at Riverside Square. The store sold practically everything. Arthur was often heard saying, "I know I have it, I just can't find it."

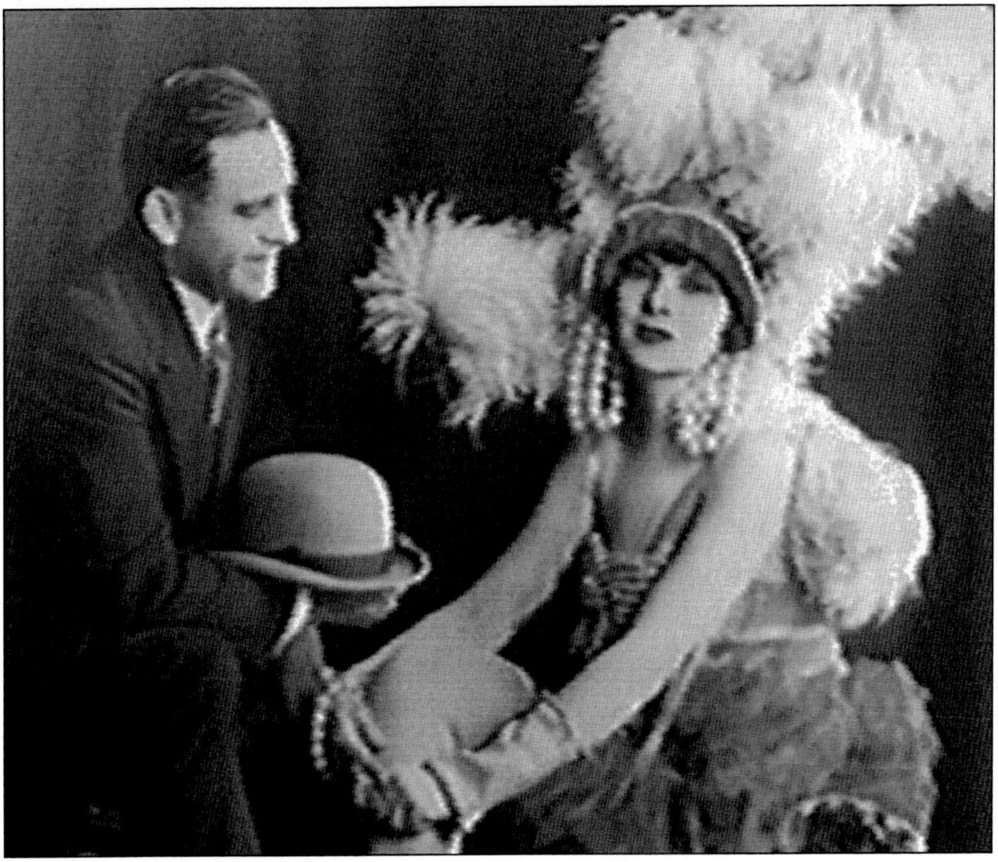

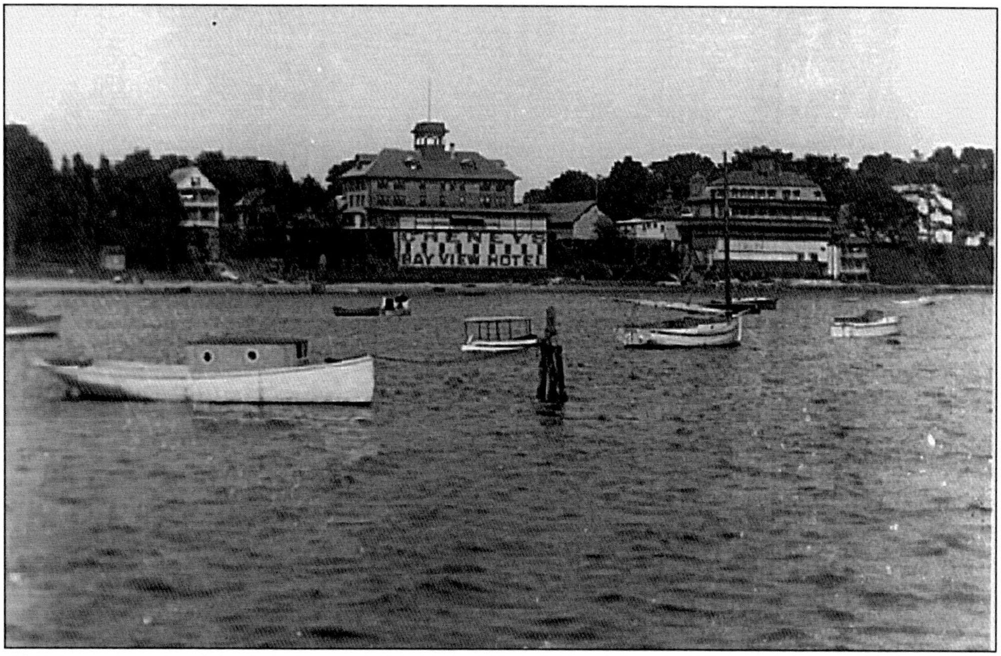

The Bayview Hotel directly at the edge of the Bay was one of many built in Riverside at the end of the nineteenth century.

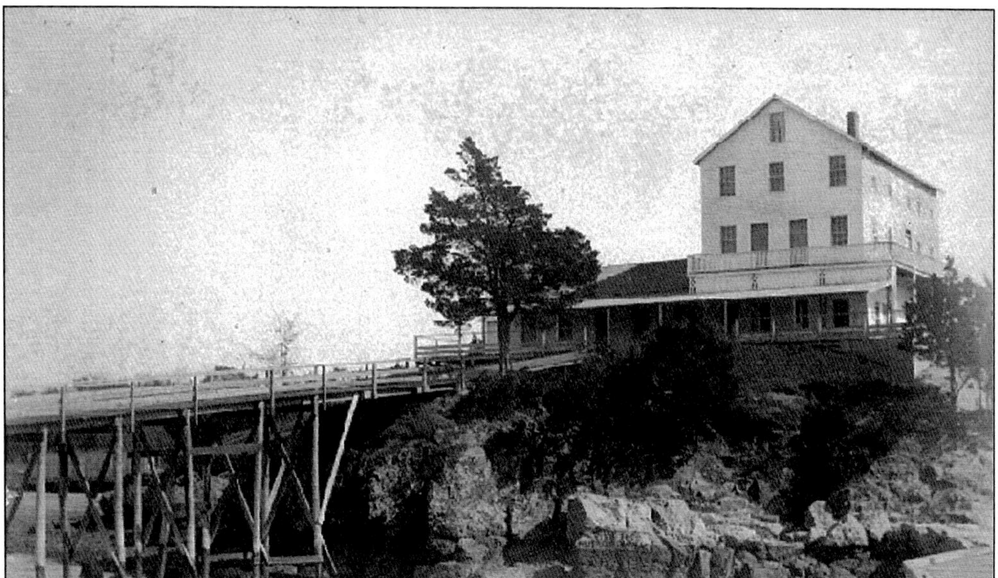

An early photograph of the shore dinner hall known as the Pomham Club shows the building's proximity to the shore with a dock to accommodate visitors. Today it is the site of the Stonegate condominiums.

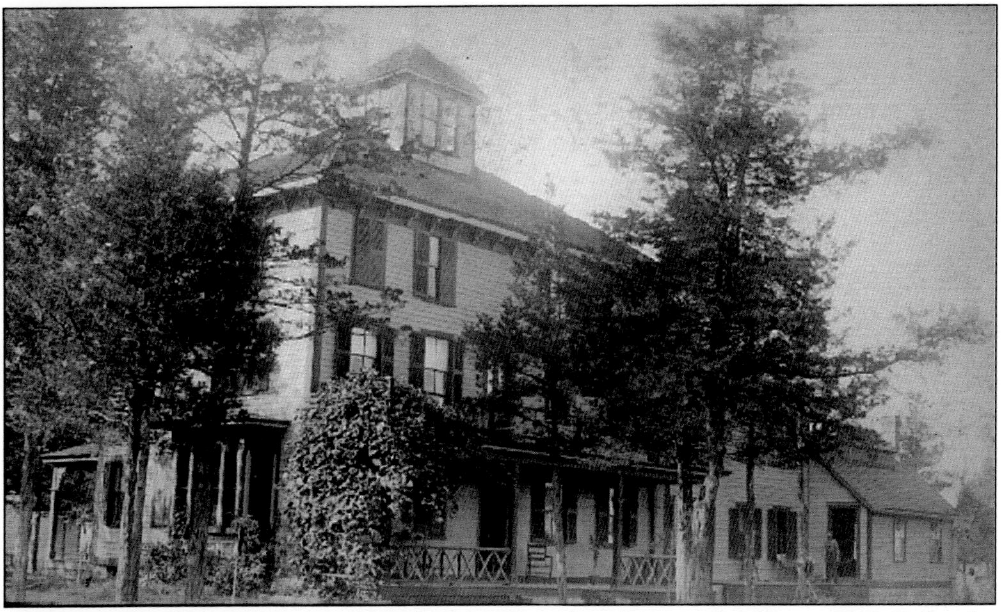

The Paton Hotel was located on Lincoln Avenue in this photograph taken c. 1886. Today the building stands divided into two sections just off Lincoln Avenue and in the Maze.

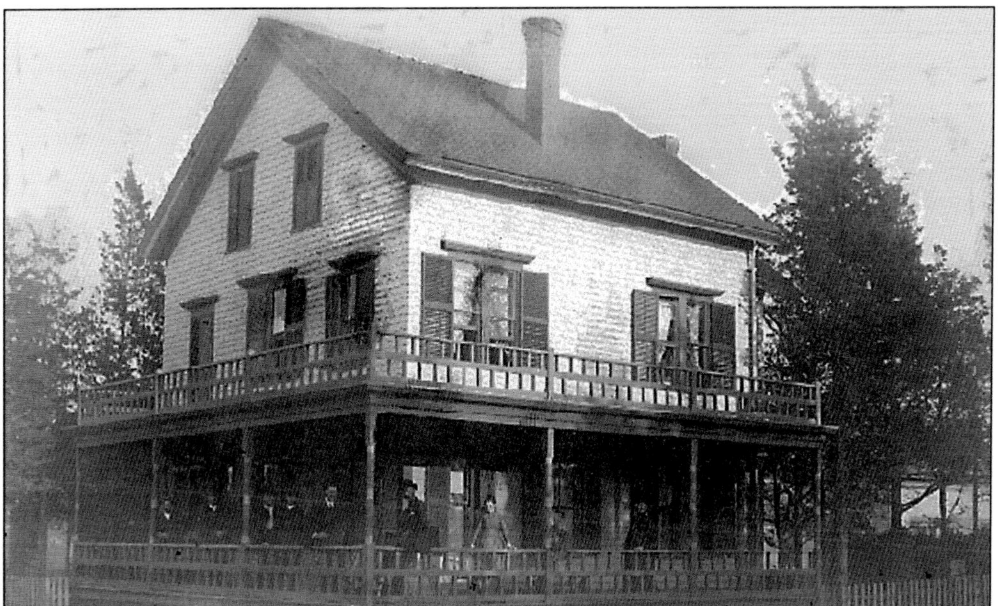

The Will Johnston Guest House was photographed in 1886. During the busy summer season rooms were hard to come by, so private homes were pressed into service.

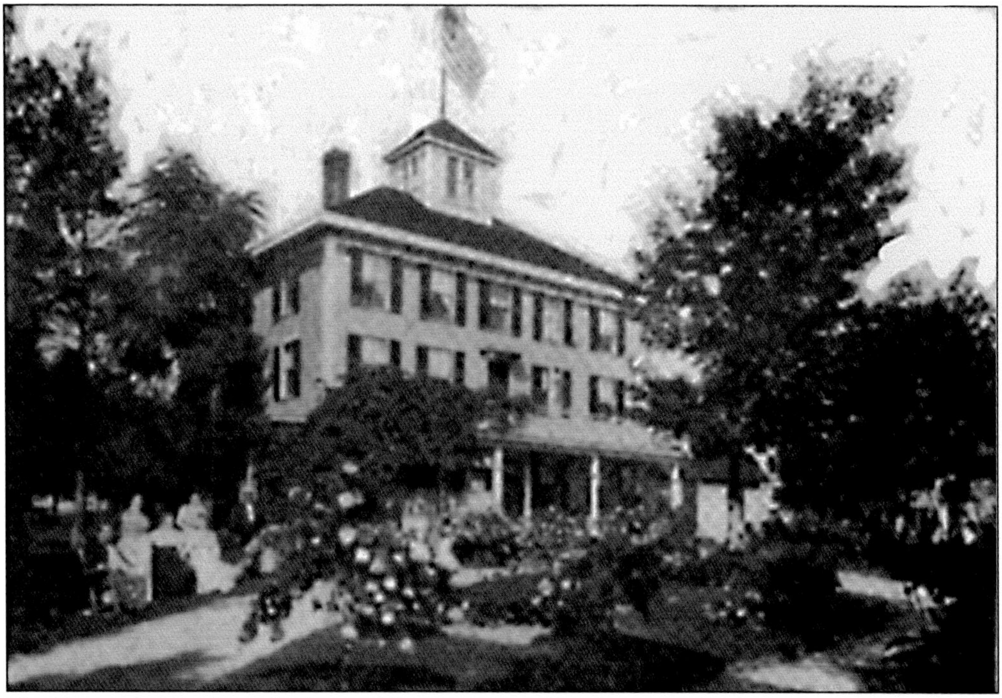

The Riverside Hotel was built *c.* 1870 on a piece of land surrounded by Narragansett Avenue, Maple Avenue, Oak Avenue, and Cypress Street. It was four stories high and had a porch on three sides that was about 15 feet wide. It was moved by schooner and barges *c.* 1880 to Nantucket and re-erected. It burned shortly thereafter.

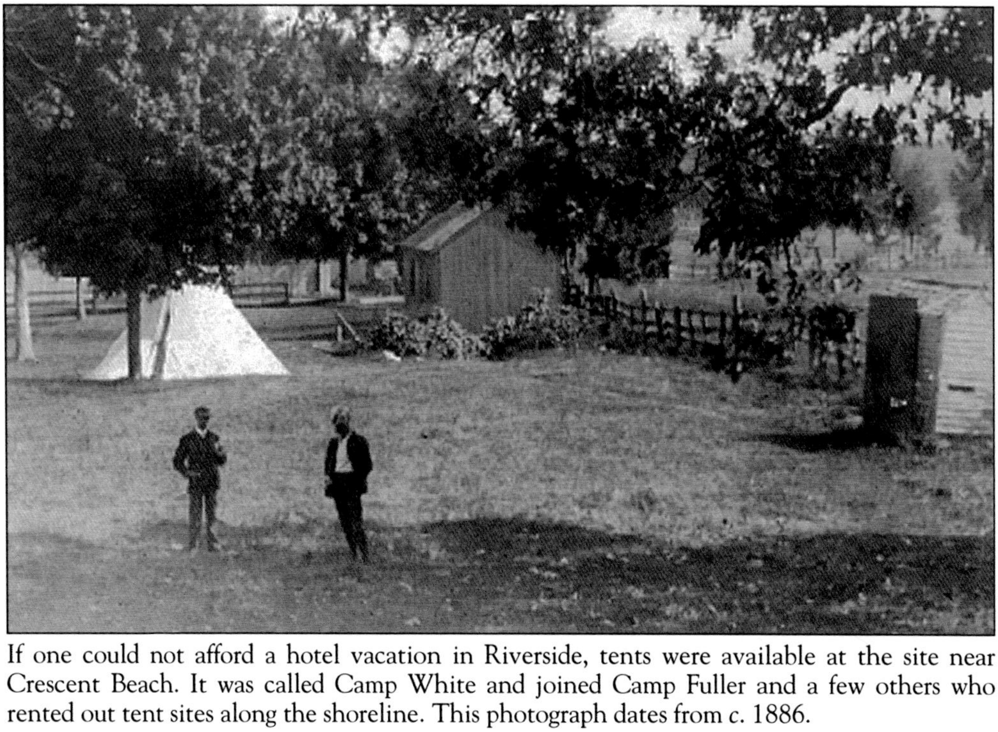

If one could not afford a hotel vacation in Riverside, tents were available at the site near Crescent Beach. It was called Camp White and joined Camp Fuller and a few others who rented out tent sites along the shoreline. This photograph dates from *c.* 1886.

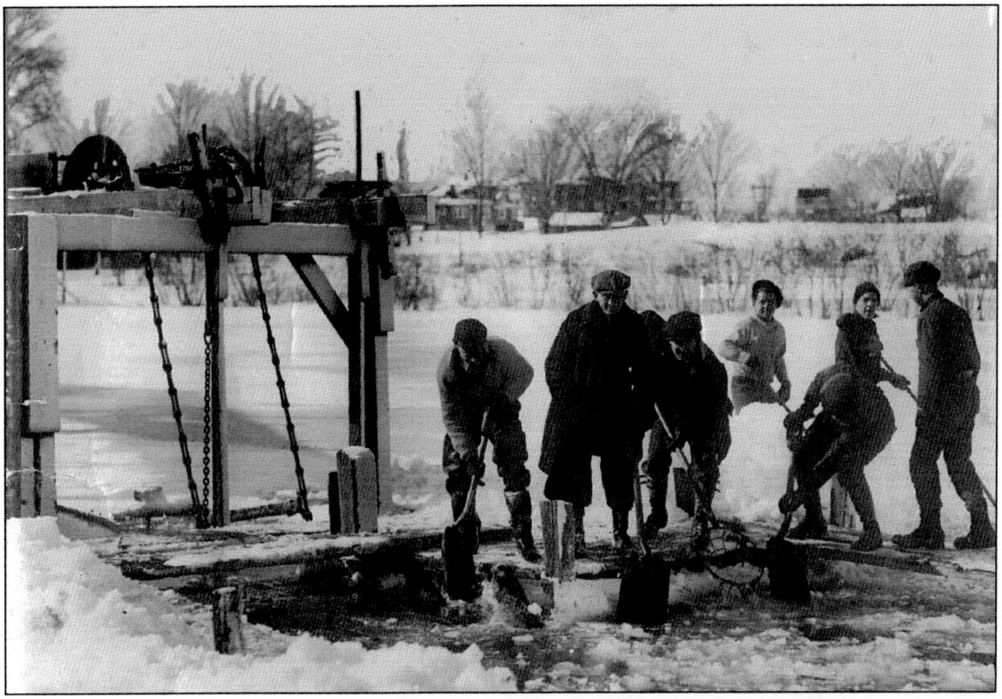

With so many hotels, restaurants, and clambake halls in Riverside, Edward Bowen saw a need for an icehouse to supply the tourist colony through the summers. He excavated an area near a brook on Willett Avenue and developed Bowen's Ice House and pond. Schoolboys would cut the ice in winter after school for around 10¢ an hour and load it by horse and wagon into the icehouse, which was built *c.* 1900. Mr. Bowen sold ice from the site and also delivered it by ice wagon throughout Riverside.

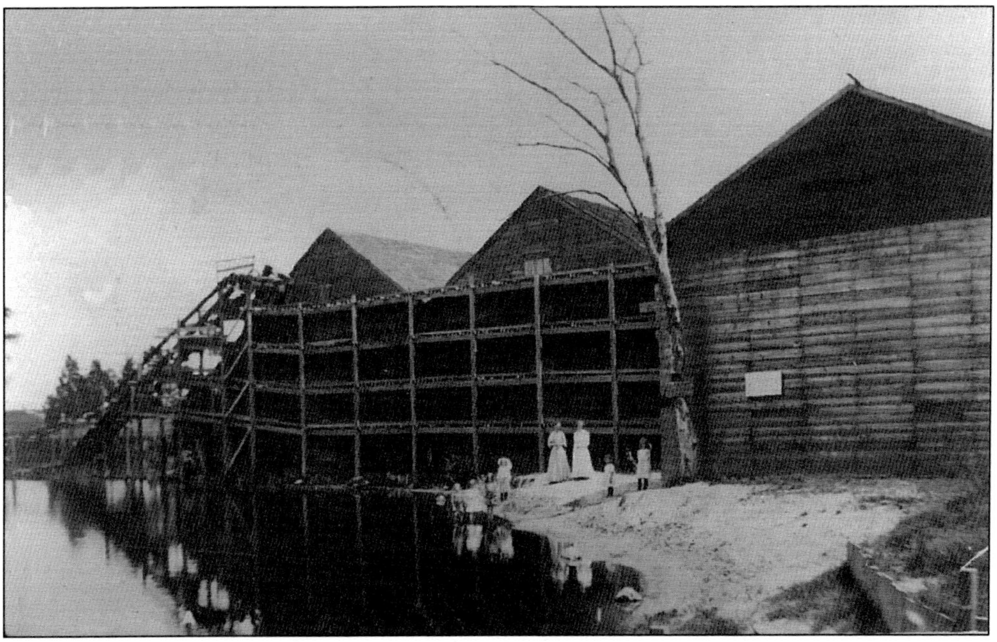

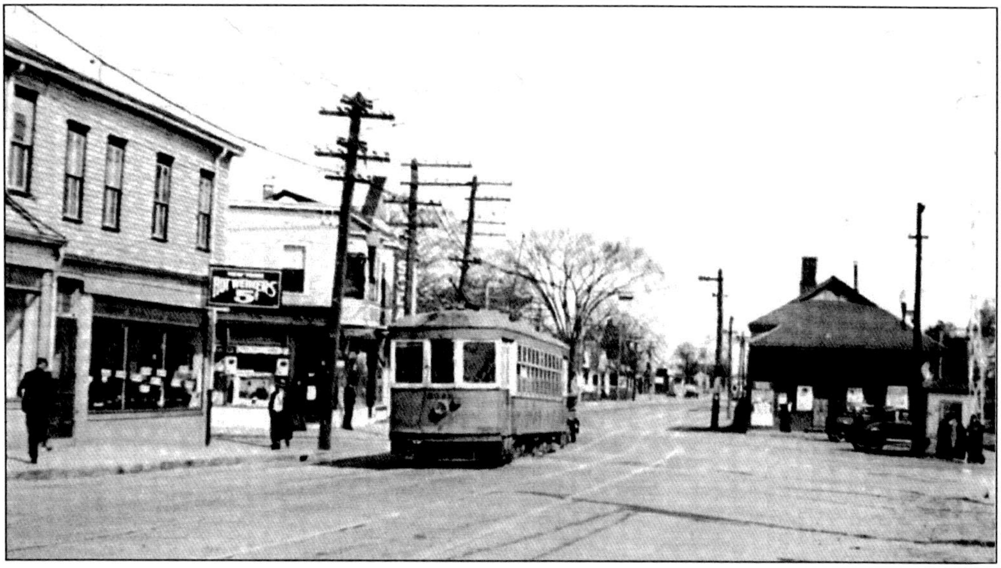

Trolleys made hourly runs from Providence to Crescent Park passing through Riverside Square. The year was 1933.

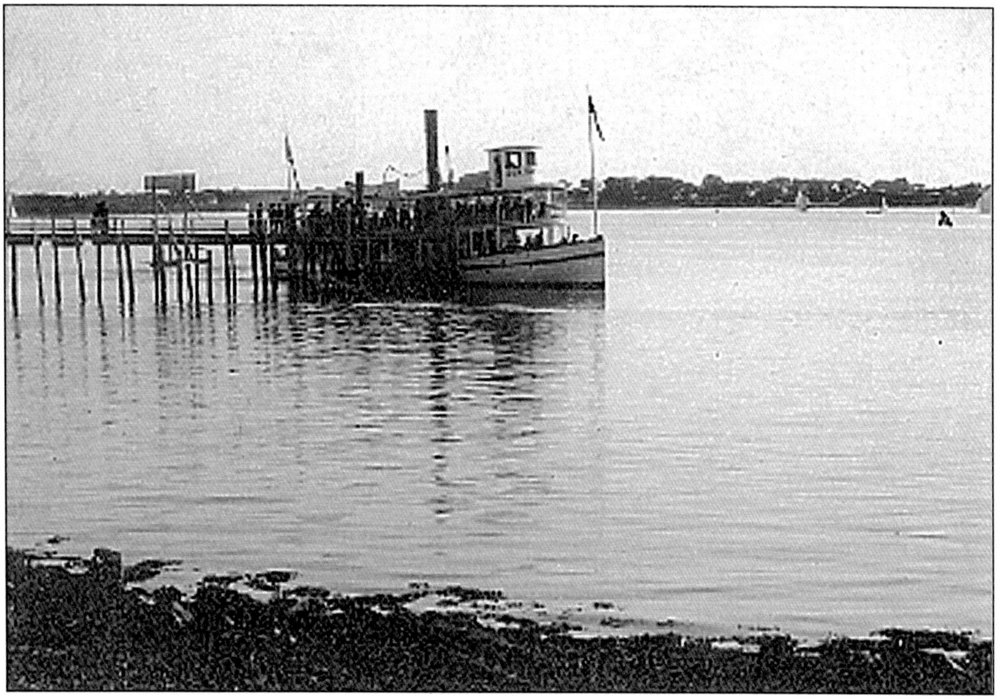

The steamer *General Bartlett* was one of many that sailed from Providence to the amusement parks during the summers. This photograph dates from 1886.

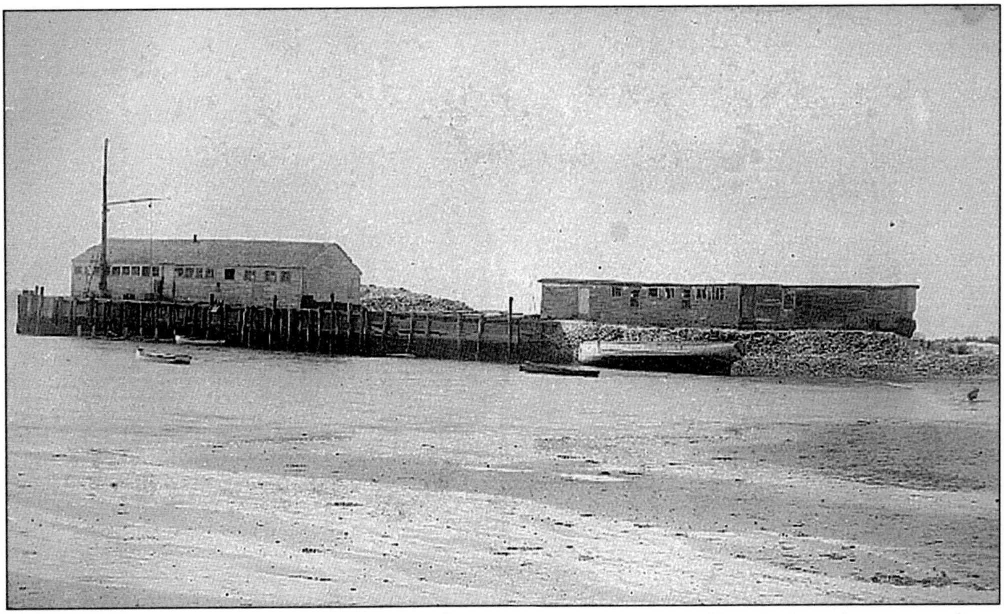

In the 1880s farmers whose properties abutted the shoreline would hitch their horses to plows and plow the beaches for clams and oysters every week in season. The shellfish would be stored for delivery at the Sabin Point Oyster House, seen here. The business was lucrative and gave the nickname "clamdiggers" to the Riverside residents.

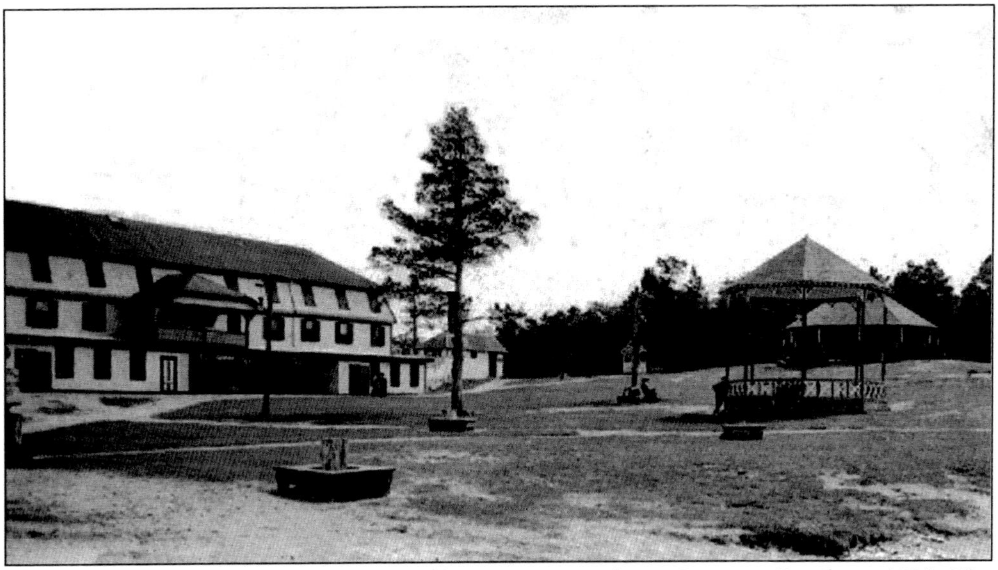

The Crescent Park Hotel was the only large structure above Crescent Beach in 1885. The beach was so named for its crescent shape. No one could foretell in 1886 that a tourist explosion was to take place later that year at this site.

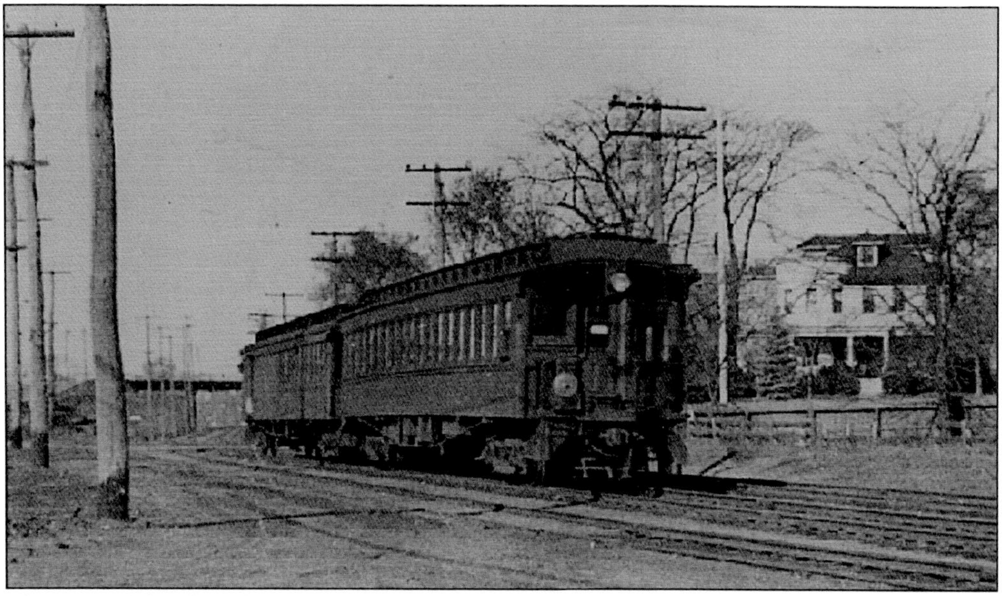

The Consolidated Railroad ran electric trains from Providence to Riverside Square in about thirty minutes. The train also continued on to Barrington, Warren, and Fall River.

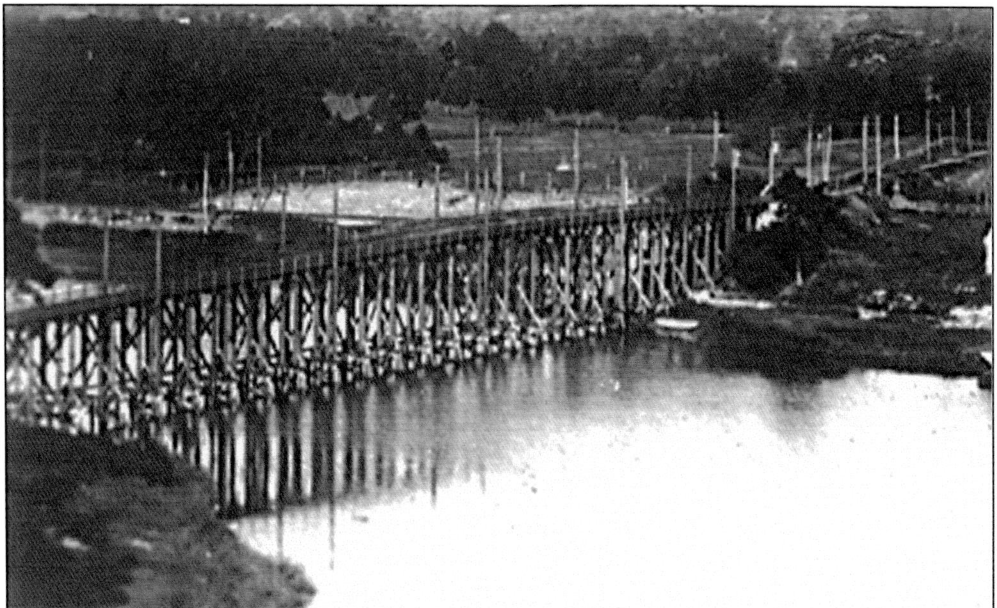

The electric trolleys passed over this trestle, which extended from Crescent Park to Washington Road in Barrington and went over Bullocks Cove.

Six

"The Coney Island of the East"

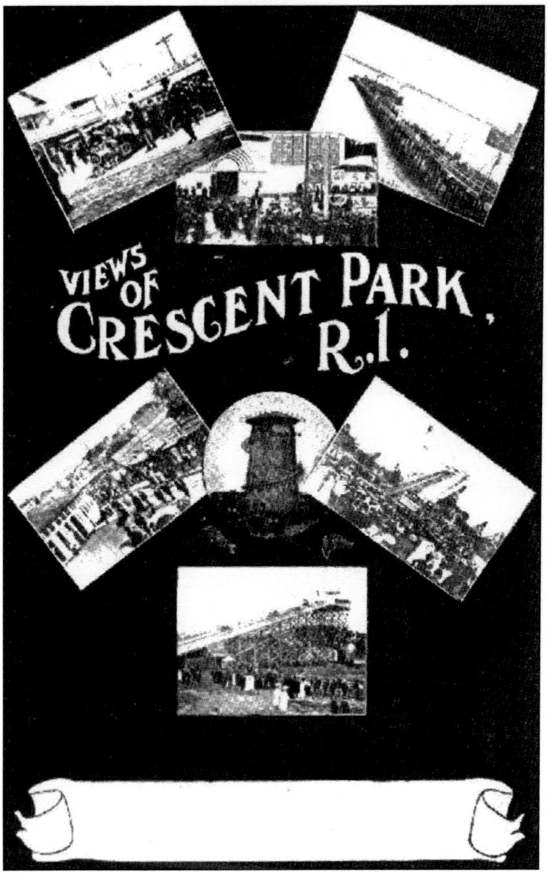

Little did anyone guess that with the building of Crescent Park, followed by Boyden Heights and Vanity Fair, Riverside would become known as "The Coney Island of the East." Up until 1886 tourists came to Riverside for the beautiful beaches and the great clambakes, the cool breezes and the beautiful boat rides to the area. Between the steamers, the trains, which started running about 1850, the trolley cars, horse-drawn buggies, and the large moving wagons that converted to transportation on weekends, there was easy access to the area.

In 1889 George B. Boyden saw an opportunity to develop an amusement park beside the Crescent Park Hotel. The hotel owner was unhappy because he did not desire a honky-tonk area next to his hotel. Mr. Boyden built a merry-go-round at the shore along with bathhouses, a shore dinner hall, and a long dock to accommodate the steamers. Business boomed! In 1893 electric trolleys delivered customers right into the park, conveniently located next to the hotel.

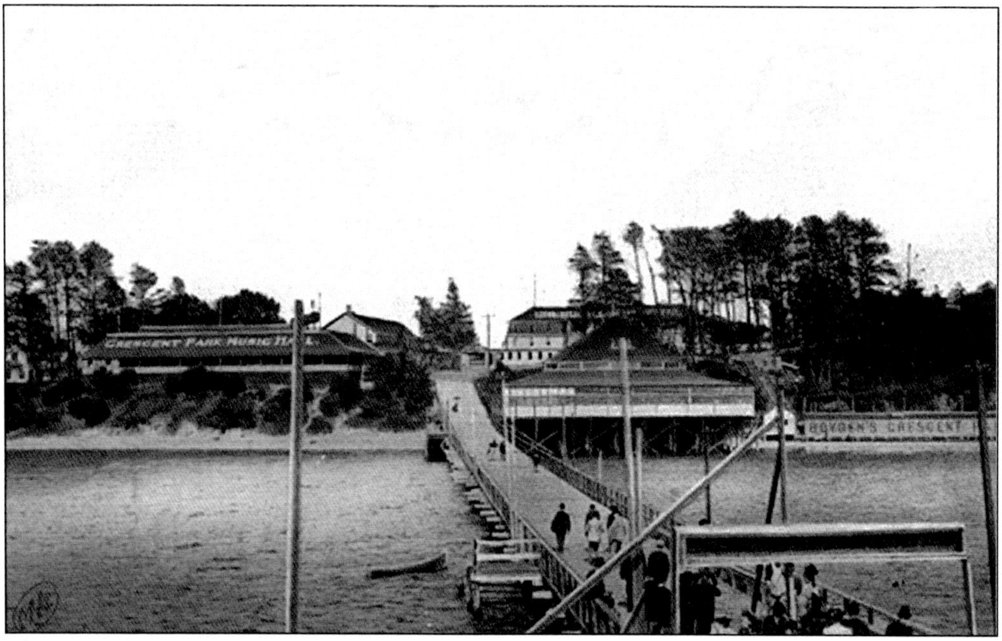

This is Boyden's Crescent Park as it appeared to a traveler alighting from a steamer at the end of the pier. The first carousel and boathouses are to the right with the hotel roof showing behind the carousel and the shore dinner hall to the left.

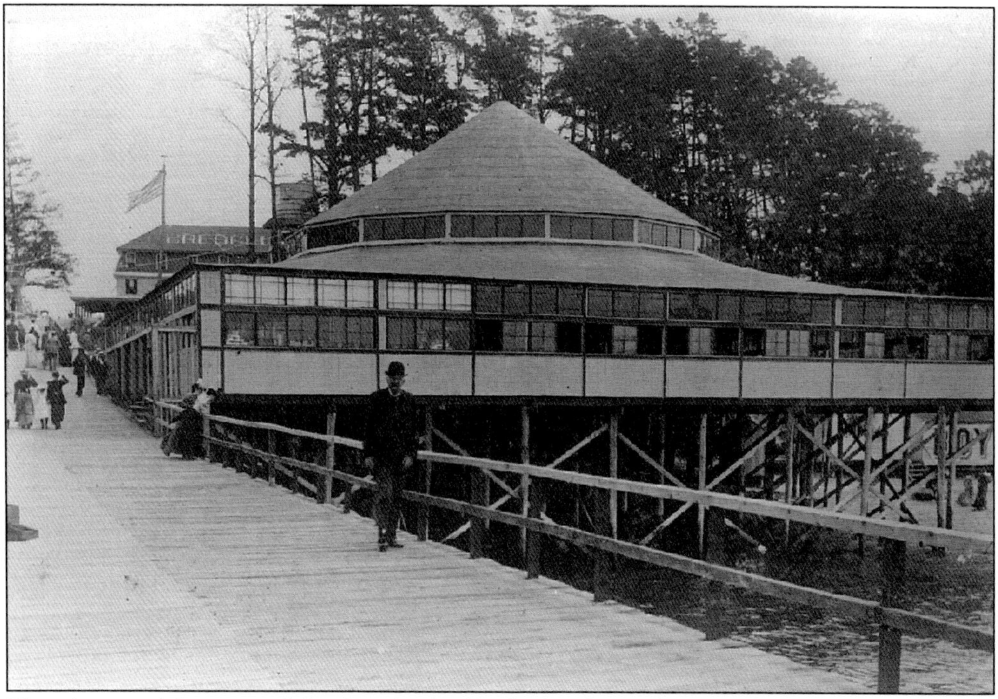

This closeup of the carousel that Boyden had built also shows the roof of the hotel with the flag flying in the background. The year is 1910.

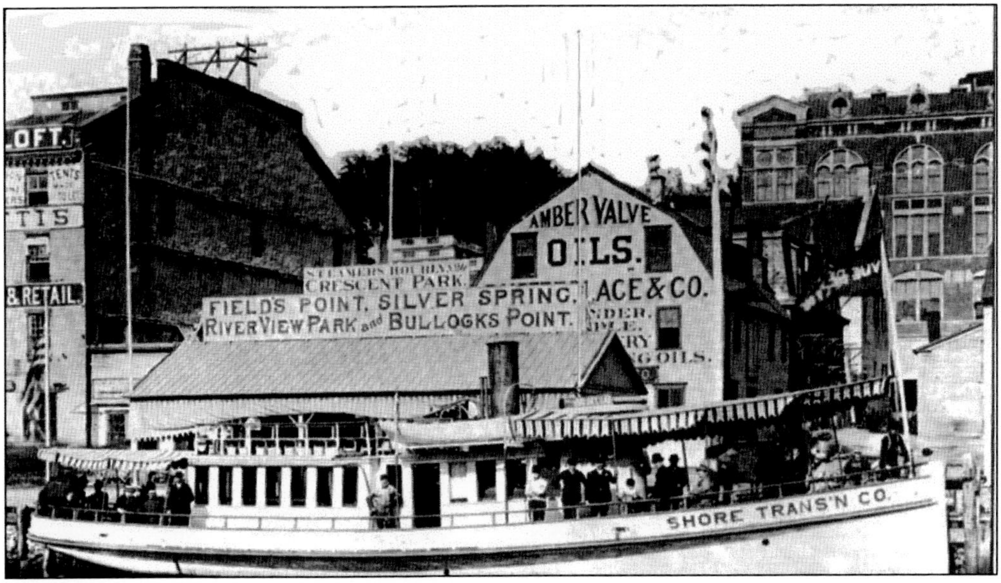

The steamer *Vue de L'Eau* picked up passengers on the south Water Street docks, just one block below South Main Street in Providence. A sign on the roof advertises the stops along the East Bay. Infantry Hall is the large building in the right background.

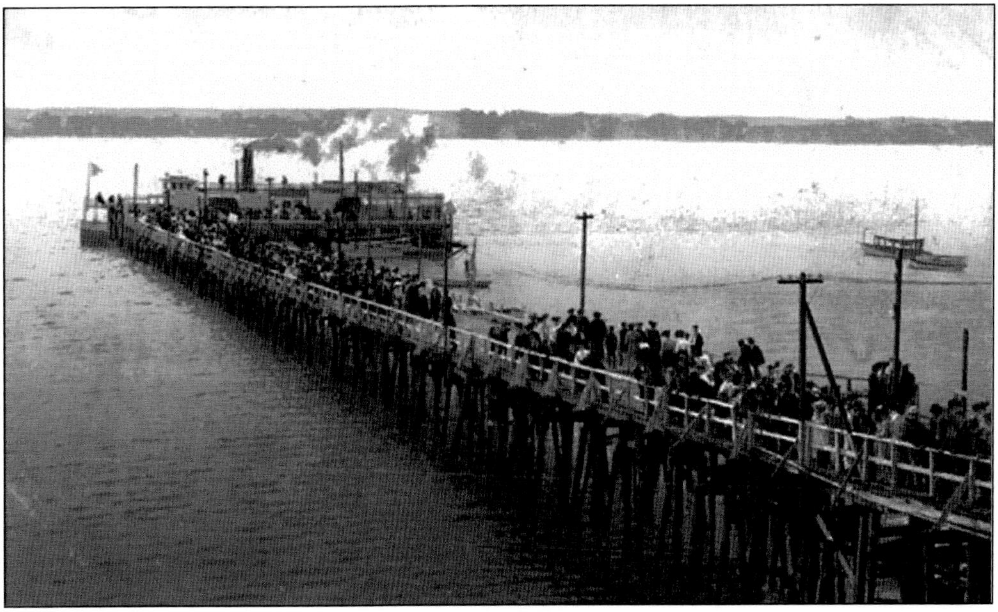

The steamer arrives at the crowded Crescent Park Pier.

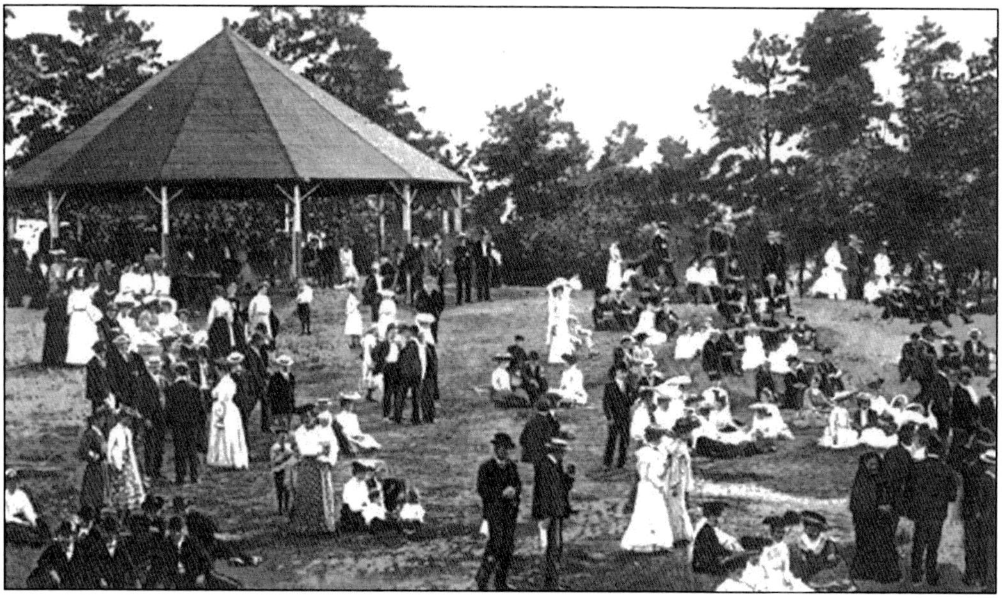

Visitors enjoy a band concert on the lawn of the Crescent Park Hotel *c.* 1900.

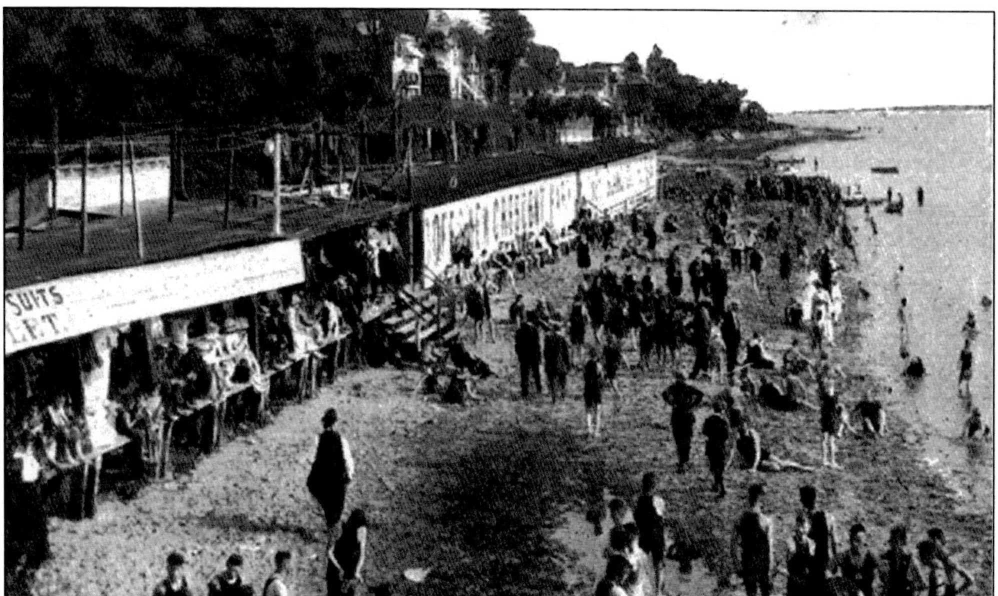

Bathers enjoy Crescent Park Beach *c.* 1910.

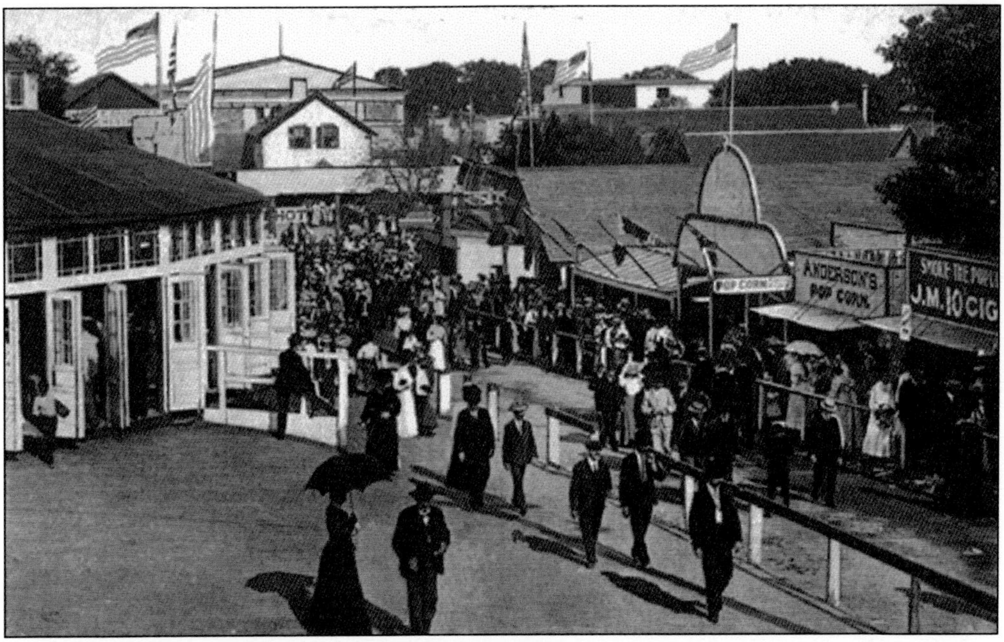

The Crescent Park midway as it appeared after 1895 when the Looff Carousel had been built.

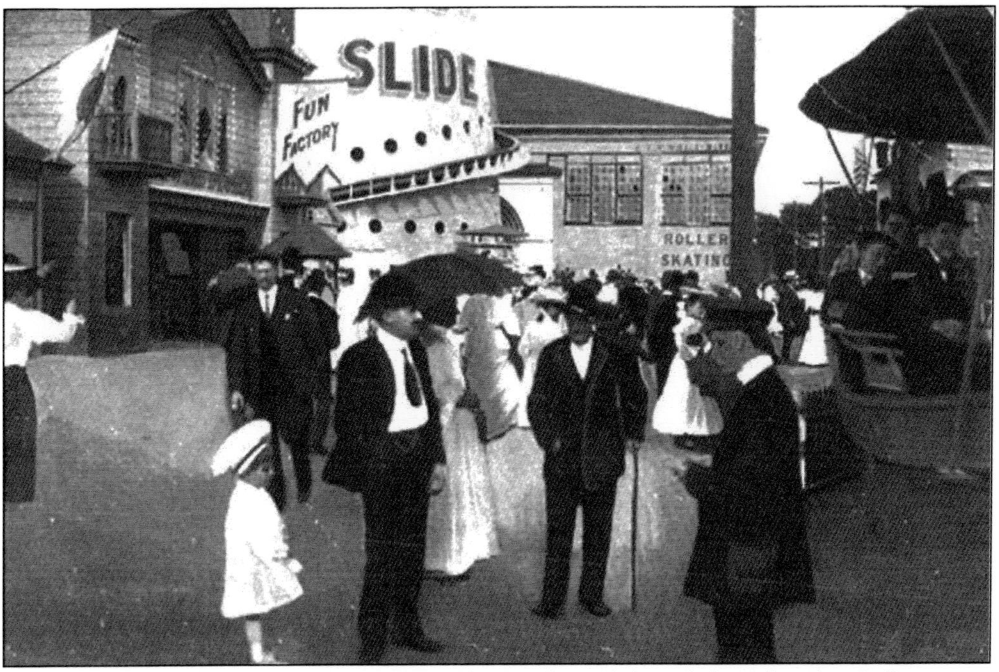

This is a view of the midway about 1900. The Bamboo Slide and the Alhambra Ballroom are in the background.

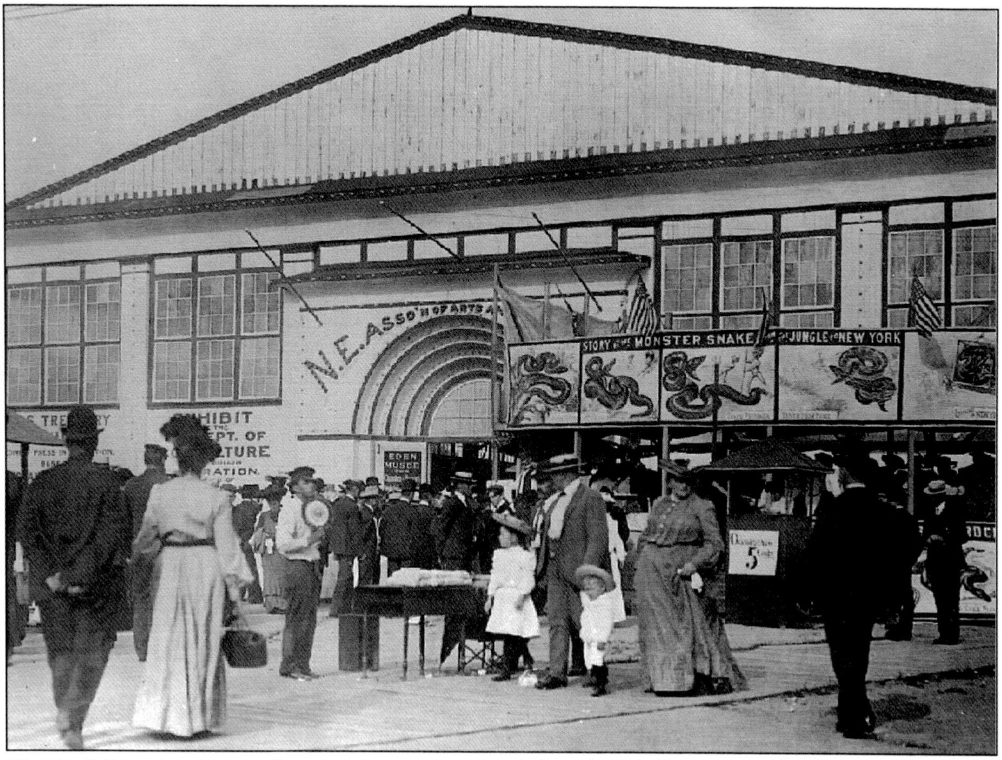

The building that was to become known as the Alhambra Ballroom was built originally as an exhibition hall in 1903 for the Second Annual New England Association of Arts and Crafts, Inc., Exhibition. The name is seen here painted over the main entrance.

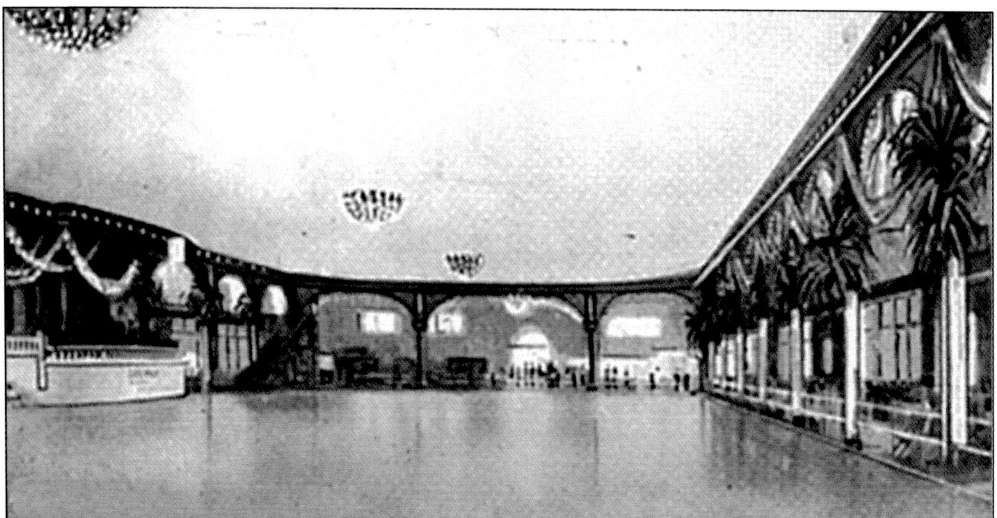

The Alhambra Ballroom was busy every weekend for dancing and large meetings. In the 1920s many name bands brought the "big band sound" to Rhode Island. During World War II, sailors from Newport mobbed the area for the great dancing and entertainment that the park provided.

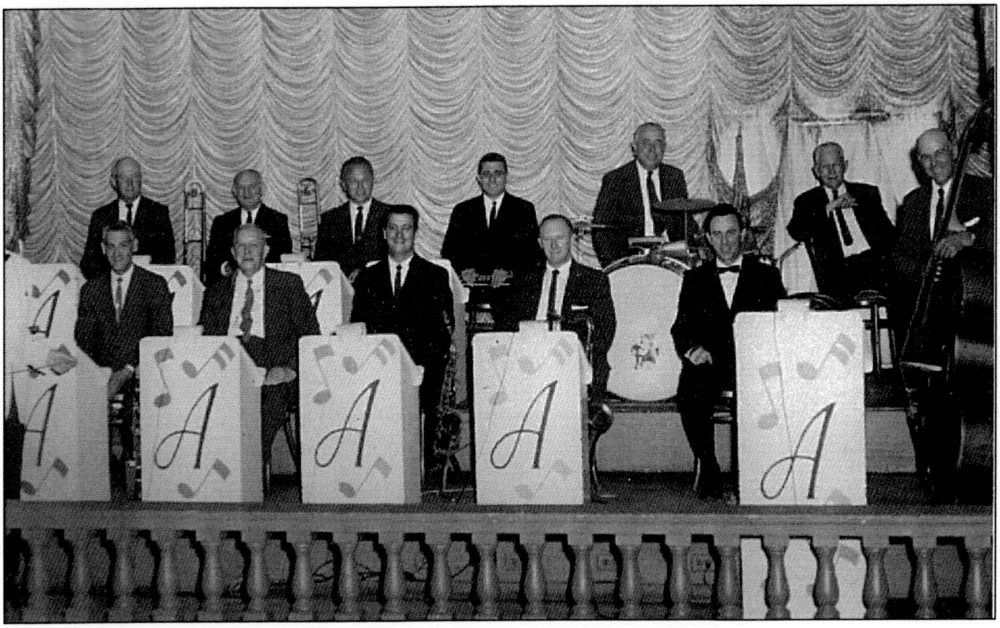

Charlie Weygand's Band performed frequently at the Alhambra Ballroom.

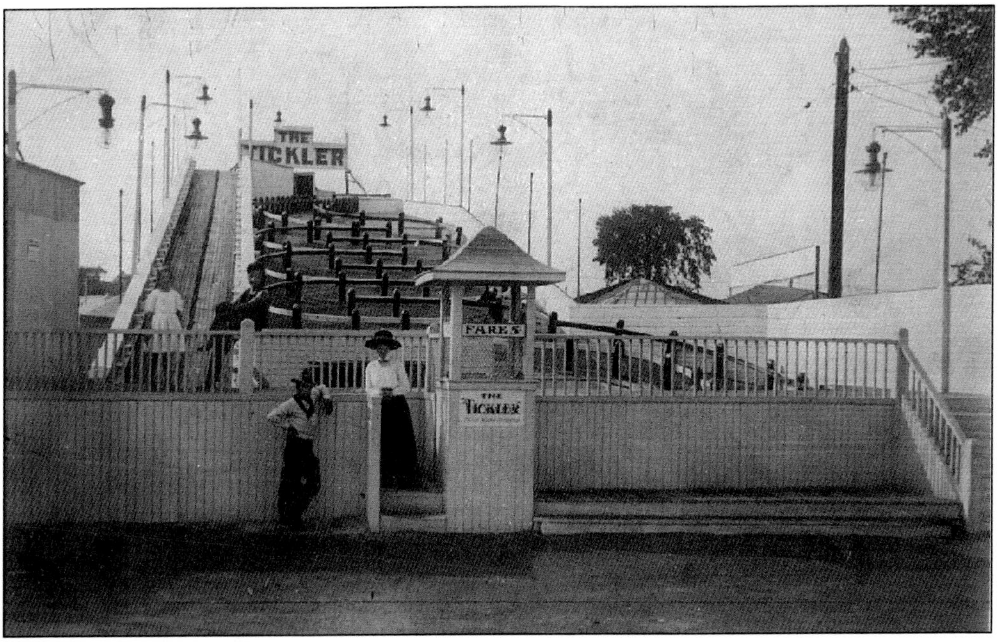

"The Tickler" was a popular ride at the park about 1900.

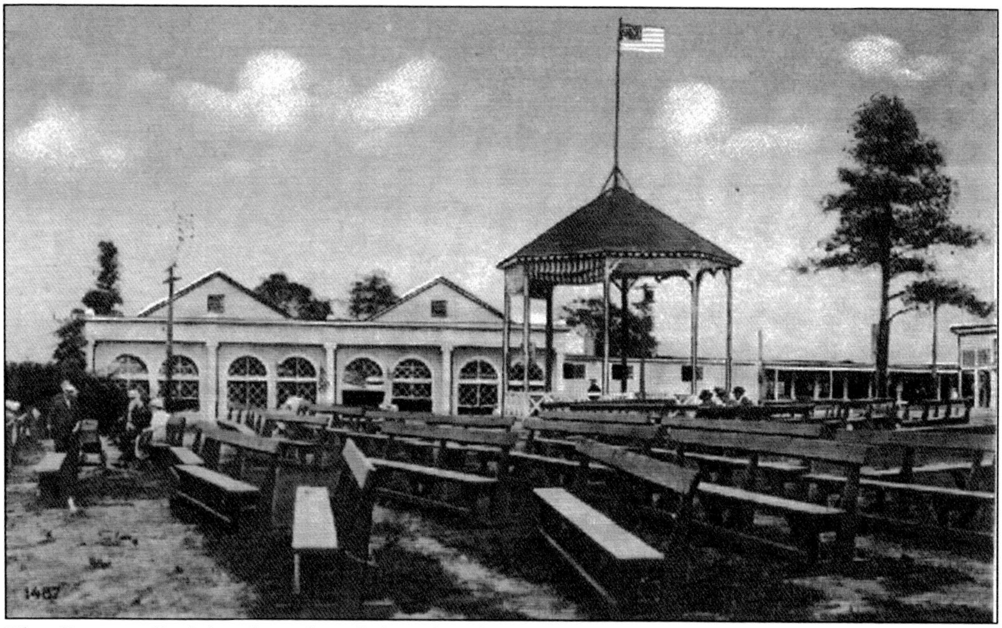

The Crescent Park bandstand, with benches for sitting, is ready for the next concert c. 1900.

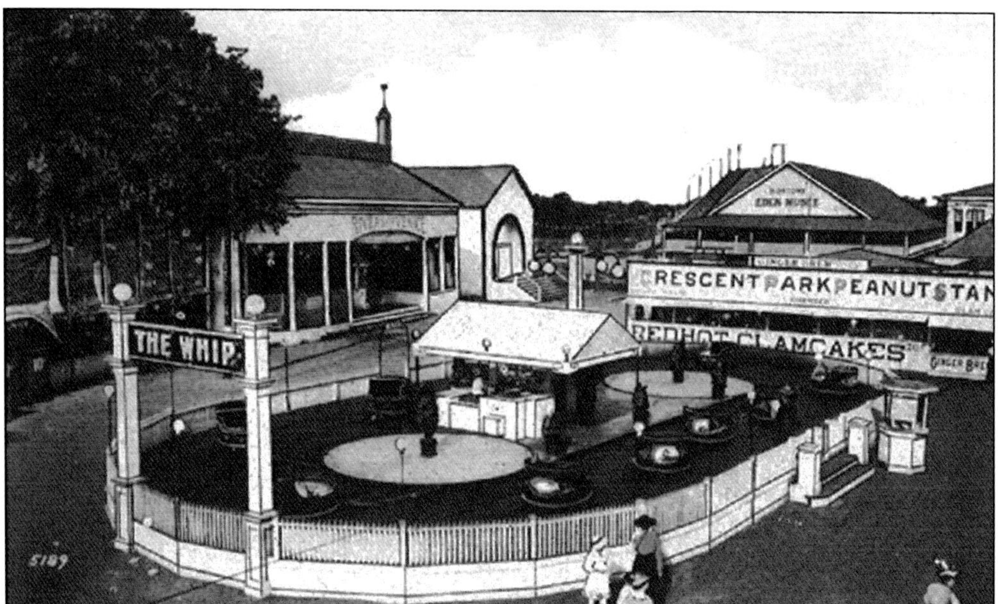

A popular ride at the park was "The Whip." The Crescent Park peanut stand is in the background.

Senior Citizen Discount Day is nothing new. Tags like this one were used for the elderly on special days at the park.

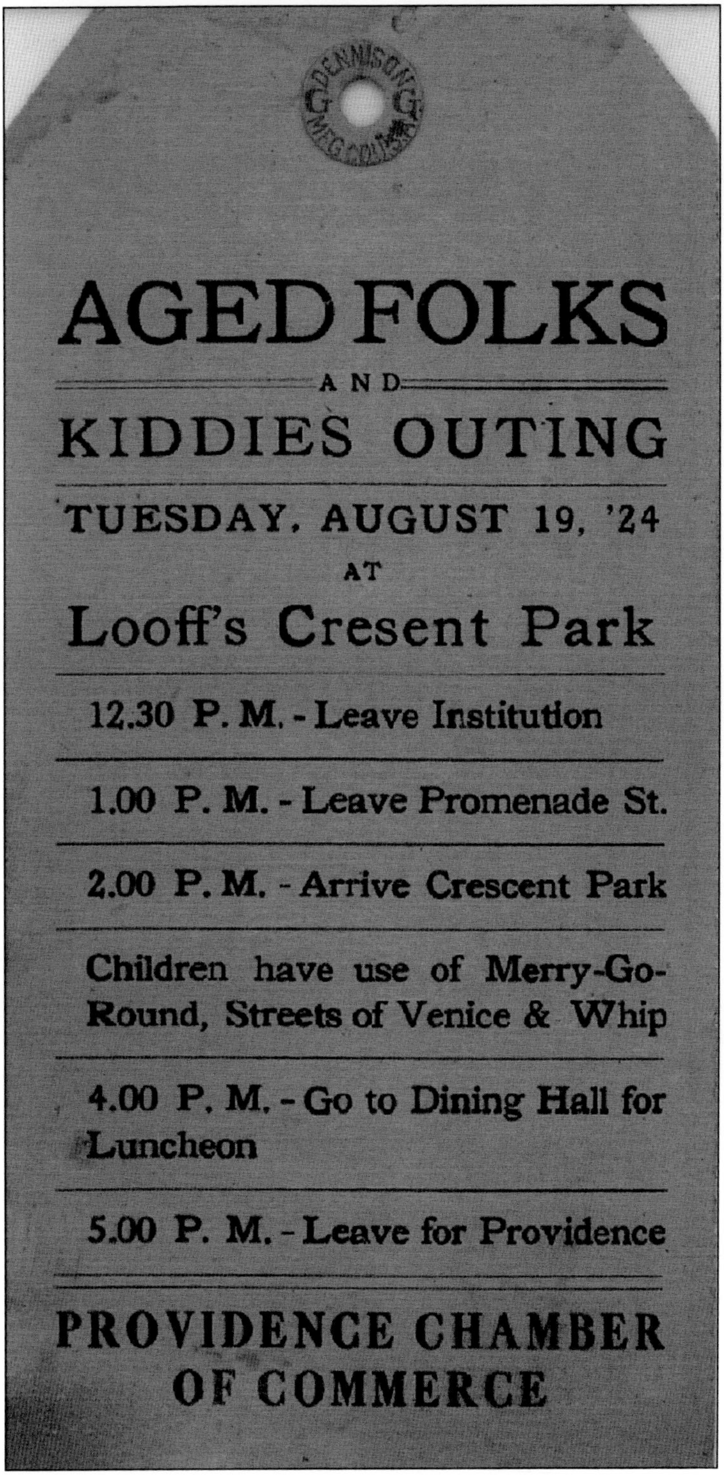

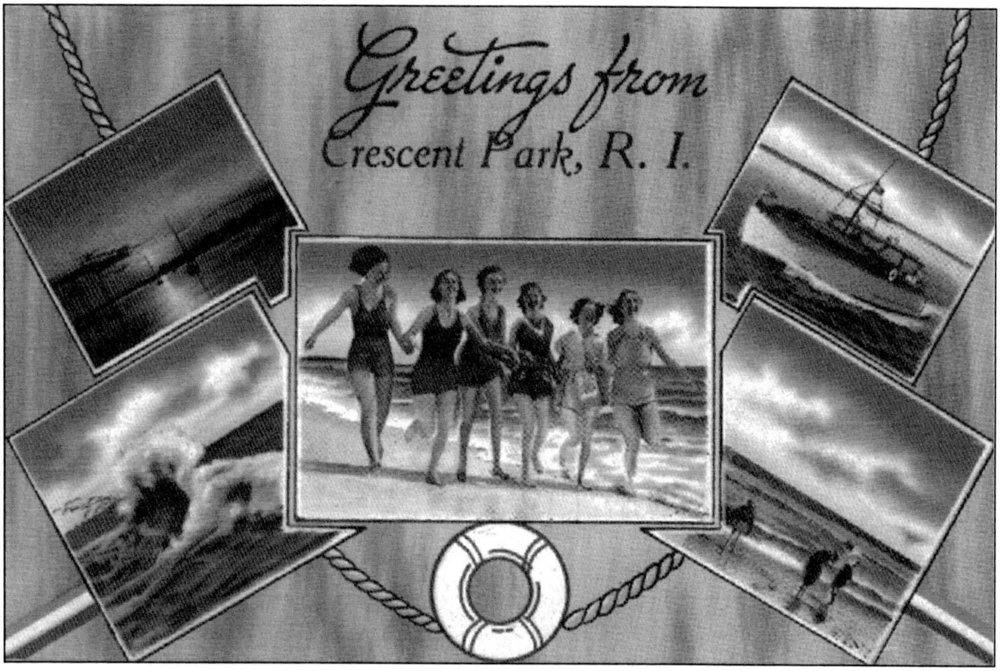

Postcards of Crescent Park from 1889 to the present are prized by collectors because Crescent Park as an entity no longer exists. These cards date c. 1940.

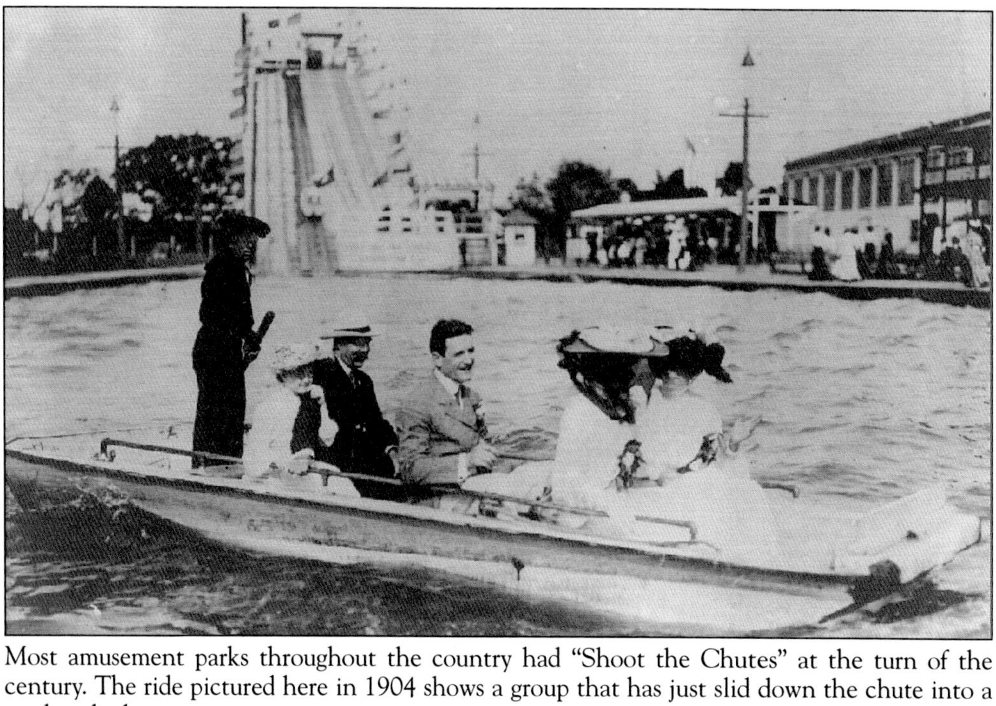

Most amusement parks throughout the country had "Shoot the Chutes" at the turn of the century. The ride pictured here in 1904 shows a group that has just slid down the chute into a pool at the base.

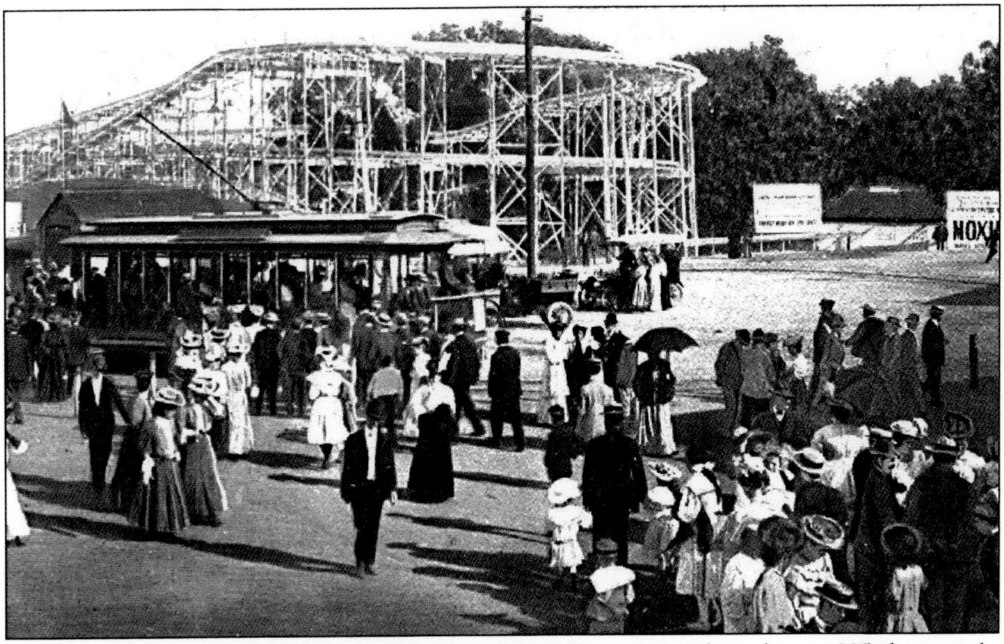

An open bloomer car rides right up to the front of the roller coaster ride in this *c*. 1905 photograph.

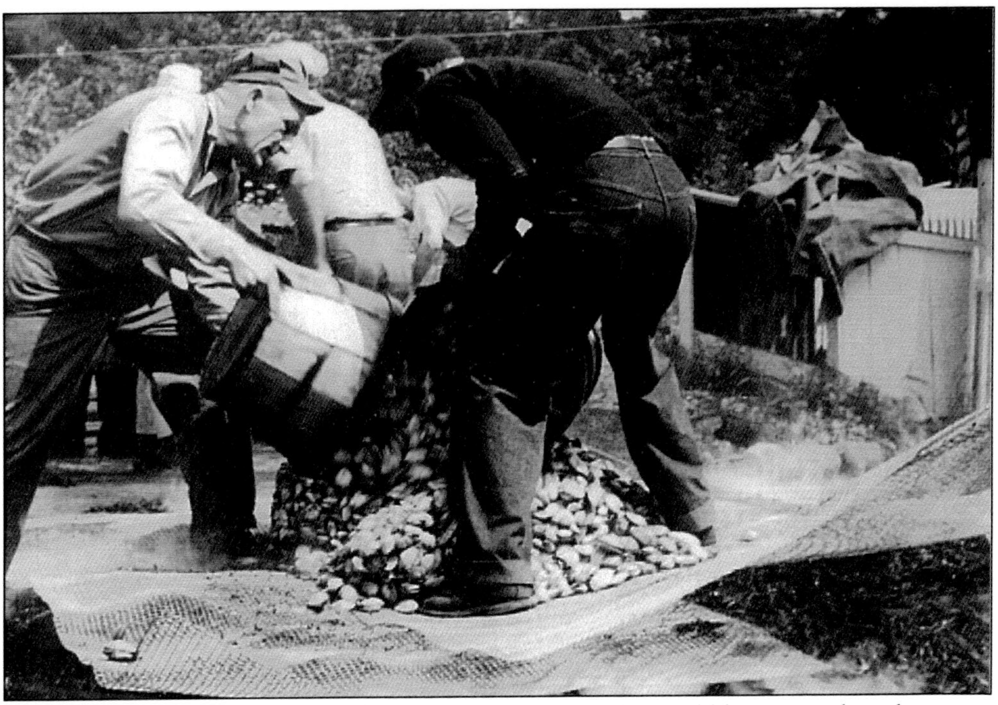

Everyday that the shore dinner hall was open, the clambake would be prepared outdoors in a huge pit.

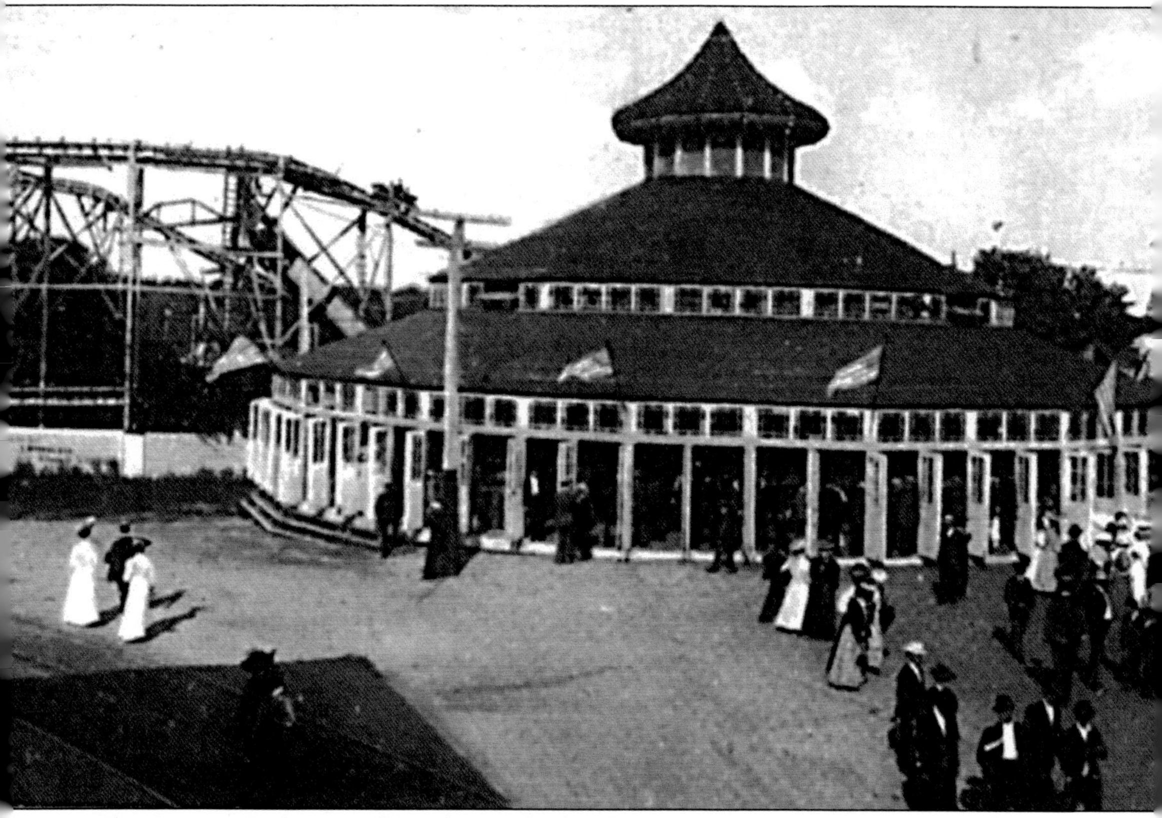

The Crescent Park carousel is a famous landmark in East Providence and is on the National Register of Historic Places. Charles I.D. Looff, a German woodcarver who came to America when he was seventeen, specialized in the making of carved carousel horses and merry-go-rounds. His fame spread throughout the country. Looff moved throughout the country setting up workshops beside carousels where his workmanship could be on display. He came to East Providence *c.* 1894 and built the carousel that still stands today in Riverside. His workshop was behind the carousel and connected to it. He bought Crescent Park from a Mr. Harrington, who had purchased the park from Mr. Boyden a few years earlier. Looff's daughter Helen married Charles Simmons, and they and their family continued running the park after her father moved to California. The Looff carousel celebrated its 100th birthday in 1995. Thanks to the perseverance of a few stalwart supporters of the carousel, it has been preserved for posterity and is being restored to its original splendor.

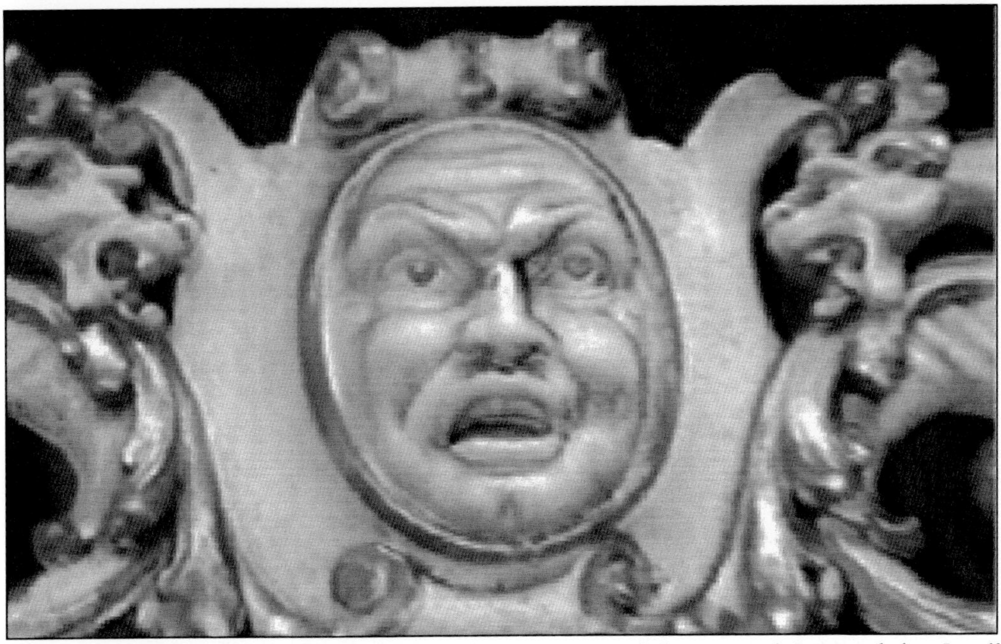

There are many wood carvings decorating the top crown of the carousel. It is said that Looff carved his own face in various moods on several surfaces of the carousel, this being one of them.

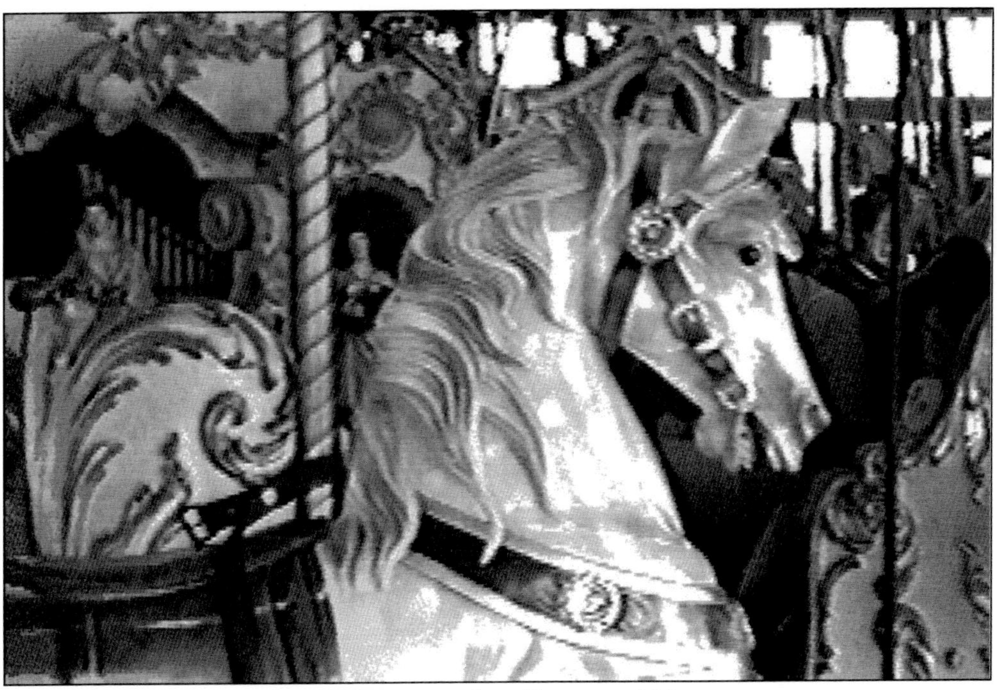

One of the horses restored in 1995 is pictured in all its graceful beauty.

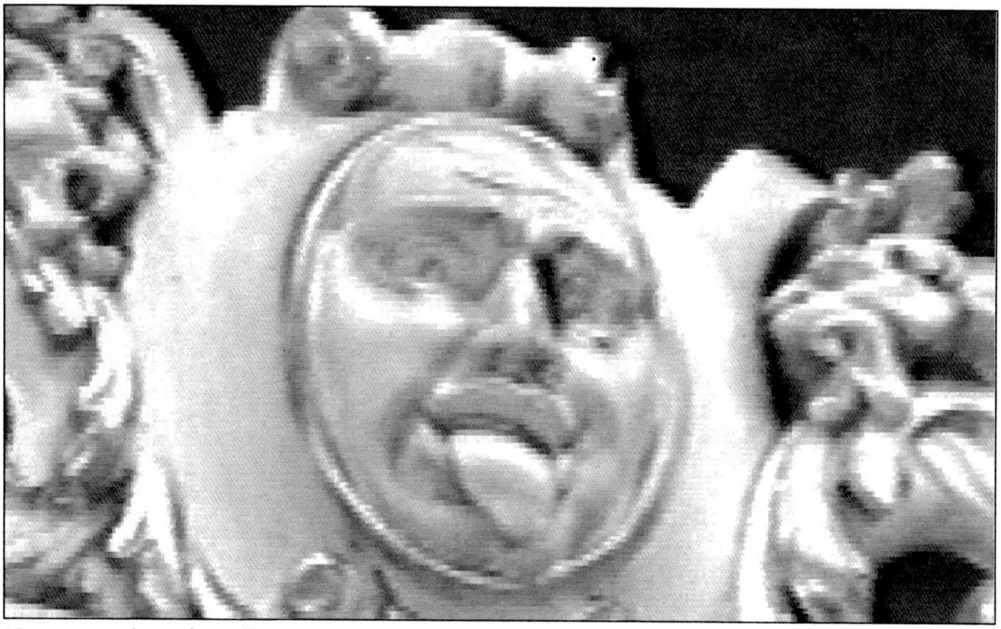

Here is another of Looff's self-portraits carved in wood on the carousel.

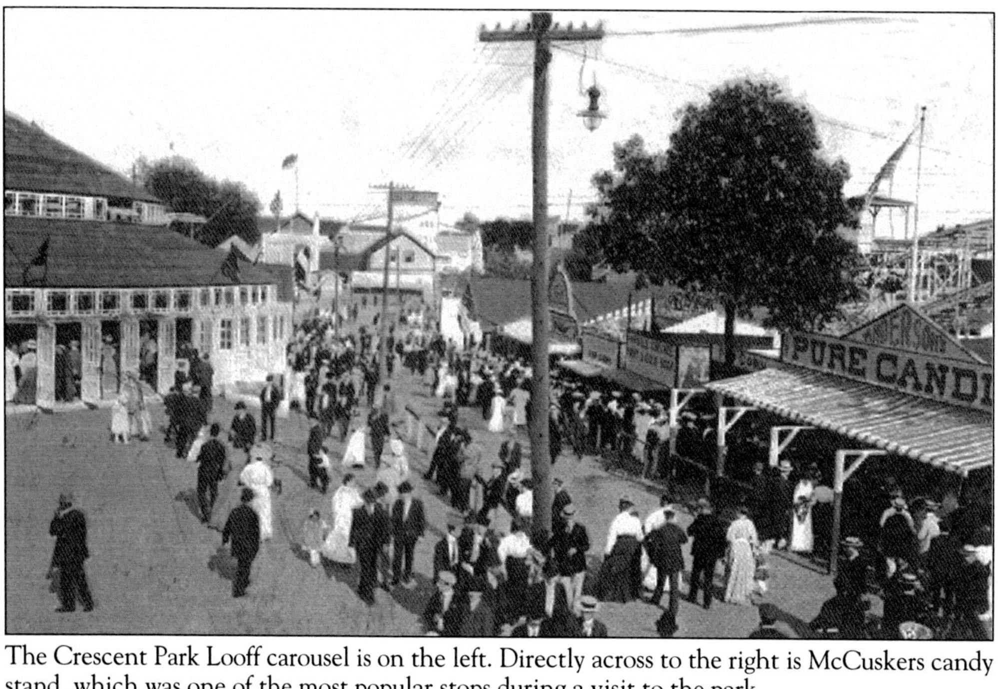

The Crescent Park Looff carousel is on the left. Directly across to the right is McCuskers candy stand, which was one of the most popular stops during a visit to the park.

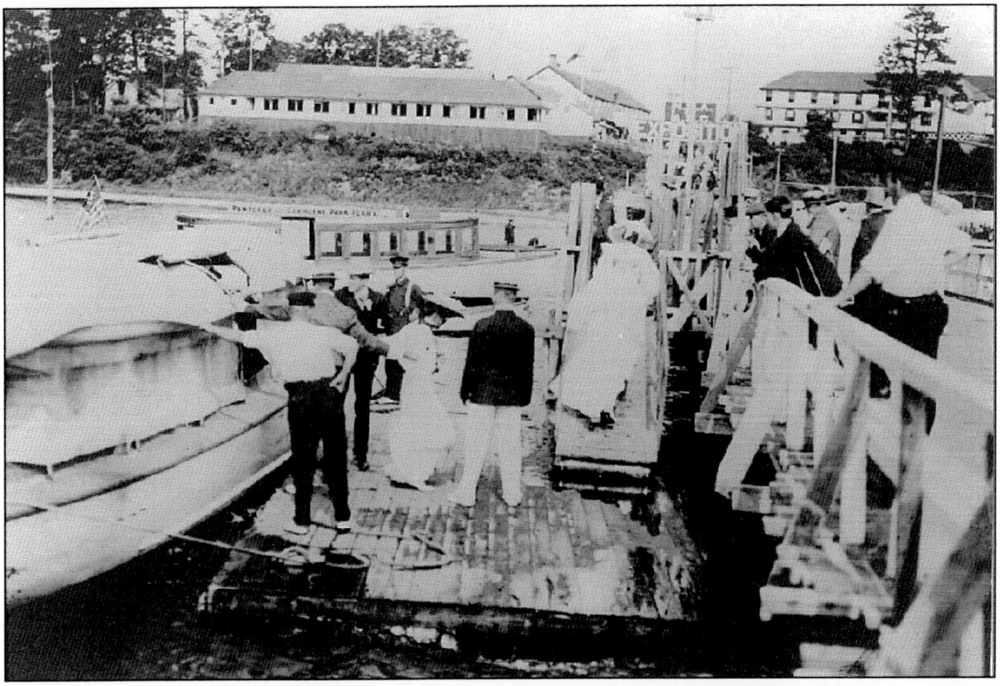

In the olden days everyone dressed up to go to the park. Some young girls stroll by the pool at the foot of the "Shoot the Chutes."

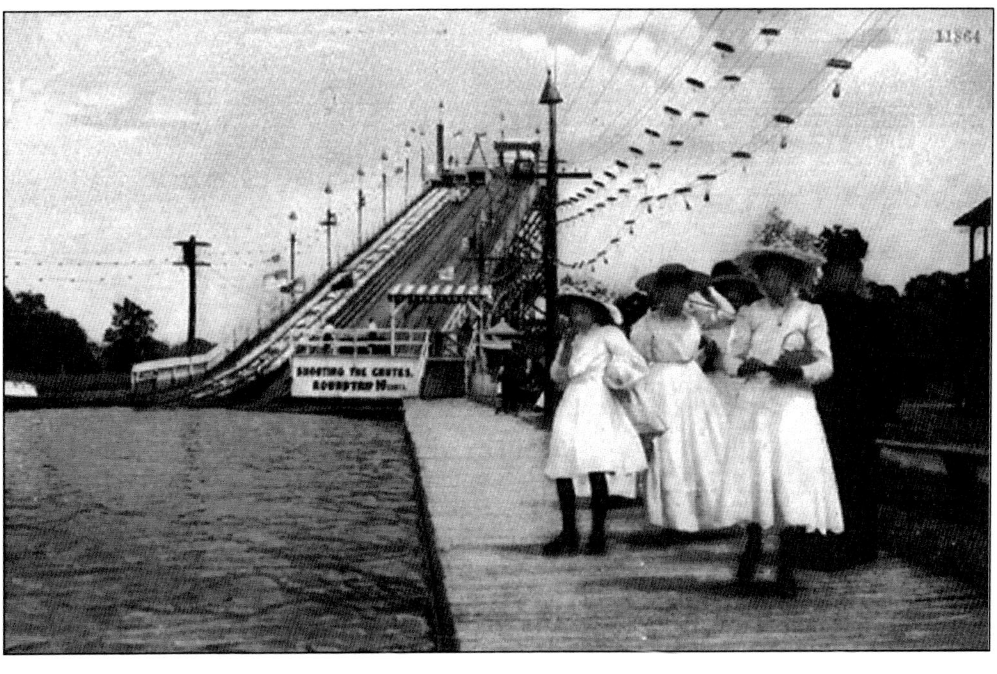

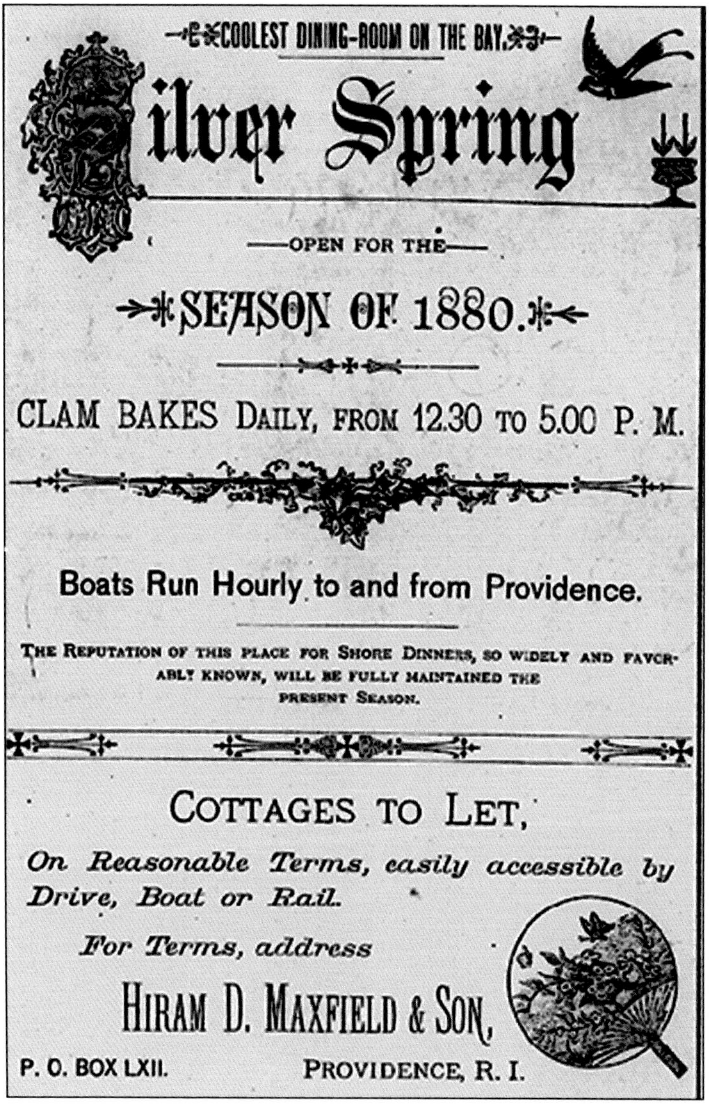

Between the Maze in Riverside and the Veterans' Memorial Parkway was a beach front area known as Silver Spring. Above is a flyer that states the advantages of spending one's vacation here and the many ways to reach the area.

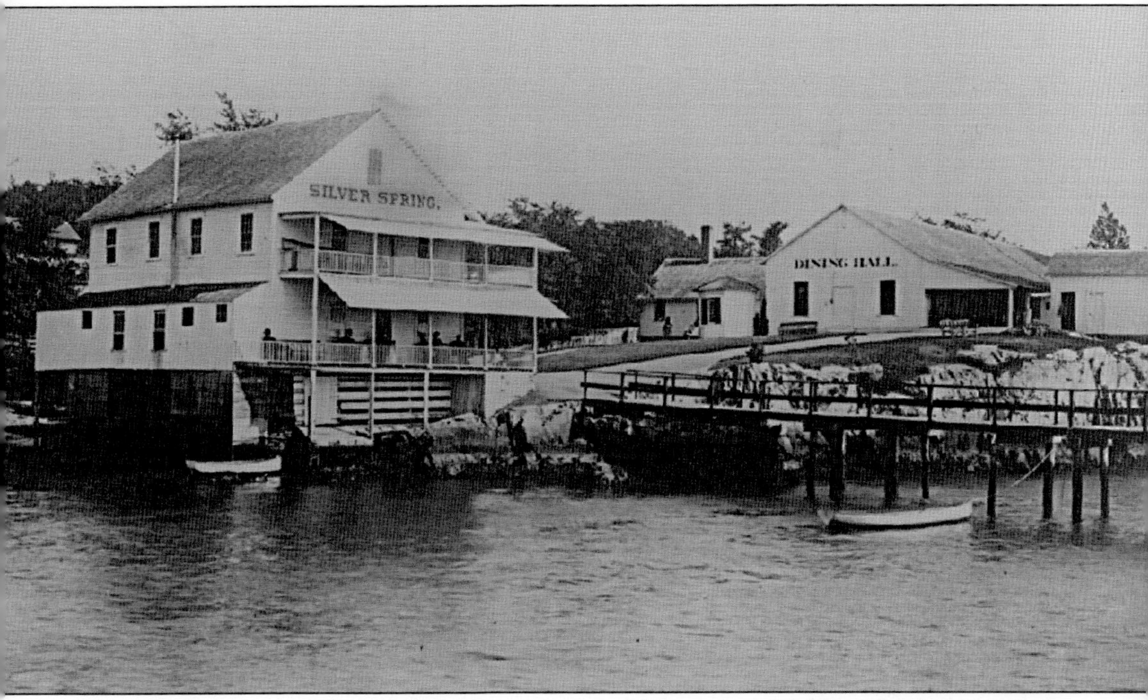

Silver Spring was one of several vacation sites available to the city folks who frequented the East Bay. The area was so named because of the many fresh water springs found here. It was a great place for swimming and boating. It was so pleasant that George Boyden, who had met financial reversals in his Crescent Park business, decided to open a new park here to compete with Crescent Park.

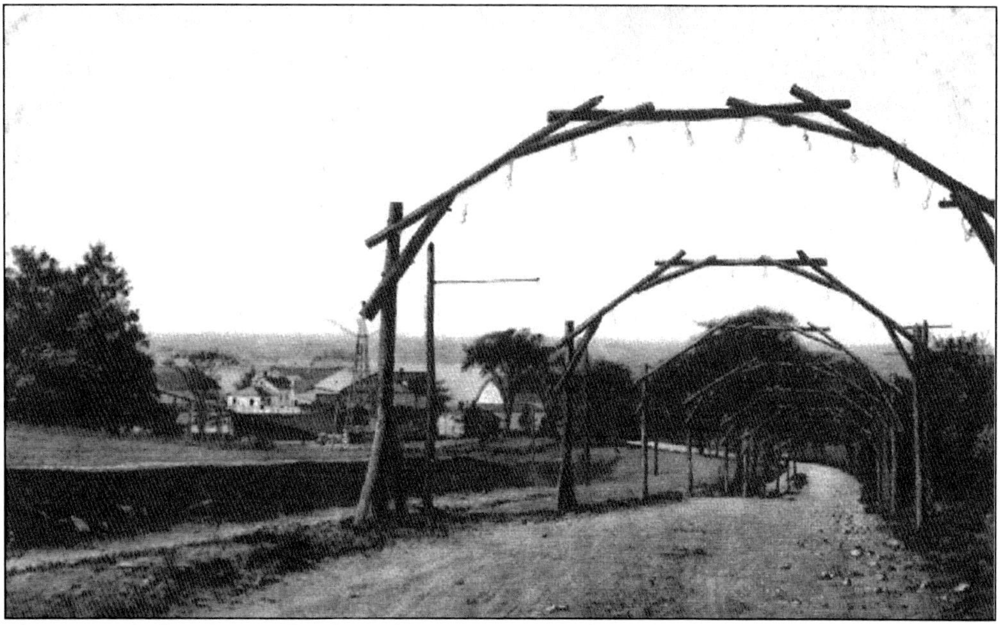

Eleven years after George Boyden's first venture into the amusement park business, he tried again. About 1.5 miles north of Crescent Park he built the Boyden Heights Park. The entry road (Boyden Boulevard today) led down a steep hill to the bayfront. There were beautiful romantic garden walkways, a dance hall, shore dinner hall, carousel, and bandstand.

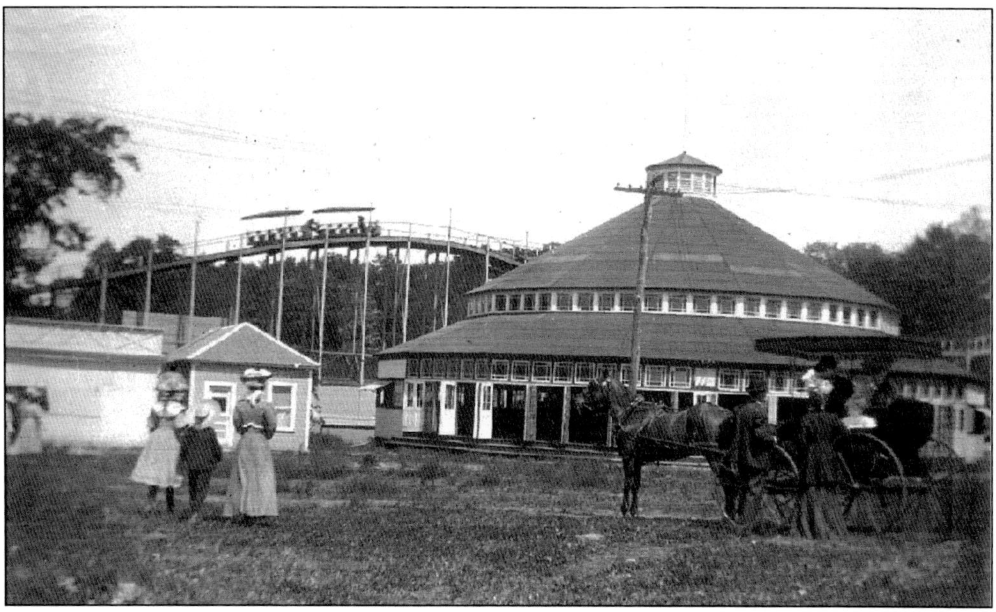

Visitors arrive by horse and buggy at the carousel and roller coaster in Boyden Heights Park in 1900.

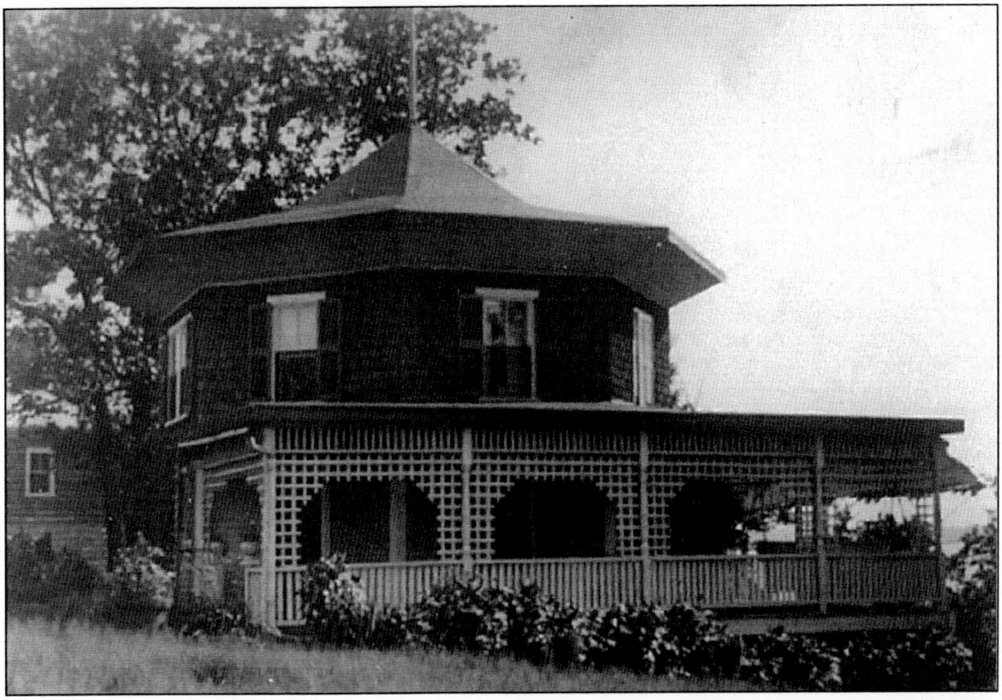

The bandstand in Boyden Heights Park is the only structure left from the park. It has been preserved and redesigned as an octagon-shaped home. It is readily recognizable today at the bottom of Boyden Boulevard hill.

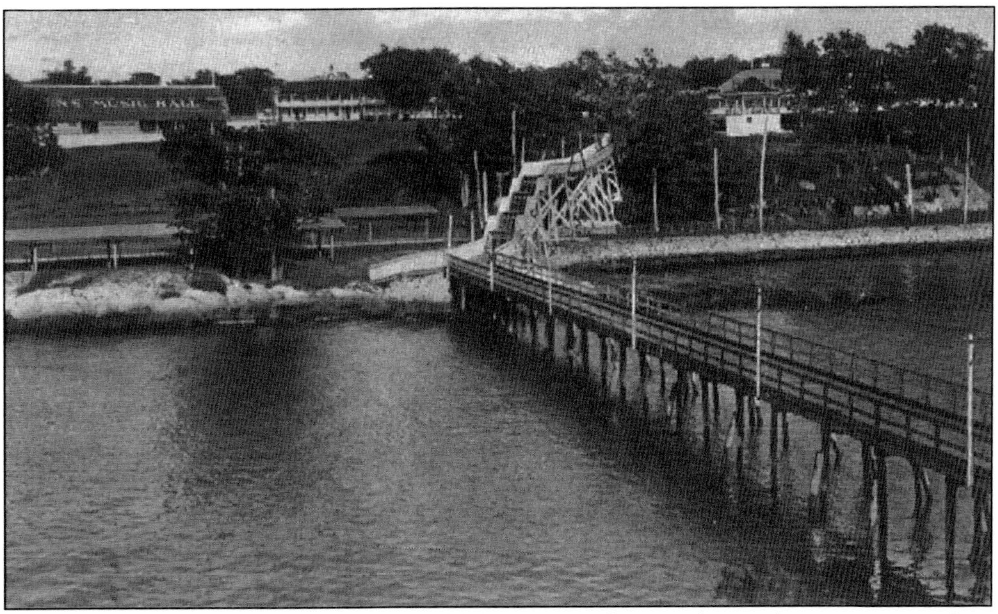

Even though Boyden's Park had a beautiful location with a good pier, the competition from Crescent Park and a new park that opened next door a few years later was too much, and Boyden went out of business for good.

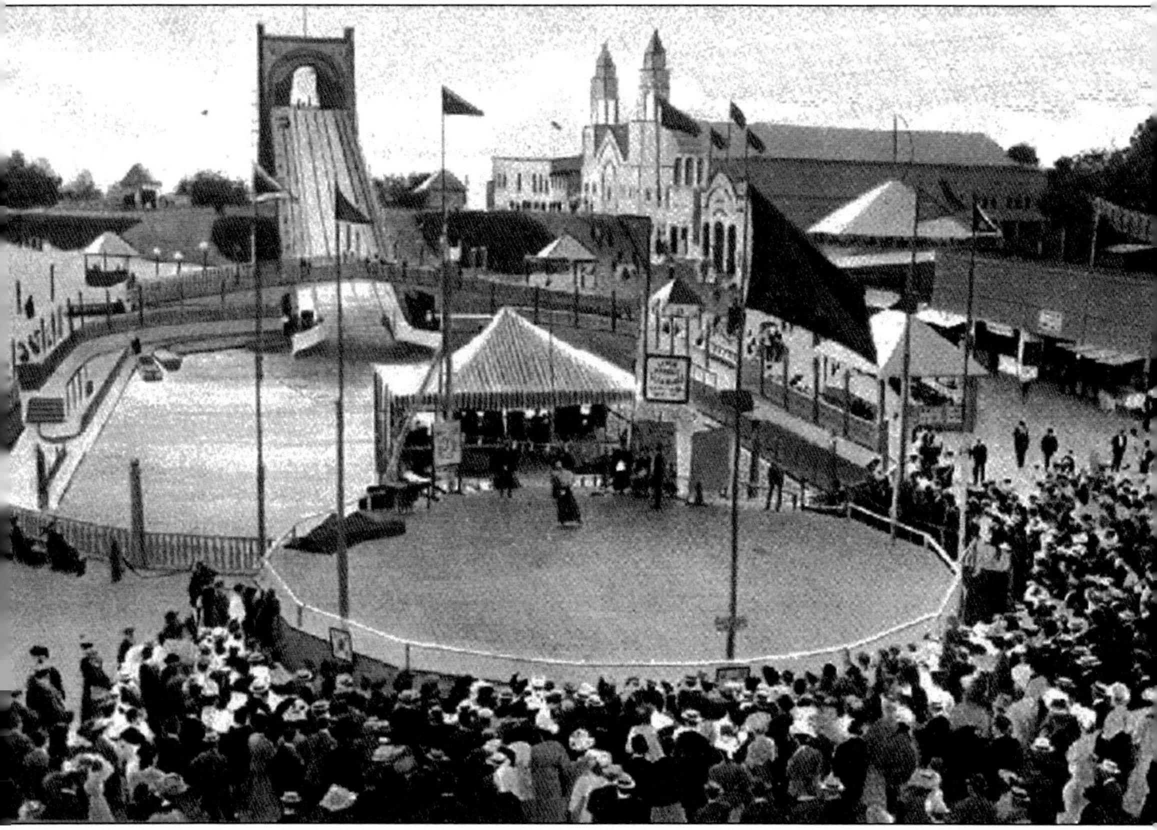

Vanity Fair was conceived by a group of businessmen in 1907 as an early-nineteenth-century version of Disney World today. It was magnificent. It had everything—performing bears, a building that was burned every hour with actors to put out the fire, a huge ballroom, and a larger "Shoot the Chutes" than that at Crescent Park, with water pumped up from the Bay. It was "bigger than life" as the saying goes, but alas, a fee of 10¢ was charged for entrance where none of the other amusement parks charged an entry fee. So, fun-loving park customers rode right past the Vanity Fair Park on Pawtucket Avenue to Crescent Park. There was even a ditty written citing the fact that there was Vanity Fair open,"but no-one is there." After enduring a "real" fire in 1912 Vanity Fair closed forever, a financial disaster.

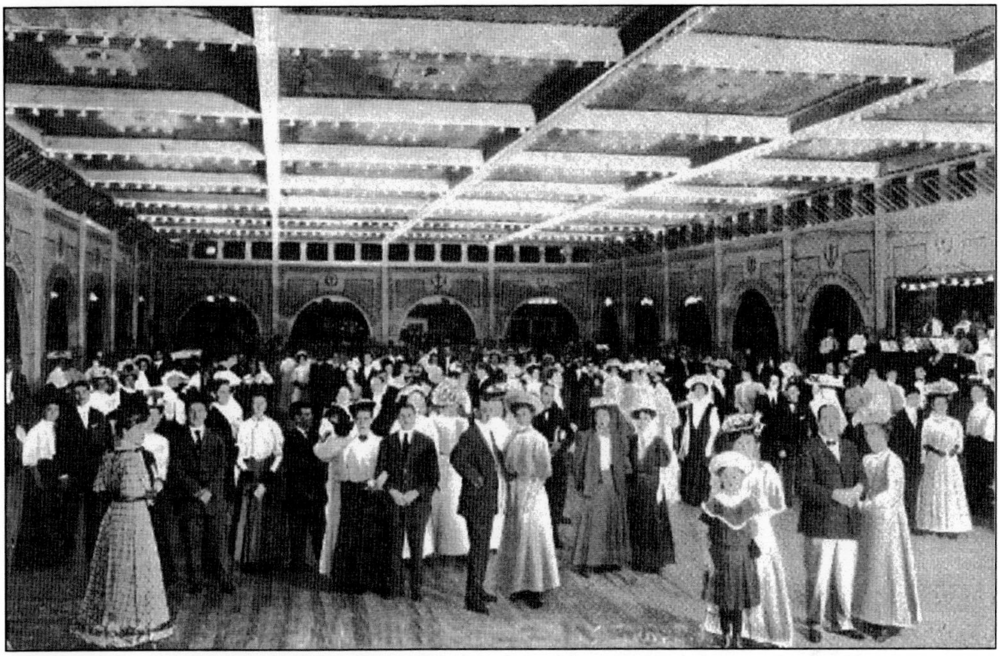

The interior of the dance hall at Vanity Fair was very luxurious.

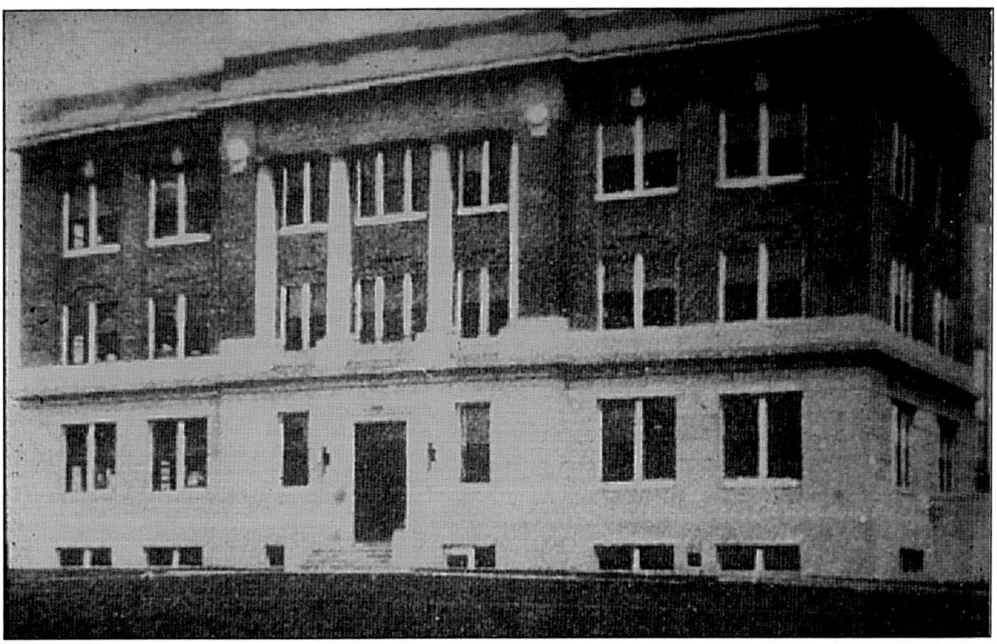

After Vanity Fair went out of business, the Esso Standard Oil Company bought the property on both sides of Pawtucket Avenue from the waterfront to the Wampanoag Trail. This office building was built on the eastern side of Pawtucket Avenue. The park site is now the Silver Spring Golf Course and the office building no longer exists.

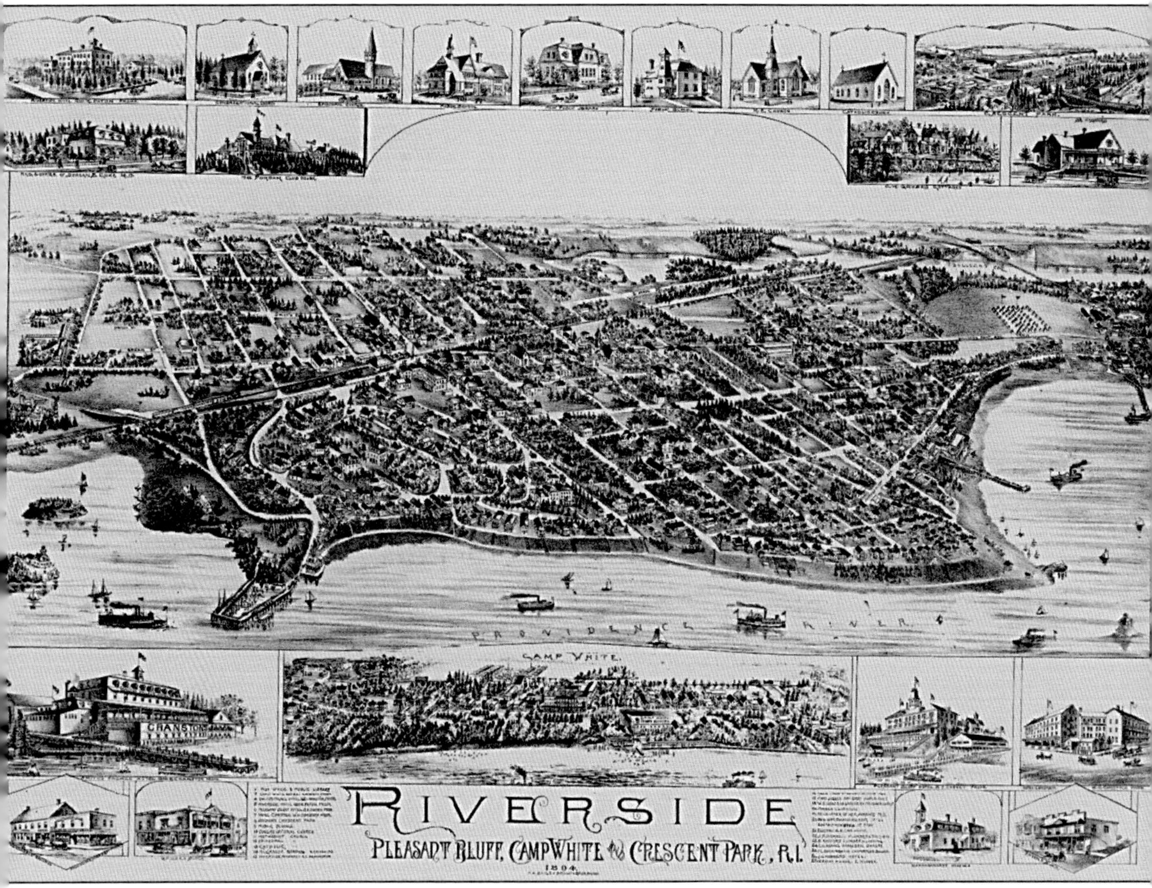

This 1894 map shows most of Riverside, which was part of the second Seekonk Purchase made by John Brown from the Wampanoag Indians in 1645. Narragansett Terrace, which would be off to the right of the map, is not pictured.

Acknowledgments

The East Providence Historical Society would not have attempted this pictorial history of East Providence if one of its members, George Adams, had not gotten the idea and sparked the enthusiasm of the society and members of the community to loan or donate photos to the historical society from which to draw on for the story. George spent hundreds of hours scanning and digitizing the pictures not only to use in this book, but to establish a computerized reference file of photographs for use in the museum. Those who loaned or gave us images were Ray Anderson, Celia Becket, Don Bowden, Ralph Bradley, Antonio Braga, Bruce Britton, the estate of Rowena Bowen, Marijoan Bull of the East Providence Planning Department, Arthur Dyer, Norm Gladding, retired school superintendent Edward R. Martin, Howard Mersereau, Alfred Rezendes, Bill Rix, Elizabeth Smith, John Soteros, Bob Tetreault, Don and Barbara Wood, and Elmer and Hope Yeau. We are deeply indebted to Jess Welt's daughter Marjorie, who made so many of his pictures available, and to Bill DeMarco for loaning some of Welt's pictures.

Extensive research that had been donated to the museum over the years in book form or as research papers was most valuable. We note here the research of Richard Lebaron Bowen, Dr. John Erhardt, Joseph Conforti, Ned Connors, Profs. Richard and Robert Deasy of Providence College, Miriam Gustafson, Caroline and Bruce Chick, Louise Healey, Pat Henry, Alvin and Gloria Meservey, the Newman Congregational Church, Sidney Paine, Gladys Panzarella, Brooks and Ruth Porter, Saint Mary's Episcopal Church, Beverly Simmons, Clint Sellew, and Virginia Whitcomb. The "Statewide Historic Preservation Report by the RI Historical Preservation Commission, 1976" was most helpful.

Many not only provided pictures, but also reference research. They include Ted Adams, John Agren, Marjorie Angell, Earl and Virginia Berwick, Ken Bridge, Don and Cathy Britton, Elsie Brown, and Barbara Crocker from the Riverside Congregational Church. Len and Barbara Erickson, Dr. Karl Holst of the Rumford Chemical Works, Fales and Ruth Peirce, Isabel Izzo, and David Kelleher had been collecting research for many years. Others were Milton and Doris Miner, Ed and Marion Coop, Ken Roberts, Lura Sellew, Charles Tebbetts, the Reverend Peter Tullis, Warren Usher, and Harold and Leroy Flint. We also owe a special thanks to Edward Serowik who is "Mr. Crescent Park Historian." He grew up with the park and the carousel and made available to us hundreds of his photographs and the stories to go with them. Taped oral histories were very helpful. We note in particular one done by Arnie MacConnell of Rowena Bowen and Warren Ivers on Riverside. Museum tapes of Bill Rix on Hunt's Mills, Eunice Russell and Hope Ivers on Kent Heights, Milton Miner of the Rumford Company, and Clint and Earl Berwick were additionally helpful.

The committee for the organization of the project consisted of Les Haworth, Dave Kelleher, Joe and Ruth McDougald, Clint and Lura Sellew, and Virginia Berwick, who all participated in the layout and captioning of the photographs. Nancy Moore computerized the captions. George Adams and Edna Anness, museum curator, edited the photographs and captions. The book was truly a team effort and a joy to achieve.

The historical society thanks all the aforementioned members or friends of the museum. Due to space limitations and the broad scope of our history, all the churches, historic buildings, and schools could not be included. Maybe a second book someday will complement this effort and include that which is missing here.